Using the Plot

Using the Plot

Tales of an Allotment Chef

Paul Merrett

Collins

For MJ, Ellie and Richie

Published in 2008 by Collins
an imprint of HarperCollins Publishers
77–85 Fulham Palace Road
London W6 8JB

www.collins.co.uk

Text © Paul Merrett, 2008
Photography © see picture acknowledgements, page 320

A catalogue record for this book is available from the British Library

Editorial Director: Jenny Heller
Senior Development Editor: Lizzy Gray
Copy Editors: Kirstie Addis and Caroline Curtis
Designers: Anna Martin and Bob Vickers
Photographers: Marie-Louise Avery, Mary-Jane Curtis and Jonathan Gregson.
Food and Props: Felicity Barnum-Bobb and Paul Merrett

ISBN 978 0 00 725261 9

Colour reproduction by Colourscan, Singapore
Printed and bound by Rotolito Lombarda, Italy

Contents

Chapter 1 | Crop Idle

If the manuscript for this book ever falls into the wrong hands then it may well end up as one of those dreadful reality TV shows: 'Tonight, on the Obscurity Channel, a new, totally original show which features celebrities living off the land for a year with no supermarket back-up. Who will you vote onto the compost heap of life?'

The frustrating thing is that my children Ellie (10) and Richie (8) would probably have loved watching this show. Unfortunately for them, though, it won't become a TV programme, which they are just required to watch. It is a family challenge *and they are required to live it!*

As you might expect, because I'm a professional chef, food is very high up our list of priorities at home. We spend far more money in restaurants than we do on any other form of entertainment and, at home, both my wife Mary Jane (MJ) and I devote a significant amount of time to cooking. Our weekly menus are always home-made with fresh ingredients. Despite all our good intentions, however, there is lots of room for improvement.

We, like most people, buy most of our produce from the supermarket. Our children's culinary quirks have forced seasonality off the agenda; and we have certainly made no contribution to the world of home-grown vegetables. In fact, my kids think soil is just dirt and, therefore, something to avoid. I have begun to realise that it is my job as a father (and a chef) to give my children a sound culinary education.

The children of chefs are no different to any others. When I had children, I naively assumed that the battles over food that my friends had experienced with their children would simply not happen in my home. I thought my kids would somehow be genetically programmed to yearn for stuffed breast of guinea fowl or rare grilled calves' livers, while utterly rejecting anything in breadcrumbs that requires deep-frying. I was horribly mistaken. Ellie and Richie have both challenged my patience to the limit with their whimsical likes and, more often, dislikes, which are aired regularly at mealtimes. If one of my social duties is to give my children a love of good food, then who masterminded my own education? (Or was I just a natural?!)

The truth is that I was probably not much better. My mum is a great cook and, certainly, my more adventurous cooking is a result of her repertoire, actually the fact that her wacky cookery used to embarrass me as a child. She would never buy anything pre-prepared that required '20 minutes at 180 degrees'. Rather, she made everything from scratch. Worse still was the fact that she wouldn't cook what I considered 'normal' food – the kind of stuff my friends were eating, like sausage and mash and burgers. Oh, no, she was busy fluffing up basmati rice or stuffing an aubergine. This simply was not very Surrey circa 1975. Nowadays, of course, this type of food is *de rigeur*, so I am immensely proud of her efforts and give her full credit for leading the culinary fusion revolution. I don't often mention the humiliation my sister Ali and I felt when our friends were served up a pork belly curry …

Two other people who had a profound effect on my culinary development were my grandparents, Dick and Marjorie (two solid grandparent names, I feel). They had a lovely cottage surrounded by a large garden, in which my sister and I would spend many happy hours. Grandpa was retired and spent nearly all his time pruning shrubs, nurturing flowers or tending to the wide variety of produce he grew each year. They were entirely self-sufficient when it came to fruit and vegetables and lived strictly by the seasons. I never once knew my granny to buy anything other than the odd bit of exotica from the greengrocer (oranges, bananas or sometimes grapefruit). Otherwise every herb, salad item, soft fruit, apple, walnut, fig and a vast array of vegetables went from Grandpa's garden down to Grandma's kitchen. It was here that Granny, a 1930s domestic science teacher, came into her own.

I reckon Marje spent most of her life in her kitchen. She was always pickling or baking or preserving. She knew every trick in the book about utilising a harvest, and I can still taste her simple and very English cooking now when I close my eyes. Looking back as an adult with children of my own, I can appreciate how lucky I was to have known this way of life and, above all, how living by the seasons, with all that one can grow, is the ideal way to live.

I realise that their efforts were not unique. Growing vegetables was an essential part of life in those days. The post-war years were full of memories of food shortages and rationing. People were careful about waste and made the most of the seasons. Ironically, when considering this, rather than looking back and feeling sorry for a generation for whom a pineapple was a major treat, I start to feel envious of a generation who went blackberry picking when they fancied a pudding!

Seasonal eating was not a lifestyle aspiration for my grandparents; it was a natural law that governed what ended up on the dinner table. As I cruise the aisles of our local supermarket happily buying green beans from Kenya and asparagus from Peru, it dawns on me that, despite cooking professionally for 20 years, I have rather missed or forgotten the wider issues concerning food. My obsession with winning a Michelin star had all but cancelled out any thought of food miles, animal welfare, seasonal cookery or the real joy of picking something and then very

simply cooking it. I realise that I should worry far more than I ever have done about where my family's food is coming from and how it is grown.

While acknowledging all this as the right way forwards for our family, I would not dare to suggest that I am at the forefront of change. I have sat at many a dinner party listening to people from all walks of life 'bang on' about food miles and globalisation, and my standard response has been to consider them the 'brown rice and sandals' types, and to turn the conversation to what I considered more 'foody' matters, such as current restaurant trends and the latest cookbooks. There is no doubt, however, that food issues are a hot topic and I have to accept that I have some ground to make up; probably the very reason for my belated conversion is that I have spent so much time in the pampered world of fine dining.

Of course, the easy option would be to buy a few books and feast on a few culinary sound bites. There are many very good books dedicated to all aspects of the great food debate and a quick check of the average politician's fingernails will probably reveal that their new-found food policy came from a book rather than a muddy field. Well, I want my family's love of food to be a genuine, muddy, hands-on experience – one that we will remember all our lives.

My own family lives a very busy, urban life. Our small city garden is kept as low maintenance as possible. We have a shed for our bikes, a bit of decking and a few shrubs. It's a lovely place to sit on a summer's evening, but we have never considered growing anything that might contribute to a meal. In fact, because of our hectic schedules, the garden is mostly 'laid to AstroTurf'. Our real lawn had started to resemble the penalty area at Griffin Park, the home of our beloved local football team, Brentford FC, from being used for footy training by Richie and his mates. With a good deal of guilt, we replaced it with shiny plastic grass. It now looks, from a distance, like a putting green at Wentworth, and the best we could do there, food-wise, is a bowl of plastic fruit.

The more I think about it, however, the more convinced I am that my grandparent's generation enjoyed a relationship with food that I witnessed as a child but have conveniently forgotten as an adult. Having discussed much of this with MJ, and she agreed that we might all benefit from a bit of home-grown produce, and adds that, as a family, we aren't particularly well placed on the 'those doing their bit to save the planet' list. We decide we will not only try to grow our own fruit and vegetables, but also start to live a more ethical existence all round. This meeting of minds is encouraging, particularly as MJ has, up to now, been the sort of person who jumps in the car and drives 300 metres to the nearest shop.

MJ suggests we start by growing a few carrots, tomatoes and beans so that our fussy children can start to understand where their vegetables come from, how natural they are and, thus, why they are so healthy. Great point, I agree, but I indicate our lack of green space. Where will we grow them?

What we need is an allotment. We talk this through and become excited at the prospect of sowing cabbages, plucking apples from our own trees and digging up armfuls of new potatoes, marking each harvest with seasonal eating. An allotment will allow me to recreate those dishes of my childhood as well as to create some new ones of my own.

It will not just be about fancy finished dishes, however. Seasonal cookery will mean dealing with an excess of produce at times, so we will also make the most of preserving, jamming, freezing and batch-cooking our bounty, as my granny did. This way we can enjoy raspberries in December or green beans in January. We will cook our food as it finds us. We are two working parents with all the commitments that go with a busy life but, rather than buy out-of-season, vitamin-deficient vegetables from the supermarket, we shall get a cheap, local allotment and grow the real version ourselves.

Chapter 2 | By Royal Appointment

Anyone who has taken the life-changing decision to get an allotment will
know that, in the last ten years, demand for allotments has escalated
beyond belief. Gone are the days when allotments were the exclusive
domain of old men, in oversized trousers held up with twine, growing
vast amounts of root vegetables. Allotments are in demand from all areas
of society: very trendy media types, posh people, very poor people, the arty
farty set ... and old men in oversized trousers held up with twine. They
all want a patch of land to call their own. Perhaps, if someone can find a
way of making serious money out of allotments, it won't be long before
supermarkets are knocked down and replaced with more plots of land
and rickety sheds.

MJ and I both feel that, with an allotment, the kids will enjoy watching
things grow and, as a result, will be more adventurous at mealtimes; we
will all spend time together with a common purpose; and we can turn
our backs on the devil of the day – the supermarket. This will not be
because we are doing something amazing, just the opposite. We are a
very normal family, with all the normal hassles of life, and we are just
trying to get back in touch with one of life's most enjoyable and
important aspects, food.

So, we register online with our local allotment association and soon we receive details of all the local sites. MJ chooses the three nearest ones and we call all three to check availability. Two have nothing available and a waiting list as long as a ball of garden twine, but the third call is rather more hopeful. A few days later we get up early for our first visit to Blondin Allotments.

It's a wet and chilly Sunday morning in November. Although the allotments are only about half a mile from our house, MJ and Ellie decide to drive down, which I feel is hardly in the spirit of things; Richie and I go on our bikes.

Our appointment is with Keith, who is the Chairman of the Blondin Allotments committee. Keith has got a beard. This makes him look like an outdoor sort of bloke. I am hoping, however, that I can avoid the facial hair and just settle for a pair of wellies.

We are shown our proposed allotment and told to think about it. It costs £27.50 a year and an (optional) extra £5 gives us access to the association's lock-up shed, where there is a variety of equipment for general use; it also gives us use of the allotments' snazzy composting toilet.

Along with these benefits, inevitably there come certain obligations and any new plot holder has to agree to the allotment rules. We ask Keith what the rules are and he replies that he doesn't have them on him. But, in brief, he tells us they are:

1. The gates must be kept locked at all times
2. Garden waste (from one's home garden) must not be dumped on the communal compost heap
3. A hosepipe can only be used if it is manned – there must be no tying it to a fork handle and nipping home for tea
4. There will be immediate eviction by the committee if one's plot is not suitably maintained

We are quite comfortable with points one to three – we will be fine locking the gate, we don't have any garden waste back home and, in a fit of greenness, we have recently given our hosepipe to my sister – but rule four has a sinister ring to it.

MJ asks Keith to what level they expect each plot to be maintained. She points out that we are new to this gardening game and may require a little leniency. Keith, sensing our apprehension, quickly explains that, if any plot is left completely unworked for more than three months, the plot holder receives written notice in the form of an improvement order. Failure to comply leads automatically to eviction. This all sounds a little overbearing to me, but, as MJ points out, with so many people wanting to rent an allotment, it would be wrong to leave a plot in disrepair. And, anyway, this shouldn't bother us at all because we are so up for the challenge that we can't imagine a day passing without a quick visit to our allotment.

Keith explains that we will meet many people on the allotments who have been 'at it' for twenty years or more so we shouldn't worry too much. He goes on to tell us that we can expect to find good soil here and that, with dedication and commitment, we will soon be reaping the benefits.

It feels strange to be standing in the middle of a huge field, in which so much produce is growing in the heart of west London. Overhead the planes are lining up to land at Heathrow Airport and, in the distance, I can see cars driving over the M4 flyover. Yet, here we are, in a small part of rural farmland Britain!

The allotments themselves are fascinating: some are beautifully laid out with rows of cabbages, beetroot, onions, potatoes; others appear to be totally neglected. Unfortunately, our plot is in the latter category. It is completely overgrown with brambles and something called cooch (or couch) grass, which I realise I shall have to find out about because Keith seems to feel its effect on growing is only marginally better than a nuclear winter. There is, however, a strip down the centre of our plot that has been cleared and covered with a plastic sheet. Keith tells us this was done the previous year by three Lithuanian students. I am not sure why this small strip among the forest of brambles and weeds was cleared or why the clearers were Lithuanian, but it does seem obvious that the reason we have been offered a plot at all is because it is not a plot at all. It will require serious attention before we start to grow anything. I had assumed

that we would be offered a previously cultivated plot which would be
'good to go', so this is a bit of a shock. What's even more of a shock is that
MJ doesn't mind in the least that we are about to accept a jungle of weeds
that would be flattered by the term 'wasteland'. She is chomping at the bit
to get digging, which I suppose I should find encouraging.

We agree to let Keith know our decision and he suggests that we look
around the whole site to get an idea of what can be achieved. As we walk
around we see quite a few people who are already working their plots,
despite it being early on a Sunday morning. I reckon there are at least
fifteen different nationalities and all age groups represented.

On our way out of the site we meet Sheila who, by all accounts, has one
of the best allotments. She is a lovely lady, and she immediately offers us
a glass of white wine. As it is only half past nine in the morning and we
have not yet had breakfast, however, we decline this generous offer. Sheila
is about sixty years old with bleached hair. She is great with our kids, and
invites them to look around at what she has grown; she even gamely
chuckles as Ellie and Richie pull up most of her carrots and trample
through her spinach. In one lovely moment she comes out of her shed
and says, 'Look at my melons', at which MJ shoots me a glance. Sure
enough, however, Sheila has grown melons during the summer, the
seeds of which are drying ready for next year. She also has chillies
growing, which is a big relief for me as it means we should be able to
have spicy food over the next year.

We eventually get home full of enthusiasm. Having initially had
reservations about the plot, I am now ready to write to Tony Tesco
immediately and tell him that I will no longer be visiting his store. It
takes MJ to remind me that our plot is one big, very overgrown patch
that may be some time off supporting the family.

Instead, we spend time strolling through our 'fantasy allotment' full
of all the things I want to cook. Seasonal asparagus, winter kale, hot
and spicy radishes (how they used to taste from my grandpa's garden),
strawberries warm from the sun, and fresh green beans. I can picture
our plot in the months to come being the envy of all Ealing as we happily

harvest our bounty of vegetables. MJ is equally upbeat, and explains to Ellie and Richie the fun that can be had from just being outdoors and at one with nature.

It's funny how such moments of family harmony can be so quickly shattered by a simple comment, this time from Ellie: 'But it's full of weeds and stinging nettles, Mum. When will they clear it up so we can start?'

'We will clear it up, of course,' is my happy response to this witty enquiry. But she is not happy and complains that chopping down stinging nettles is not how she intends to spend her weekends. MJ quickly rescues the situation by saying that Daddy will make a start on it while they are at school. I presume that this, also, must be a joke.

Keith had told us that our plot is 'ten poles' in size; at the time, I had presumed that MJ knew what this meant, so I had kept my ignorance to myself. Now we are home and discussing the allotment I ask her what a 'pole' is exactly. Unfortunately she had presumed *I* knew what Keith meant and so had decided to keep *her* ignorance to herself. We look it up in the dictionary. There, under 'the end of an axis' and 'a native of Poland', is the explanation we are looking for: a pole is a measurement of five and a half yards (about five metres). For some unknown reason this is how allotment folk choose to measure their given space. Ten poles is, therefore, actually damned big – about twenty-five square metres – so MJ suggests we split it down the middle with our friends Dilly and Doug. They have previously expressed a similar gardening urge and we will still have more than enough space to grow what we need as well as having some neighbourly encouragement if we start to flag. Our kids are also far more likely to see the allotment as a good place to go if they might run into Dilly and Doug's children up there.

As far as encouragement goes I realise we will also need help and advice in the coming months on what to plant, where, and when. MJ suggests that she rings her mum and I ring my dad, both of whom are keen gardeners. I also promise to ring Chris Williams, an old friend who is a gardener by profession. My relationship with Chris is primarily based around drunken afternoons at Lord's watching England lose cricket matches so, when I speak to him, he is a bit surprised by my horticultural awakening, but he promises to come over to Blondin to give his considered opinion on the best plan of attack.

Just as we are saying goodbye he casually mentions that I should write up my vegetable-growing experience in the form of a cookery book. When I put the phone down I am struck by the simple brilliance of this suggestion. I have always been the sort of bloke who likes to immerse himself fully in a project. I can envisage sunny days spent toiling on the land and evenings spent writing up recipes cunningly concocted from an array of fruit and vegetables. The more I consider this idea the bigger the project gets. My proposal of avoiding supermarkets, for instance, becomes less about avoidance and more about a total ban: WE WILL LIVE BY THE SEASON AND WE WILL NEVER GO TO THE SUPERMARKET AGAIN.

Later in the day I explain to MJ that it has occurred to me that I could write a book (no need to mention it wasn't my idea) on our experiences, including a selection of recipes, and that there should be a total ban on supermarkets. She immediately rounds on me saying that the whole allotment idea was a family decision and not one that I can hijack and turn into one of my doomed projects.

She is referring, of course, to my previous mission in life, which was to sell our house and move to Zanzibar (a small island in the Indian Ocean). I had researched the whole thing over a couple of weeks on the Internet and realised that, with the proceeds of the house in London, we could afford a crash course in Swahili, standard class flights and still have enough left over to buy a restaurant with some guest rooms once we were there. MJ could educate the children at home, as well as give English lessons to the island's adults. My big mistake on that occasion was to say nothing to MJ during the planning stage and then get caught at home with an estate agent valuing the house. I had even costed up the shipping of our furniture before I had said a word about my idea to her.

This time, though, I promise things will be different. MJ may feel right now that she wants an allotment 'just like everyone else' but, when we get started, she will soon come round.

Despite our differing opinions on the allotment project we are both itching to get started. MJ gives Dilly and Doug a call and the plan to divide the plot in two is agreed.

A few days after accepting the plot we are sent the keys that open the main gates. I presume the gates are needed to keep the local youths from ducking in, when no one is looking, to steal shovels and trowels; it could, of course, be to keep the allotment folk *in* lest they start sowing broad beans and Swiss chard in the local park.

The very next morning, at 7am, I am at the allotment to meet Chris Williams. As a gardener, Chris knows lots about plants and, to prove this, he, like Keith, has a beard. As he pulls up in his truck, I walk over and swing open the gates for my first visit as an official paid-up allotmenteer. As we walk down the path towards my patch, Chris points out various plants, to which he knows not only the English names, but also the Latin. We pass plots full of cabbages and sprouts and kale and I can see that Chris is already impressed with the efforts of my fellow amateur gardeners.

Eventually we reach my plot and, almost immediately, Chris's jaw drops. I ask him if he has spotted an obvious problem and he replies that, in 30 years of gardening, he has never taken on such an overgrown patch of land with a view to doing anything more than turning it into *a slightly less* overgrown patch of land.

Positive thinking is crucial on such an occasion so I explain that, when we came to look at the site, I saw a man clearing an old vegetable bed with a large bionic lawnmower-like machine. This strikes me as a fairly fast way of digging the ground once we have cleared the brambles and assorted weeds so surely we could use one of these things to 'plough' our plot.

Chris has bad news on this front. The rotivator – the name of the machine – is not a good idea where cooch grass is concerned; it chops it up and spreads it out, which means that it effectively re-sows it. It turns out that Chris has driven all the way over just to tell me to buy a spade and dig it by hand.

On the subject of self-sufficiency, Chris is scarcely more help, pointing out that it is doubtful if we will be able to survive; I have freely admitted to him that the first and last thing I have ever grown was cannabis when I was a teenager – and that died before it ever saw a Rizla!

It is almost 8am and it's cold, so cold that I am beginning to understand why so many gardeners have beards. As Chris and I walk back to the gate, he stresses again that, in his view, the best way to remove all our cooch grass is by hand, and then, as he climbs into his truck, he winds down the window to deliver one final bit of encouragement, 'If you keep removing every bit of cooch grass that springs up, you will find that, within three years, you will have got rid of the lot.' With this cheery advice in mind, I walk back up Boston Road in the freezing cold.

Back home I sit down for breakfast with MJ and explain that Chris is a little pessimistic about our chances of survival. She immediately takes the line that, if we just grow as much as we can, that, in itself, will be an achievement. I explain that this would be fine for most people, but that this is now a 'project' and the rules of it are clear – we have an allotment and we have to survive independently, with no backup from food shops.

Sensing my despair, MJ suggests that we drive up to Homebase to see what sheds they have on display. Up to this point I haven't even considered that we will need a shed, but, on reflection, it is obvious. I also wonder if we should look into buying a caravan so that we can spend entire weekends on the plot, but MJ convinces me that we should just stick with a shed for now.

A couple of days later Chris calls to see how we are getting on and I sheepishly admit that we haven't been down to the allotment since I met him there. I do let on, though, that I am up for his book idea and that I have put a proposal in the post to a couple of publishers.

Before he rings off, Chris tells me that his wife, Stella, googled the word Blondin, as she believed it was actually a person's name. It turns out she is right and he suggests we take a look. Mr Blondin was a famous tightrope walker who notoriously crossed the Niagara Falls on a tightrope in 1859. He didn't stop there, though; he crossed it again and again, each time using a different theatrical variation: he carried a man across on his back; he pushed a wheelbarrow across; he did it blindfold; and he even did it on stilts.

Blondin performed at Crystal Palace in 1862 where Charles Dickens declared, 'half of London is here eager for some dreadful accident'. Nice. Blondin did not grant Mr Dickens his ghoulish wish; instead he pushed his five-year-old daughter across a 55-metre high rope in a wheelbarrow. It took an intervention by the Home Secretary to stop him repeating this particular version.

All of this is very interesting but seems to have little to do with cabbages. Stella, however, had discovered that he eventually moved to England and ended his days on Northfield Avenue, which is the main road just off which are ... you guessed it, Blondin Allotments. With a list of achievements like his, the very least I would expect is a large bronze statue. Instead there are 112 amateur vegetable gardeners working on an allotment named in his honour. And now, I am one of them.

Although we are yet to really make an impact on our small section of the Earth's crust, I am busy reading up on food issues big and small. My new-found passion is fuelled by well-wishers. I receive text messages from my dad, who reads *Nature* magazine, telling me of a crisis in North Sea fish stocks; I receive emails from friends with pictures of phallic-shaped vegetables (this possibly says more about my friends than it does about my green agenda); and a friend, Greg, drops off a book that he suggests I read. The book, called *Not on the Label* and written by Felicity Lawrence, explores the truth about supermarket food. It's the sort of book I would have run a mile from just a short while ago but now I am hooked – it makes fascinating, yet scary, reading. I have never fully realised the impact these large superstores have on all areas of our lives, and, by the time I have read the introduction, I am already a committed eco-warrior!

Feeling particularly militant I drive off to Tesco for the last time. Inside the shop I already feel like a stranger prowling the shelves, despairing at the labels of origin on the beans and tomatoes, and all that packaging, all those air miles. As I drive away from the shop I note those things I shall miss most:

> Tesco cheese and pickle pork pies
> Tesco Finest vanilla ice cream
> Tesco Finest dry-cured bacon
> Tesco Finest cider
> Tesco pancetta and Parmesan sausages
> Tesco Finest cookies

But, despite the loss of these, I make a point of sitting down with the family to discuss the idea of buying all our cleaning stuff, tinned food, dry goods and sundries from local stores, so that we need not physically enter a supermarket for one year as of now.

The trouble with MJ is that she lacks the true heart of a subversive. She will not suffer for the cause and tells me in no uncertain terms that she won't rule out supermarkets; her reason is that they are convenient – so much for her militancy. She does look pretty fired up when she tells me this, so I compromise by agreeing that dry goods, tins and general 'stuff' can still come from the supermarket, but we should start to buy all our meat, fish, bread and vegetables (until our production line begins) from local shops.

As MJ and I continue our conversion to the church of culinary Puritanism, we can't help noticing that our children are somewhat underwhelmed by the whole thing. Up to this point we have not really canvassed their opinion on the whole allotment 'Should we/Shouldn't we' question, because we have been so sure it will be good for them. They do think it will be great meeting their friends at the allotment, but they are already voicing concerns about having to eat all the vegetables that Dad is so convinced he will grow.

Over the years, I have spent a lot of time encouraging, coercing, even bribing and ultimately forcing my children to eat well. Vegetables are often the source of our discussions. On one occasion I explained that they had to eat their vegetables, if only from a health point of view. I went to great length to explain the 'five portions a day' rule and pointed out, when they argued, that this wasn't my idea, that it was actually a government initiative. Still they argued, and, in utter desperation, I told them that, if they didn't like what I was telling them, they should write to the Prime Minister Tony Blair – or the Queen for that matter – and take up the issue with them.

The next morning I came down to breakfast to find the following letter written by Richie to the Queen:

To call his bluff I made him address an envelope and send it. Then we got back to normal, resuming mealtime conflicts and bribery. Two months passed and then, through the letterbox, fell an envelope addressed to Richie and emblazoned with the royal stamp. We could hardly believe what we saw when Richie opened the envelope. The Queen herself had written back. I'd show you the real letter here . . .

....but unfortunately her majesty only gives vegetable consumption advice on a strictly one to one basis and won't let me print the letter, so you'll just have to take my word on it (lest she chop off my head.)

The truth is that the letter was actually written on behalf of the Queen by the Senior Correspondence Officer who said that the Queen thanked Richie for writing and that she thought it was thoughtful of him to tell her that I want him to eat more fruit and veg. She then suggested Richie look up information on the web about what children should be eating. Funny, I had never pictured the Queen surfing the 'net'.

She then mentioned that she was going to forward Richie's letter to Patricia Hewitt MP, the Secretary of State for Health. Well, sure enough, soon after we received the following letter (which the Department for Health is very happy about my showing you here):

(DH) Department of Health

Our ref: TO00000114105

Richmond House
79 Whitehall
London
SW1A 2NS

Tel: 020 7210 5812

Mr Richie Merrett

Dear Mr Merrett,

Thank you for your letter of 29 March to Her Majesty The Queen about eating fruit and vegetables. As The Queen's Correspondence Officer told you in her response, your letter has been sent to the Department of Health for reply. I am sorry it has taken a long time for you to receive an answer from this Department.

The Department of Health thinks that it is a good idea for people to eat at least five portions of different fruit and vegetables each day. The 5 A DAY message is that all types of fruit and vegetables count. Fresh, frozen, chilled, canned and dried fruit and vegetables, 100 per cent juice and smoothies can all be part of your 5 A DAY.

An adult portion of fruit or vegetables is equivalent to about 80 grams. However, some foods, such as fruit juice or smoothies, count as only one portion, even if you eat or drink a lot.

If you look at the website www.5aday.nhs.uk, you can find out lots of information about fruit and vegetables, and you can even download a chart to make sure you are eating five portions a day.

I hope this reply is helpful, and that you are starting to enjoy eating delicious, healthy food.

Yours sincerely,

Daniel Spinner
Customer Service Centre
Department of Health

By then vegetable consumption was a hot topic in our house – any green thing served was eaten 'because the Queen says so'. And I hope to keep it as a hot topic.

While bribery and torture can work in getting children to eat vegetables, however, I still hope that the best way to 'sell' vegetables to the young is to pick them fresh and cook them with care. A strawberry fresh from the plant and still warm from the sun will always taste better than a bought one, and the same will apply to a cabbage and even the dreaded sprout. My job is to convince my children of this.

Forget AA Gill or Michael Winner. Ellie and Richie are my toughest food critics. Yet, with the allotment now secure, I believe it is only a matter of time before garden-fresh vegetables are getting the Michelin treatment and being eaten with glee!

MJ and I have big plans for the allotment: we discuss dishes we love and note the vegetables we require as we discuss a growing plan. By this time next year we will be 'grow your own' bores who turn up at friends' houses for dinner with a pointed cabbage and half a kilo of broad beans instead of a bottle of wine.

Nothing can stop us now.

Chapter 3 | The Ealing Project

Despite our early enthusiasm, Christmas has come and gone without a single trip to the allotment. We have thought about going but the festive season just kept getting in the way.

Strangely, however, both MJ and I have demonstrated our commitment to the future in the form of Christmas gifts. My main present from the kids is a portable gas stove. MJ tells me that it is for making tea, but I have bigger ideas. We will carry out 'from earth to pot' experiments with all the vegetables we grow by eating them as soon as they are picked.

My gifts on the other hand are seriously 'correct'. I have done most of my shopping on the Centre for Alternative Technology website. MJ is the main beneficiary of this environmentally aware shopping spree and I shall always remember her joyful expression as she unwrapped: her new water siphon especially designed to remove 'grey' water from the bath to use on the garden; a reusable J cloth; a notepad made from elephant shit; and a (reusable) string bag for shopping – in local stores obviously. She just looked so happy.

When it comes to the allotment itself, the truth is that, since we got the keys, we have not found, nor made, the time to visit. MJ is retraining as a teacher and I am at the pre-production stage of a TV series called *Ever*

Wondered about Food..., which will be filmed during February. We are
both simply too busy, and are perhaps slightly daunted by the task ahead.
To compound the situation, the temperature has plummeted to minus
two degrees and the thought of digging in this weather is too much
to bear.

The trouble is that we are constantly reminded of the allotment. Each
time we drive down Boston Road past the gates that lead to Blondin,
one of the kids will call out, 'that's where the allotment is' (or 'lotment,
as Richie calls it). MJ and I just grimace and mutter empty promises
that contain the words 'next weekend'. It is now two months since we
inherited our plot and it's hard to ignore Keith's echoing words about
eviction after three months of neglect.

That cold November morning we had been filled with so much hope
for the future – a future full of vegetables – and I had worked hard
over Christmas convincing MJ that my allotment project, including a
supermarket ban and a book of our achievements, was a good idea.
She had only come around when I had received a positive response
from HarperCollins about publishing a book – she couldn't bear to
crush my excitement, I expect.

In early January I had gone to meet a lady at HarperCollins called Jenny
who had bowled me over with her enthusiasm for my book. She fully
agreed that a supermarket ban should take place and I had confidently
told her that I would start right away. This had been somewhat foolhardy
as we hadn't lifted a single nettle, let alone planted anything, and now,
another month on, I am beginning to envisage a cookery book with no
recipes and no story.

Our weekly trips to the supermarket are carrying on unchecked. At first
I had refused to go myself, but now even I am resigned to the fact that,
until we get the allotment up and running, the supermarket is our only
hope.

Towards the end of February, we have Dilly and Doug over for lunch (no
prizes for guessing where the ingredients came from). As we sit around
the table, the conversation drifts into choppy waters when MJ mentions

the allotment. It comes as a huge relief to learn that they have also not visited their half of the plot and are wrestling with the desire to pack it all in before they start.

At meetings like these, you need a leader, someone who stands up and bangs their fist in defiance of the gloom. I'm not about to lead anyone anywhere, but my wife is made of sterner stuff. She leans on the back of the chair and makes a stirring speech along the lines of, 'We will conquer this patch of land. Paul's even going to write a book and he's never going to a supermarket again – ever. And we are behind him one hundred per cent.' It does the trick; all of a sudden we are four gardeners around a table ready to dig at a moment's notice. We all agree that we will get down to the allotment and show our mettle … next weekend.

It is March – and still bloody freezing – when we take our first visit to the allotment. We have now had the plot for over three months and have failed to scupper a single weed. Dilly and Doug, and their children Eddie and Sylvie, join us so that we can divide the one very big plot into two smaller ones as per the original plan. Standing, shivering, in the middle of a frozen jungle that we have been silly enough to pay for, we agree ends and decide that a shared shed shall be the dividing line.

Our plot is so overgrown that it's difficult to know where to start; the whole area is a mass of tall grass, brambles and nettles. I feel the best way forwards is to go home, make a nice cup of tea and sit down in the warm to devise a plan of attack, but MJ counters that meetings simply get in the way of progress. We have brief words before she grabs the only shovel we own and starts randomly digging like a woman possessed.

As this is really the extent of our garden tool kit my choices appear to be limited to standing in one spot and shivering, or standing in another spot and shivering. Eventually I decide to make a fire with the kids. One of the points of this mad folly is to give the kids a bit of outdoor life, so we collect as much wood and dried grass as possible and are soon all standing, hands held out, around a blazing fire like some 1970s workforce at odds with our employers.

As the day wears on, it becomes increasingly obvious that we need some sort of plan if we are going to defeat this tangled, weedy corner of Ealing; even MJ, when she joins us around the fire, has to admit as much. MJ, Dilly, Doug and I decide to concentrate on a small area that will eventually be the spot for our shed. The next two hours are spent pulling up brambles and digging down six inches until we have a relatively flat space.

A shed is a vital addition to an allotment; everyone who has an allotment has a shed. It means we can begin to buy some tools and store them on-site, and also that we will then have somewhere to shelter from the more extreme weather.

Sheds, of course, are joked about as some last domain of male authority, a place where a bloke can go when everything gets too much. I have never thought of myself as the shed type but, as I look at the patch of cleared ground, it is easy to get excited about the structure waiting to stand there.

We are the allotment that is furthest west so our shed will be like an outpost in the other west. The wild one. I start to ponder the whole shed thing and realise that I could really get used to having a shed. I then consider the five things I need in my shed:

1. A radio – for football results, the *Today* programme and *Woman's Hour*
2. A kettle – for making tea
3. A camping stove – to boil the kettle (to make that tea)
4. A chair – well, you can't stand during your tea break; it might have to be collapsible
5. A barbecue

The other thing every allotment worker has is a compost heap. These come in various guises. Some are simply piles of vegetation left exposed to the elements; others are elaborately constructed from old wooden pallets; some are even the more modern type – a green plastic drum with a removable lid.

We have the latter variety – MJ had accepted the council's offer of a subsidised compost bin and had given it to me for Christmas (ooh, lucky me!). After some discussion, we decide to put the compost bin at the outer edge of our plot. MJ feels that it might pong a bit during the summer, so we shouldn't put it too near to where we will be working.

It's worth mentioning that, as well as a shed and a compost bin, there is something else that marks a gardener out from the crowd – his or her wardrobe. It includes: stout sensible boots; lightweight practical trousers with lots of pockets; thermal shirts (preferably with a checked pattern); waterproofs for wet weather; and thick socks. This is the type of clobber you will find yourself wearing should you take up the challenge to 'grow your own'. Incidentally, this is also the sort of clothing over which I seriously considered divorcing my parents when I was young, so I have tried to avoid it at all costs!

The following Saturday, nursing a monster hangover, I go to watch Brentford crush Barnsley (3–1). Over a Friday night beer, Chris, his wife Stella and I discussed all things horticultural, and I awake to find not only that I have a serious headache but also that I have in my pocket a list of tips on: growing tomatoes, killing slugs, types of weedkiller and building sheds. It seems that I can't escape the allotment, even while drunk!

As the haze clears, I remember talking enthusiastically about the task ahead. Chris listened intently as I told him that we have begun the ground assault. He agreed that a shed is absolutely vital and pointed out that we will also need to start thinking about garden tools.

Stella asked if we had planted anything and I had to admit that, so far, I have only thought about clearing our space because that, in itself, is such an immense task. She suggested taking it bit by bit. Her view is that we might be spurred on once we have something in the ground. This is probably very true but the thought of actually planting anything has seemed further off every time I have considered it.

It had taken Dilly, Doug, MJ and me the best part of a day to clear a relatively small patch for the shed, so I am already beginning to redraw the ground rules of our project. I consider pushing back the whole self-sufficiency thing to next year, by which time I hope all the weeds will have been removed. Stella's suggestion, on the other hand, will allow us to clear and plant a certain area and then move on to the next section.

After the match, despite still feeling a bit rusty, I join MJ, Ellie and Richie for a spot of digging with some new shovels. We all dig for a solid three hours until at last the base for the shed is fully dug and we can lay down the reclaimed paving stones that will act as the foundations for our yet-to-be-purchased Homebase shed. This small measure of progress is encouraging and we soon begin to tackle another small corner of the plot just as Stella had suggested.

It fast becomes apparent that weed clearing is, quite literally, the tip of the problem. The patch of land that is now free of brambles and nettles has all sorts buried in it – we have uncovered glass, metal rods, bricks, medicine bottles (why?), gardening gloves (six pairs), shoes, rusty beer cans (lots of these!), and other assorted rubbish, and it feels as though we have inherited a landfill site rather than an allotment.

I am sure there are some who would feel that all this preliminary work makes the eventual harvest more rewarding. MJ and I, however, reckon eating vegetables minus the graft is just as rewarding, and we can't help wishing we had inherited a recently vacated and lovingly cared for plot that had only just been dug over and maybe had a mature pear tree in one corner.

Back at home the allotment is also having an effect on our daily lives. As the project develops I am finding myself thinking more about our life in general. Every news bulletin seems to include some further evidence of the environmental destruction of the planet. I have long been aware of this but now, as I begin to live in tandem with the earth (well, I *have* dug a couple of holes), I realise that there is possibly a bigger effect to be had from the allotment than simply putting food on the table.

MJ agrees with me that we, as a family, could make a bigger contribution to the planet-saving drive than we currently do. We have long been
recycling paper, glass and plastic, but, to be honest, we could increase our
efforts. I resolve to change all our light bulbs to energy-saving ones as
soon as I can and, in the meantime, I sit the kids down and deliver a
stirring lecture on the need to switch off lights when they leave a room
(to be honest, this is a bit rich coming from me as I am possibly the worst
offender in the house). I also advise the children to consider the amount
of water they use. I sound like Al Gore as I stand in front of these two
slightly bewildered children describing scenes of a sun-baked African
village where children ('much younger than you') are forced to walk miles
to a waterhole or pump before carrying a heavy container of water all the
way back to their home. Once again, the irony of my speech is obvious
– I have never once turned a tap off while brushing my teeth or put the
plug in when washing a saucepan. However, I am not the first great leader
to fail to practise what they preach and I do at least intend to change
forthwith. From now on, baths are banned unless it's your birthday and
teeth must be brushed with no more than a cup of water. Ellie is horrified
to learn that the toilet will only be flushed after number twos and that
showers have a three-minute maximum time allowance.

By this point, my children are quite used to my sudden bursts of
enthusiasm over some life-changing project or another and it is obvious
that they see these new house rules as nothing more than Dad's latest
rant. However, they look quite shocked that their mum is in full
agreement, rather than raising her eyebrows as she normally does
when Dad goes off on one.

I really think that, if we are to be self-sufficient from our allotment, then
we should embrace the whole lifestyle package. One clearly cannot expect
credit for growing a carrot if one's bin is stuffed full of plastic. With my
convictions sharpened to peak condition, I turn up for a meeting at
HarperCollins. I had known Jenny was behind the supermarket ban, but,
when we discuss my green credentials, it soon becomes apparent that a
spot of token recycling will not be tolerated. I will not be allowed to write

a book about green living unless I do in fact 'live green'. It occurs to me that I may have rather over-egged our green credentials and that actually we may not stand up to scrutiny, but there's nothing like a challenge, and my family are more than up for it.

Back at the plot, work continues. The shed base is ready, the compost bin has had its first delivery (a salad Ellie and Richie refused to eat!) and now the task of carving out and digging our first bed can begin.

This involves hardcore digging. Each spade load is a mixture of earth, stones and bric-a-brac. After a whole Saturday toiling on the land we can dig no more. It's back home for a quick supper then straight to bed for all of us – Saturday night and I'm in bed at half past nine. Vegetable growing sure is one crazy lifestyle!

A day's digging can make you feel fairly healthy – you are outdoors and it's good honest physical work – similar to running a marathon (I expect). It's the next day, however, that puts those healthy thoughts in perspective. Needless to say, I wake the following morning to find my hamstrings are so tight that it feels as though they have been tuned overnight by the ghost of Jimi Hendrix – I can't scratch my bum let alone touch my toes.

I eventually drag myself from the bed, go downstairs and almost immediately have a row with MJ over the allotment. I say we should have a day off; she disagrees and says she seriously doubts my commitment. Having said this, she grabs the kids and storms off to the allotment. I mooch about at home feeling a bit guilty for an hour or so and, in the end, think the best thing to do is to go down to the allotment, eat a slab of humble pie and show a bit willing.

I eventually manage to lift my leg high enough to get it over the cross-bar of my bicycle and, with a genuine feeling of goodwill, I very slowly make my way up Boston Road to the allotment. Dilly and Doug are there starting on a bed their side of the divide; MJ is digging away and all the kids are charging about, filthy, and having a great time.

Having told MJ that I am sorry for my anti-allotment tendencies and reaffirmed my commitment, I grab the shovel and, with a look of resolve in my eye, I throw myself into the task in hand. On the third dig I fall to my knees in complete agony – I literally crumple up; my back clicks and gives way and I am so sore I can hardly move. I have been there for ten minutes and am now reduced to a writhing wreck. I feel a complete fool as MJ and Doug carry me to the car to take me home.

But what makes the experience so much more humiliating is that, after I have been carted home, MJ returns to the allotment where she meets Keith, the committee Chairman. He obviously takes pity on this poor husbandless woman digging her vegetable patch and offers to bring over his rotivator; he proceeds to clear half the plot in ten minutes.

It's bad enough to be humiliated in such a way, but we have also used a rotivator to clear cooch grass, which is exactly what we were told to avoid doing. I had told MJ Chris's warning about spreading the cooch grass, and she had quite obviously ignored my advice.

To make matters worse, Keith tells MJ that, since it's March, our first bed should really be put aside for potatoes as they are due to be planted soon. On the back of this, MJ has bought three bags of seed potatoes on her way home … at bloody Tesco. Now the very shop we are working so hard to avoid, has sold us the first thing we are going to plant.

I ask MJ what variety of potato she has bought, determined to pour scorn on whatever strain she has got (huh, Desirée are *so common*, we'll simply have to take them back), but she finds that the labels aren't attached so we don't even know what our potatoes are. I am away from the project (due to a serious industrial injury) for two hours and, all of a sudden, the whole thing has gone tits up.

There's no doubt that allotments are dangerous places – I see the osteopath three times in one week. On my first visit, Mal next door literally has to carry me to his car and slide me in horizontally across the back seats, before driving me up to the Old Isleworth surgery. It is obvious to me that Stuart the osteopath had rarely seen a man as badly injured and he has to draw on all his experience to gain me just a little comfort. He uses gels, manipulation and acupuncture to relieve the pain. I am not able to walk, sit, lie or stand with any comfort, though sympathy at home is, quite frankly, in short supply.

A few days later I go to our local garden centre with MJ. She has spoken to her mum about our imminent potato patch and has been told that, before we plant them, we should get some manure dug in. My back is still so sore I can hardly get in the car, but I manage to hobble about pointing at the things I think we should buy before returning to the car and collapsing once more. People give me very strange looks as I sit in the car and watch my poor wife load three twenty-kilogram bags of manure into the boot!

After lunch we return to the allotment, where MJ digs in her manure (not *her* manure obviously – we are not that green yet) and plants our unknown variety of potatoes that she has so carelessly purchased from the supermarket. I am still way off 'planting fitness' and, to be honest, I feel that, since she has taken the decision to buy the things regardless of the fact that we have not done a stitch of research on the topic, she can darn well plant them. I (slowly) terminate weeds with a (very light) can of (hopefully green) weedkiller that we bought.

We arrive home to a phone message from Doug saying that he is picking up the shed and we can put it up the next day. This will make going to the allotment a whole lot less hassle as we can leave stuff there.

The next morning my back is still sore but I am determined to get the shed up. I meet Doug at the allotment at 11am and we get cracking; cracking probably isn't the right word as we make painfully slow progress. We have purchased the cheapest shed in the shop (1.8 x 1.2 metres/6 x 4 feet); it is tiny but it still takes us the best part of four hours to assemble. This is not only because the assembly instructions have been written, I reckon, by a dyslexic foreign teenager on work experience at B&Q, nor completely due to me being bent double with a serious back injury, but also because of the never-ending stream of goodwilled advice from our allotment neighbours. The gist of this advice is as follows:

1. Face the shed into the prevailing wind (north?) or else it will blow away in a high wind
2. Have the door on the south side so that we can sit outside when the sun shines
3. Have the window facing south southeast (or something) so the rain doesn't get in

As neither Doug nor I have a compass on us, we decide to just get the thing erected and take our chances with nature. Having put it up we realise that good old B&Q has given us the wrong size of roof boards and we are about six inches too short. Rather than go all the way back to the shop, we decide to bodge it together with a couple of redundant floorboards that we find lying about; I feel this represents the green option both in recycling the floorboards and also in terms of saving fuel emissions by not driving back to the shop (actually, we simply couldn't be arsed to go all the way back – sometimes 'green' is the easy option).

During the final stages of construction the kids join us and Sheila pops over to chat to them. On seeing us finishing the shed, she delivers the most useful advice of the day – always remember to keep an emergency bottle of wine hidden in the shed in case there is a thunderstorm. This gem apparently comes from her experience one time when she was stuck in her shed for almost two hours without a drop to drink!

Despite the shed being in place, the allotment continues to feel like it will never be conquered and, as a novice, it's really hard to see it taking shape. It is now April; the only things we have planted are a few potatoes, and the part of the plot that isn't knee-high in weeds is still so strewn with rubble that it will take days to clear.

On top of all this, it turns out that on the Friday when I got very drunk with Chris, he apparently offered me (and I accepted) 50 cubic metres of topsoil. This is great – it is good quality soil and will help our digging efforts – but 50 cubic metres weighs around 6 tonnes and I have one wheelbarrow and a bad back. If it comes soon I shall have to tell MJ to shift it, which could see me on the receiving end of a spot of domestic violence.

Allotments aren't all about marital strife and industrial injury though. We now have crops in the ground, something to look forward to. Ok, so they weren't quite planted to plan but at least they're in the ground.

The fun in this vegetable growing game is in the anticipation. Having sown our potatoes, it is hard not to start imagining what I will cook with them. The potatoes are of an unknown variety – they could be new potatoes, waxy or floury – so, for the time being, I am content just to imagine eating as many chunky chips as I want.

Chapter 4 | Read What You Sow

Back pain doesn't really have an upside but, in my case, having been banned from digging for seven days by my osteopath, I at least have the opportunity to do some reading and research into this allotment business.

Over the years I have accumulated a mass of cookery books, which has cost me a fortune. Where gardening is concerned, I am reluctant to do the same, so we decide to rely on four or five books for advice. I now see the chance to get stuck into each of them. As with any subject, each writer has his or her particular take on the gardening question. I don't really know which books are the best to buy, so the following short list is simply my choice rather than the ultimate selection:

1. Geoff Hamilton – *Gardeners' World Practical Gardening Course*
I don't know where I got this book but it's been on the shelf for ages. Geoff was a man who liked to lean on a hoe and gaze wisely at the camera – he reminds me a bit of my grandpa with his checked shirts and sensible shoes. He writes quite well and doesn't presume the reader is already an expert; he includes lots of pictures, which is helpful, though a little intimidating as his vegetable gardens are totally perfect.

2. Dr DG Hessayon – *The Vegetable and Herb Expert*
It would be tempting to dismiss anyone who called themselves a
'vegetable expert' as a horticultural megalomaniac, but he is a doctor
and that must mean he's well qualified. The book is basically a page
per vegetable, and outlines growing methods, pest control, cooking
advice (steady on doctor – my territory), and varieties of plants.

3. Alan Titchmarsh – *Gardeners' World Complete Book of Gardening*
Everyone knows Alan Titchmarsh. I met him once when I was working
at The Greenhouse (the restaurant, that is), and he was a charming man.
His books are very informative and you feel you can trust him (people
say this about Delia Smith with regard to cooking, and they do share the
same haircut). His outlook is a more modern one than Geoff's so it will
be a good balance.

4. Edward C Smith – *The Vegetable Gardener's Bible*
This book claims to contain all you need to know about successful
vegetable growing; however, I seem to have fallen for the word 'bible'
in the title. Cookery writers have employed the same trick – *The Bible
of French Cookery* or *French Culinary Bible* would be obvious titles – but
generally they are written by people who spend two weeks a year in
the Dordogne and claim to know all there is to know about French
cookery despite the fact that they wouldn't know Marc Veyrat if he
married their daughter. (Actually, thinking about it, Alan Titchmarsh
has done *Songs of Praise* so, from the Divine's point of view, he would
get the nod on using 'bible' in the title.) Anyhow, to get back to Mr
Smith's book, every subject from soil testing to pruning is covered
with helpful step-by-step pictures.

Pictures are a really important element because you really do want some
idea of the final result before you start to dig (or whisk).
    All of these books contain fabulous pictures of finished vegetable beds
burgeoning with peas, beans, tomatoes and just about any other vegetable

you can think of; this can, though, leave one a little frustrated if, like us, your vegetable plot currently consists of a shed, a compost bin, a potato patch and a vast uncultivated area. All the books do, however, give practical advice on starting out, and it is obvious to me that we should give some thought to how the finished plot will look.

There are more ways than one to plant a cabbage, apparently, so it is important to think ahead. At this stage two questions need to be answered:

1. Are we the 'plant in row' traditionalist types, or are we going to have raised beds?
2. How are we going to deal with crop rotation?

I turn first to the issue of raised bed versus traditional row sowing. My grandpa's vegetable patch was a succession of perfect rows, each one a different vegetable – this is the 'row' method and it allows the gardener to walk between the plants to weed and water. The modernists are not satisfied with this tried and tested method, however, so they have come up with a new method called 'raised bed' growing. Here, one builds the bed up above ground level and then sows in blocks so that, when mature, each plant is touching its neighbour (sounds like a dodgy council estate!), thus producing very high yields. This is apparently done in narrow beds so all watering and weeding is done from the edge of the beds. Geoff Hamilton is a 'plant in rows' man and he does look like the type you can trust, but Titchmarsh reckons one shouldn't overlook the block planting method and he's done OK for himself, so the jury is still out.

Next up it's crop rotation. All the books agree that crop rotation is a must. This is for two reasons: if a bug knows that every May his or her favourite food will be in abundance then he or she just sits and waits for the harvest to begin, so crop rotation thwarts pests and disease; secondly, certain plants sap the soil of certain nutrients so, if one sows a different type of crop in a plot each year, the nutrients remain at a consistent level.

This is all well and good but here's the snag – the authors can't agree on how many beds one should be rotating. The vegetable expert Dr DG Hessayon suggests three beds – roots, brassicas and 'others'. Geoff

Hamilton enjoys a little more rotating with four beds, though one of these he suggests is for permanent crops (as yet, I am not sure what permanent crops are). Compared to these, Alan Titchmarsh takes a 'radical' view suggesting (correctly, in my opinion) that both DG Hessayon's and Geoff Hamilton's systems require equal space for each crop type, which can result in yielding slightly more root vegetables than is fashionable to eat. He, however, has a picture of three beds with an enormous list down the side of the page showing what he is growing, including nasturtium, Florence fennel, rocket and coriander (Geoff will be turning in his grave at this list: 'Where are your turnips and swede, Alan lad?').

My gut feeling on all the above is to sit down with MJ and decide what we want to eat, then group the list into types of vegetables and take a view on how many beds we can logistically chop our allotment into. We both agree to limit the rotational beds to three: legumes, brassicas and root vegetables will all get a similar sized bed and be moved to the neighbouring bed the following year. On the row versus raised bed issue, I decide to go with tradition – and the seemingly easier option – and sow at ground level in rows.

Further reading reveals that permanent crops are those plants that are only planted once: rhubarb, soft fruit, perennial herbs and asparagus all need a permanent site. I reckon that, if we concentrate on getting these beds dug and planted, at least we will feel we have made progress. My plan is to line these beds with old floorboards so they are defined in area; this will also make the digging feel more achievable.

With my osteopath's digging ban now at an end, and having read up on the relevant topics, I am ready for some serious allotment action. I get up full of enthusiasm and head to the local garden centre. As I walk towards the entrance, I have the same feeling of excitement and anticipation I used to feel as I approached HMV. Now, rather than wondering if I will come out with an Otis Redding CD or one by Bob Dylan, however, I have string and nails on my mind. Actually 'String and Nails on my Mind' does sound like it could well be a track by Bob Dylan, but this is a complete coincidence.

I have never been good at sticking to budgets and I decide that I will
buy everything we need to kit out our shed on this one visit. String, nails,
wire, hooks, soil-testing kit, forks, trowel, rake and a very necessary pink
barbecue set are all purchased and then carted back to Blondin. The afternoon is spent hammering in nails and hooks and putting up shelves and,
by the time I leave, the shed is beginning to look like it is a real gardening
shed, albeit with very shiny tools. The pink barbecue is given to Ellie and I
promise to teach her how to cook on it.

The Easter holiday arrives and with it comes the first serious sign of
dissent in the camp. Ellie and Richie are far from thrilled to learn that Mum
and Dad intend to spend most of the holidays moving things on at the
allotment. I think they both feel that they are the victims of a huge con. Back
in November, when we explained to them what an allotment was and why
we should have one, I seriously played up the plus points (as anyone would
when trying to encourage an unconvinced third party). I promised them that
the allotment would be huge fun: bonfires, digging big holes, picking
strawberries, pulling carrots, finding frogs, having barbecues; in truth, the
only things ticked off that list so far are bonfires and digging big holes –
and there are only so many holes you can dig with a smile on your face.

At this rate, I realise that they will hate the place by the time we have it
up and running, and this will be a serious crisis. We are so keen for them
to enjoy the allotment. Yet, if we are honest with ourselves, we have to
admit that we would have felt the same at their age – the difference is
that our parents wouldn't have cared. We do care, though, and it has
always been important to us that we all enjoy the allotment.

MJ points out to them that part of our reason for taking the allotment
was out of guilt. As children, we had both enjoyed a childhood in the
countryside with all the freedom that brings. We had seen the allotment
as going some way towards giving them that outdoor life that we had

deprived them of by deciding to live in London. What we had possibly not recognised was that our kids might be urbanised beyond repair. Allotments are as foreign to them and their peers as the current Arsenal football team. As Ellie explained: why would they want to go to the allotment when they could be playing on the PlayStation? So, while MJ and I are both free spirits who have settled in London through convenience, our children are Londoners born and bred. We have given birth to Chas and Dave!

Obviously, there are times when the call of the allotment is simply too strong to resist and, at these times, you just have to drag the kids there kicking and screaming, but we have discovered that there are ways to encourage the children to get involved. You can sit the little darlings down and calmly explain that the planet is in trouble and needs our help; possibly they can be convinced that the outdoor life that is on offer is one that can enhance their lives way beyond the reach of a Game Boy or an iPod; or you can simply resort to bribery ...

Easter Monday starts with coffee and hot cross buns, and the conversation centres around the fifth family member – the allotment.

'Well, kids, where would you like to go today: Chessington World of Adventures or the allotment?'

'Oh, Dad, not Chessington again. Let's go and dig.'

That conversation never took place over breakfast because, right now, my children would rather go to school than the allotment. I offer several packets of football cards and a kilogram of chewy sweets but still they complain so, in the end, MJ suggests that we can go to Chessington later in the week if they come to the allotment today, and they finally yield. This is great, but how do we get them there tomorrow? We shall soon be offering skiing trips or safaris if we continue to up the stakes.

The day starts with a trip to the garden centre (I am rapidly becoming a regular), where we buy some paint for the shed – chosen by Ellie. Then we meet Dilly and Doug and their children at the allotment.

Progress is being made. MJ and I have started digging an area of about eight feet (2.4 metres) square, which will be our asparagus bed. The problem is that we are still having to sieve every spadeful for debris – I feel like I'm a pastry chef once more sieving icing sugar (though this is a lot more heavy!). An entire morning is devoted to this thankless task and this is just eight square feet.

I finally finish off the asparagus bed and then MJ and I make a start on the rhubarb bed. While we dig, the kids all paint the shed – it is lavender and marine-blue stripes, and is, without doubt, the smartest construction on the entire allotment site (personally, I wanted to do red and white stripes in honour of Brentford FC but I was overruled). They have done a great job and, by the time we leave, most of our allotment neighbours have come over to admire their work.

One of them, John, tells us of an allotment hosepipe ban put in place by Ealing Council, despite it being only April. I get the impression he sees this as nothing less than botanical murder by the council but, frankly, with nothing planted bar potatoes, we couldn't care. So, despite this news, and after what has been a really good day, we fire up the barbecue. As we eat, we can see the progress we have already made: a potato patch, a compost bin, a very smart blue and purple shed, an asparagus bed with freshly sieved soil, and a rhubarb bed half finished. And all this domestic bliss for just the price of entry to Chessington World of Adventures.

The following week school restarts and MJ gets back to work, leaving me lots of time to spend at the allotment. I finish digging the rhubarb bed and get it manured and lined with floorboards; one of my neighbours is a builder called Richard who does loft conversions, so I have now got easy access to as many floorboards as any gardener could wish for.

I also line the asparagus bed, which we have raised as a trial of the raised bed system. I have spent many hours now reading all I can about this succulent vegetable. It's one I'm desperate to grow but, one of the reasons asparagus can be so expensive to buy is that it takes the farmer three years to produce a crop he can sell. For the first two years after planting asparagus must be left untouched. Dr DG Hessayon, author of *The Vegetable and Herb Expert*, warns the reader that taking even one spear from newly growing asparagus can have catastrophic consequences. This is all well and good, but what Dr Hessayon forgets is that I am a man with a mission – I need asparagus recipes in my book and I, therefore, can't wait three years for it to grow.

By now I am totally absorbed by the allotment and have started turning down weekend trips to visit friends and family, opting instead to carry on digging. The weather is improving, the dark days of a freezing barren wasteland seem far away and the whole project now feels under control.

One Sunday morning over breakfast the kids ask the inevitable question: 'Do we *have* to go to the allotment today?' My response would have been a gruff 'definitely', but MJ got in there quicker than me. She suggests that they have their own vegetable bed where they can plant exactly what they want. She adds that she will help them dig it and Dad will buy the plants the next time he goes to the plant shop.

My initial plan had been that everything we grow, wherever possible, should be from seed, but I can see MJ's point and I refrain from pointing this out. If we can fuel their enthusiasm, it's worth relaxing the rules so, after breakfast, we give them a gardening book and tell them to make a list of what they want to plant. This list, when complete, looks something like this:

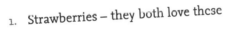

Dad's Shopping List!

1. Strawberries – they both love these
2. Pumpkins – because they want to grow one bigger than the world-record pumpkin
3. Tomatoes – because Richie likes red things (not because they are better to eat, but because they are the same colour as Manchester United)
4. Marrows – again, no culinary basis but big is best
5. Cauliflower – Ellie loves cauliflower cheese (Richie loathes it, incidentally)
6. Bananas – Richie opened the book at the greenhouse page and won't take no for an answer

I am trying hard to embrace MJ's cunning plan and show willing but, when I read their list, it's hard not to give just a small lecture on the principles of plant types and crop rotation. I bite my lip just in time.

When we get to the allotment MJ immediately stakes out a small bed, about ten by five feet (3 x 1.5 metres) and starts to dig the kids' vegetable patch and, to my amazement, they are happy to help.

During the afternoon we have some visitors; our next-door neighbours Gill, Mal, Jake and Joe come down to give us a hand. With four adults now digging, we make real progress. The sun shines and I am soon stripped to the waist. Vegetable gardeners need a weathered look about us because we are the outdoorsy types!

The extra help means that we not only finish all the beds on the go but we also start and finish a soft fruit bed and begin on bed number two of our three rotational beds – things are seriously moving on. When we come home I immediately have to apply aftersun to my back because it is so badly burnt, and then I collapse into bed.

Twelve hours later I am back on site and proudly gazing at our plot. I take stock of where we have got to:

Potato patch – rotivated (against my better judgement) and planted
(variety unknown). This is bed number one of our three rotational beds
Asparagus bed – dug, 8 x 8 feet (2.4 x 2.4 metres), raised and lined with boards
Rhubarb bed – dug, 3 x 3 feet (0.9 x 0.9 metres), lined with boards
Soft fruit bed – dug, 12 x 5 feet (3.6 x 1.5 metres), lined with boards
Kids' bed – dug, 10 x 5 feet (3 x 1.5 metres), lined with boards
Herb bed – dug, 2 x 3 feet (0.6 x 0.9 metres), lined with boards
Rotational bed two – under construction

OK, so we haven't actually planted anything except potatoes so far, but, with all these beds ready, we are just one shopping trip away.

We have three gardening centres near us, if you include Homebase, which I don't because it is owned by a supermarket. So, we have two gardening centres near us and both are good for the more general gardening requirements, but, when it comes to plants – especially the permanent crops – they can be a little lacking in choice. For example, if you are a chap who wants a blackcurrant bush, your local garden centre will no doubt obligingly flog you one, but, if you are a chap like me, say, who has done nothing other than read about blackcurrant bushes for the previous six nights, that is different. That marks this chap out from your common or garden blackcurrant bush customer, as this chap is obviously well up on *Ribes nigrum* and he simply won't take the first bush he is offered. This chap needs a garden centre with a choice befitting his knowledge. In fact, this chap needs Wisley Garden Centre.

Wisley Garden Centre is the Wembley Stadium of garden centres. It is run by the Royal Horticultural Society and is situated just off the A3 in Surrey, just 30 miles away. I don't actually want a blackcurrant bush at all – that is just by way of explanation – but I do have a rather particular shopping list gleaned from my previous six nights researching soft fruit, herbs and asparagus. In addition, my dad has recommended I try Wisley for all my permanent crops.

I have not seen my mum for some time – mainly because I am now a full-time vegetable gardener – so I suggest we meet at Wisley. She naturally thinks I am going all that way to meet her (which is fine until this book is published) but really I have plastic in my pocket and some very empty-looking vegetable beds to fill. I also have a detailed list:

Rhubarb – three varieties. The books recommend getting different
  varieties to prolong the season
Raspberries – these come as summer- or autumn-croppers. I want
  summer-croppers so that we can make summer pudding. Apparently
  raspberries can suffer from ill health, however, so a benefit of going
  to a place like Wisley is that they will be certified 'virus free'.
Blueberry bushes – two varieties are needed to ensure pollination
Gooseberry bushes – these come as a dessert variety (which is sweet) and
  a culinary variety, which tastes sharper. I am not sure whether we will
  eat them from the bush or make jam so intend to buy both
Herbs – I intend to buy a general selection

Strawberry plants – my favourite are the Gariguette strawberry so I will
look for these. I also love wild strawberries – we call them *fraises des bois*
in the kitchen – which are tiny strawberries with an intense flavour. The
gardening books call them Alpine strawberries

Asparagus crowns – Edward C Smith, author of the religiously endorsed
Vegetable Gardener's Bible and one-time front man for The Fall
(possibly not), suggests buying the male hybrid plant, which is
apparently better than buying mixed sex asparagus

All of the books I have read have made the point that you should buy
plants from a reputable supplier. This doesn't just apply to raspberries; you
shouldn't buy plants on the cheap, and you should even be wary of well-
meaning old ladies at the allotment offering plants that they say they have
raised from seed. You have to buy the right thing for position, climate,
and culinary requirement, but also, crucially, for its disease resistance.
Failure to do so can result not only in a poor harvest but also in an out-
break of death in the flowerbed.

With all this in mind, I head off to Wisley full of enthusiasm. I can't wait
to buy the plants and get them dug into the sandy soils of Ealing. I meet
my mum outside and, after a quick cappuccino in *le café* (that contains lots
of people in woolly jumpers and sensible shoes), we head straight for the
shop, where I promptly part with one hundred quid on books. Then it is
off to the plant department.

Mum suggests that we stroll through the manicured gardens that Wisley
boasts alongside the nursery shop, but I decline. What she doesn't understand is that I am not interested in orchids and rhododendrons; I am a
vegetable man through and through.

The nursery is all I had hoped it would be. They have a huge array of
plants and at least two types of each variety. From my list I manage to get
the following:

Malling Jewel raspberries – a summer cropper and 100 per cent disease
resistant

Blue Crop blueberry and Northland blueberry – to aid pollination

Herbs – lavender, sage, pot marjoram. I could have bought more types of herb but my trolley was too full. (Curiously, you don't grow pot marjoram in a pot.)

Honeoye strawberries – I have bought this Honeoye variety from my vegetable supplier at work before and they are right up there with Gariguette for flavour. Apparently I am a bit late for Alpine

Rhubarb – early and late varieties (Red Champagne and Victoria)

There are a couple of things I do leave without:

Gooseberry bushes – these are not sold at this time of year unless container grown, and they don't recommend container grown (naturally – this *is* Wisley after all), so these remain on the list

Asparagus crowns – I can't find these until, at the checkout the lady says they are on the far wall; by this time, however, I have seen my bill and decide to quit while still solvent

At this point, however, I can't wait to get back to the site and plant my purchases so I ditch Mum at the checkout and head back to Blondin. One small blip along the way is that I have totally forgotten to buy the plants that Ellie and Richie want to plant in their bed. I am halfway home before I realise my mistake and can't turn back. I know that if I turn up empty-handed, however, I will be accused of only caring about what I choose to plant, so I make a small detour to our local garden centre, which feels like a corner shop after my Royally Horticultural experience. Nonetheless, I am able to pick up everything on their list – a list incidentally that does not feature words but pictures of vegetables, drawn by Ellie a couple of nights previously. It takes a few moments before I decide whether I should buy pumpkin plants or an orange tree!

I carefully leave the children's plants to one side so that they can dig them in themselves, and then get started on the crops I have bought. I feel a real sense of responsibility as I dig in these permanent crops. These plants won't be yanked out at the end of the season and moved elsewhere; these plants are in the ground for life. As I plant the impressively straight line of raspberries, I wonder how many allotmenteers will enjoy their fruit long after I am on the compost heap.

The plot looks so good with things finally in the ground. I know the guys back home will want to see this big development so I take some photos on my mobile phone to show them. Back at home I also find myself fretting like a new parent that the raspberries won't take or the rhubarb will be unhappy where I have put it, but, really, I tell myself I have done my bit for them and now it is their turn to repay the favour.

These plants should all be in early enough to produce some fruit this year, which is hugely encouraging, because, at the moment, we have nothing to show for our efforts. The supermarket ban I tried to impose now looks ridiculous. As MJ points out we would all be dead of scurvy had we actually followed my plan. Personally, I have actually been trying to use local shops for fruit and vegetables but I am not convinced that they are any more in tune with the seasons than the supermarkets are. I recently asked my local shopkeeper if his vegetables were in any way local, and explained my desire to reduce food miles. He said that they were; they came from Covent Garden wholesale market each morning – which frankly misses the point, but I couldn't be bothered to argue with him.

The thought of producing our own fruit is very exciting. It reminds me of long hot childhood summers spent picking raspberries, blackcurrants, redcurrants and gooseberries with my sister in our grandfather's garden. We would pick kilos of fruit that my granny would then turn into jams, fools, jellies and preserves. The books advise that we don't pick any rhubarb this year because we have to allow it to establish itself. However, MJ's standard (and most delicious) dessert is rhubarb crumble, so I have promised she can make one batch later in the year.

Apart from the potatoes, all the now-planted crops are permanent – they come back each year and don't wish to be shunted around the plot. Our rotational beds cause a little more angst because they cover a greater area so getting the beds sieved and cleared of all the debris is a mammoth task. We have, however, made some progress. We have potatoes in one of our three rotational beds and a second bed for legumes is well on the way – this bed will be for beans, tomatoes, spinach, lettuce and leeks. This leaves just one space uncultivated. As soon as we can sort this one out we will plant brassicas.

Geoff Hamilton says in his book that, because we have inherited such a poor plot, it is important to enrich the soil with manure just as we did with the potatoes we planted. To this end I buy copious amounts of well-rotted farm manure from the garden centre (I have bought some crap in my life). It also seems that one should spread on a general fertiliser, so I use Grow More pellets. I am not really sure how organic these are but, right now, I have bigger responsibilities than saving the planet – I need to move this venture along swiftly and I will take whatever measures I have to!

The additional books I purchased at Wisley are proving, with one exception, most useful. By far the best is an RHS one, cleverly titled *Fruit and Vegetable Gardening* and written by Michael Pollock. It contains detailed information on plants as well as diagrams on pruning and general tips. This will definitely be a much-thumbed book. On the other hand, one is now on my 'books to be avoided' list. It is by Robin Shelton and is called *Allotted Time*. The book is basically a journal written by some bloke who has never gardened before (sound familiar?), and he takes the reader on a month-by-month journey through the gardening year. I only read about three pages before I begin to think that the book I am struggling to write has already been written. I realise that, if I read any more of it I will be become despondent, not least because his seems to be so much funnier than mine. Recent news has featured a legal battle between Dan Brown and some chaps who claim they have already written *The Da Vinci Code*. The case is threatening the release of a film of the book. Will a similar scandal hit the gardening world with allotment holders taking sides between me and Robin Shelton? While we sling organic manure at each other in court, a host of actors led perhaps by George Clooney (set to play me, of course) await the go ahead to release the blockbuster *Brassicas Quest*. My saving grace is that, as far as I can tell from the book, Mr Shelton is no cook, so at least I have him on that one. The book is now hiding in my sock drawer.

Chapter 5 | iPods and Asparagus

As a chef I am lucky enough to go to some really interesting foody events. Not long ago I was invited to Dorset to present the Dorset Food Awards and give a small talk on regional cuisine. The evening was a big success and afterwards, the organiser, Fergus, suggested I might like to return for the World Nettle Eating Championships. Unfortunately, I can't make it to this important event, but it has given me an idea.

Despite having cleared half our plot, we are yet to eat anything from the place and this is a constant source of frustration to me. I have considered stealing vegetables from our allotment neighbours but this really isn't in the spirit of things (and anyway they would all find out when I publish the book). But one thing we can eat that is growing in profusion is stinging nettles.

A few years ago, while head chef at The Greenhouse in Mayfair, I put nettle soup on the menu and it was a huge hit. What is a little embarrassing to acknowledge about this, however, is that I *bought* the nettles from a vegetable supplier. Nettle soup is actually a well-loved dish on the continent, but it is obvious that, if I am caught at home cooking nettles for human consumption, my children will be on the phone to Esther Rantzen at ChildLine quicker than you can say 'dock leaf'.

However, if I am careful to knock up the soup when no one is home, then I can probably pass it off as pea soup, and no one will be any the wiser.

One morning, therefore, I go down to the allotment with a pair of rubber gloves and a dustbin bag and start collecting nettles. They grow mostly along the borders of the allotment against a wire fence. With my Marigolds on, I am able to sift through and choose only the youngest, tenderest nettles; back home I turn them into a brilliant green creamy broth that everyone agrees is the best pea soup they have ever tasted. Sensing my moment of triumph, when the last spoonful has been eaten, I proudly tell them the truth – at which point Ellie bursts into tears and says her mouth is 'sting-y'. Who cares about mouth ulcers when we have just eaten our first allotment meal? I wonder what cooch grass is like?

I quite enjoy my solo trips to the allotments, and during the week the plots are relatively quiet. Our most immediate neighbour there is Andy, who seems to spend days on end at the allotments but never on the same plot. While we have nodded a hello in the past, I have not ever had a chat with him, so, when we pass on the path one morning, I make a quip about which plot he might be working on today.

Andy explains that he is the Vice Chairman of the Blondin Allotments committee and, as such, he regularly checks the entire area and looks over plots that seem to be falling behind in terms of maintenance. I had never realised that our closest fellow gardener is part of the Blondin secret police.

Although we have moved the plot forwards in the past two months, I am aware that our initial start has been anything but convincing, so I ask him if we have violated the rules by not coming to the plot from December to March. He, surprisingly, replies that quite the opposite is true and that, in fact, they are all rather impressed with our efforts. Furthermore, Andy lets slip that one of the adjacent plots to ours is on the hitlist and, if the owner is evicted, we might be offered a plot extension. This faith in us should be heartening but, having worked so hard to get to where we are, I am not sure if I could start all over again on another bit.

We say our goodbyes and walk off in opposite directions. It's good to get to know a few people at the site because a day's digging can be a lonely life. At first, although Sheila and Keith had been friendly, few other people acknowledged us as we walked to our patch but, now we have proved ourselves as hardcore, green-fingered regulars, we have been accepted into the clan.

Sheila always calls hello as we come through the gate and invites the kids over and Keith will come over for a chat, and John – a plot away from us – is also a friendly chap, and there is the most charming West Indian woman who always stops me and asks when I'm next on the telly. My standard response is to joke that she should forget all about that CCTV appearance on *Crimewatch* and not say a word to anyone; every time she laughs as hard as the first, which is very kind.

On the other hand, several of the plot holders have erected large fences made of poles and bits of wood around their plots and these guys tend not to be the 'good morning, nice day' types. They appear to have barricaded themselves in. Then there is Mr iPod Man, who sings out loud while he works. He is usually bent over planting or digging and, while I have never worked out who he's listening to on his iPod, it is obviously a band that he knows well, because he is always in full song whatever the time of day.

I have yearned for an iPod for ages. Every birthday for the last three years, I have hoped in vain to spot the Apple logo as I tear back the recycled wrapping paper. So far, no joy, but now I am head gardener I feel it might be time to treat myself.

I once heard John Major describe writing his memoirs as a cathartic experience. Frankly, I am finding writing my book completely frustrating. Digging, however, now *that* is truly cathartic. Some of my best times at the allotment have been spent with just my rambling imagination and a shovel for company. One morning, having nodded a hello to the iPod man, I take my shovel and start to dig rotational bed number three. It strikes me that, if I were to get an iPod, I could spend many a happy hour listening to what I please as I dig and sieve the land. The trouble, I have found, is that, as your children get older, they start to complain about the music that's played in the car – 'Dad, is "White Riot" really appropriate for us to be listening to?' – and then, worse still, they demand music of their own. Ellie now insists on the Black Eyed Peas (at least it's a vegetable reference) or some blokes called McFly, and she inevitably gets her way. Suddenly the allotment offers me a way out of this musical rut – if I were to buy an iPod I could cycle down to the allotment and listen to Neil Young without someone calling 'this one sounds the same as the last one' from the back seat.

iPods are a wonderful invention and, as I ponder the possibilities, it strikes me that there could be a vegetable version of this wondrous gadget. Just imagine this. You desperately care about the environment. You also wholeheartedly agree with the environmental issues surrounding food production, such as the air miles it is flown and the use of pesticides, but you are simply too busy working to play a 'hands-on' role in the environmental movement. Perhaps you are a long-haul pilot with a busy schedule or a lumberjack working away from home in the Brazilian rainforest, or simply someone who doesn't like dirt under their finger-nails. If this is you, then you need iPlot.

The investors and I buy a huge patch of land (perhaps Wales) and we carve the entire area into allotments, each with its own shed, compost heap and water butt.

You, the ethical wannabe, contact us and we assign a plot of land exclusively to you and give you a small piece of software through which you can download vegetables 24 hours a day. We then run out and plant your download to order before delivering it to your door when it's ripe and ready to eat. Perhaps after a few beers you will fancy downloading a few carrots, a marrow and a plum tree. No problem. We at IPlot will get them dug in. For the specialist gardener there is the whole range of obscure vegetables to enjoy with just the simple click of a button. Salsify, artichokes, sea kale and red carrots will all be available for immediate download. And with coordinates provided by Google Earth you can tune in and watch your garden grow. One click of a button and out rushes some chap with a watering can. You can tend your virtual plot while down the pub, on the train or even while on holiday …

OK, so I've overdone this digging thing lately. What I need is a night off.

I have arranged to meet some friends, most of whom are chefs, for a quick beer. The problem with chefs, though, is that quick beers don't really exist. We spend the first part of the evening catching up. I tell them of my allotment project, promise all of them a box of vegetables as soon as I can manage it and, before I know it, it is three in the morning and I am lying in the back of a black cab.

MJ had told me not to be too late home so, as I stumble into bed, I know I will need a good excuse if I am to be granted a lie-in. Though in-car map reading, forgetting birthdays and impromptu hangovers can all lead to domestic disagreements, the next morning I discover that, even if I haven't come up with a good enough excuse for a lie-in, the allotment provides the perfect solution for the hangover issue at least.

I hop out of bed as if I refused every one of the fourteen bottles of beer I was offered the night before. Maintaining this look of sobriety, I declare that a visit to the allotment is well overdue, and that I shall go without delay. With a quick stop en route to buy a Mars bar, a cappuccino and a newspaper, I whiz down to the allotment, set up my camping chair, doze, read the paper and listen to the football on the radio before rubbing soil on my hands and returning home. And you thought you could walk a tightrope, Mr Blondin?

Back in the real world, the late April sun is drying out the earth and making the digging of the rotational beds that bit easier. Each of the three will measure approximately 18 feet by 10 feet (5.5 metres by 3 metres). I suspect that each year we might try different crops within each bed, but the principle of grouping a type of crop together, and moving it along one bed each year, remains. The various books seem to overlap in advice on which vegetable goes in which group, however. For instance, Dr Vegetable Expert puts onions in with his legumes, while the Royal Horticultural

Society put onions in with their roots. We make up our own minds on these arbitrary points by letting the chef decide – an onion to me in the kitchen is a root vegetable and so be it. So, we finally have a list of which vegetables we are going to put in each of the rotational beds:

Bed number one – roots
Potatoes
Carrots
Onions – spring, pickling and
    large
Beetroot
Parsnips
Garlic

Bed number three – brassicas
Cabbage
Broccoli
Kale
Cauliflower
Radishes
Brussels sprouts
Swede

Bed number two – legumes
Beans – runner and broad
Spinach
Lettuce
Tomatoes
Sweetcorn

Having worked out what vegetable gets grown where, however, we have to re-read all the books to see what vegetable gets planted when. It turns out that 'just about now' is the answer to the above question, certainly when it comes to the bed of legumes; it is late April and runner beans, broad beans, tomatoes and sweetcorn are all in need of sowing.

The books also advise that most of these plants should be started off at home, so we make yet another trip to the garden centre, this time for plant pots and potting compost. I thought that growing your own vegetables was supposed to reduce the cost of living but, right now, it's costing us a bloody fortune and we still haven't eaten anything home-grown.

At home Ellie, Richie and I cover the table with bin liners and set about sowing seeds. They are actually far better at it than I am. Whereas Ellie easily manages to sow each tiny tomato seed dead centre in its little pot, they are far too small and delicate for my wacking great hands. Peter Schmeichel would make a useless gardener.

Within a couple of weeks our fledgling plants are ready to be transferred to the allotment and we all drive down to Blondin. All three passengers have a tray on their knees full of little plant pots, each containing a potential supper. While MJ and Richie plant up the seedlings, Ellie and I plant spinach and lettuce straight into the ground. I haven't yet managed to grow anything but I already know that, when I do, I want it to grow in a straight line, so we put a bamboo cane across the bed and crawl along it placing each seed with great precision.

Before long our entire legume bed is a mass of baby plants about which I worry constantly. My dad had explained that watering at the beginning of the day is far more beneficial than a midday water so each morning my first job is a pre-breakfast dash to the allotment to water the plants.

One morning, while I am busy watering and generally minding my own business, a lady from a plot not too far away comes over to chat. She is obviously a gardener with some years' experience and she immediately realises that I am a complete novice and therefore must be in need of tips – lots of them.

It is almost impossible to carry on watering when you are having a conversation but I do my best and, even in this department, she is on hand with some useful advice. She advises me to purchase a hoe at my earliest convenience. Apparently hoeing breaks up the earth and allows the water to penetrate the ground, thus reaching the roots of the target plant rather than forming a small temporary pond a little further down the bed, which, to be fair, is exactly what is happening to me. She is actually a little incredulous that I don't already own one. I feel like telling her that I am new to all this and, while she has spent the last ten years fretting about bindweed and parsnip germination, I have been busy having a life. She doesn't look the sex, drugs and rock 'n' roll type, however, so I keep my opinions to myself and leave to buy a hoe!

My other mission at present, since I failed at Wisley, is to buy and plant asparagus in our inaugural bed. During the digging of the asparagus bed I had continued to read up on this wonderful vegetable and now feel I am more knowledgeable. Asparagus, or *Asparagus officinalis* to give it its full title, is a fussy customer. The books advise me to prepare the soil by adding lime. It turns out that different plants require a different pH factor; in other words, some plants like a limey soil and others like an acid soil, while most sit somewhere in between. This is good information, but only if you know what pH your soil is in the first place. Luckily, help is never more than a vegetable patch away on the allotments and Andy tells me that our soil is relatively neutral, which means we definitely need to add lime.

The books also advise removing all weeds and stones because these can cause bent spears, which can be particularly annoying to the cook (don't I know it?). As well as this, the Royal Horticultural Society book urges top dressing of the soil. This apparently means sprinkling on a general fertiliser; however, the book warns the – by now terrified – novice asparagus grower that too much fertiliser will cause excess nitrogen and, guess what, old fussbags asparagus doesn't like too much nitrogen.

American Edward C Smith also knows a good deal about asparagus cultivation – at least this is his boast in *The Vegetable Gardener's Bible*. He advises lining each trench with something rather frighteningly called triple super phosphate. I buy this at the garden centre – it is very slightly cheaper than cocaine! As I go to tip it in I wonder whether it was an organic addition to my plot. The box suggests that it might not be but my serious desire to see my asparagus flourish means I decide to ignore the plight of the planet on this occasion and add it anyway.

To drive the knife home, so to speak, the RHS book reminds the reader that slugs and snails can damage the crop, as can the worryingly named asparagus beetle. All this, and you can't even make asparagus soup with seared salmon and crème fraîche until the third year after planting!

But I am still determined to grow it so now, with my bed ready, I am on the hunt for asparagus crowns to buy. Planting asparagus seed is not that simple, so most of my books recommend planting what is known as a crown. This is actually a one-year-old root stock, which is then transplanted.

I don't have time to drive back to Wisley and am unable to get asparagus crowns locally so, in the end, I hit the button marked Google and type in 'asparagus for sale'. There are lists of people all over the country queuing up to sell me asparagus. I note three numbers and hit the jackpot on the very first call. I phone a farmer in Kent who sells asparagus crowns and explain to him that I have a bed dug and have added lime. I ask him if I should plant the crowns next year after the soil has had a chance to settle and develop, but he tells me, in no uncertain terms, to plant it this year, saying, 'We could all be dead this time next year.' This is alarming news and I am not sure if he made the statement as a sales tool to encourage me to buy asparagus, or whether he may in fact be a witch doctor with some uncanny foresight of the future. Anyhow it works, and I purchase ten crowns from him. A year ago I knew nothing about asparagus cultivation but now I find myself having highly technical discussions on the subject. I ask him if the ones I am purchasing are male hybrids, which he assures me they are (both of us know that you don't want female asparagus depositing red berries among your crop and spoiling next year's harvest – though I have to admit I never have quite found out why).

A few days later my asparagus arrives. I have not been to the allotment for several days because, thankfully, we have had a bit of rain so watering has not been an issue. I arrive at the allotment with half an hour put aside to plant my asparagus only to find a weed epidemic in full flow. This is what happens if you fail to visit the allotment for even a short period. I immediately start hoeing all the beds including the proposed asparagus site and then turn to planting the asparagus.

This humble fern represents far more than a tasty excuse to consume hollandaise sauce; the asparagus is the yardstick by which I shall measure my gardening success. I have spent long nights reading about this fussy perennial and, as I approach the planting stage, I feel nervous lest my knowledge should come to nothing more than a barren bed of earth.

The crowns of the asparagus themselves are the size and shape of a small octopus but, unlike octopi, which are best tenderised by beating against a rock, these plants need to be lovingly handled and spread out in the trench with care. As with the raspberries and other permanent crops, these are only planted once so I feel that the pressure is on.

I discover also that runner beans are only slightly less troublesome in the planting department than asparagus. They require some imaginative structure on which the runner beans can climb so, one Sunday morning, the family all troop down to Blondin where we meet up with Dilly and Doug and their children. MJ is on watering duty while I am putting my maleness to the test with a spot of DIY bean-structure building. Runner bean supports – an aid to the climbing bean plant – are an opportunity for a gardener to show his more practical side. I remember that, when I was young, my dad made his by fixing a stake in the ground and securing a metal hoop at the top. From all the way round the hoop he then ran twine down to the ground. The beans climbed up the twine. My grandpa on the other hand was more of a traditionalist – he made a wigwam out of canes and let the beans climb up these.

We do not have the room for a wigwam structure and I have no metal hoops so I can't replicate my dad's. Instead I make my own version by putting a cane into the ground at either end of the bed and then joining them by another cane, which acts as a crossbar. I then tie canes either side of the crossbar coming down to the ground at a slight angle.

Once this is in place, Ellie and I dig holes and plant the three-inch-high plants at the base of each cane. We then plant more rows of broad beans, spinach and leeks, while MJ and Richie dig in some sweetcorn plants.

I mark the rows with a line of string over the planted line of seeds, with the string held taut at each end by a short piece of bamboo. When the plants start growing we will obviously be able to see them but, until they push through, the string will act as a reminder to us all that there are things happening below ground level. This isn't my own idea but one I have copied directly from our allotment neighbour John, who seems to know his stuff. Actually, MJ and I are always very careful to walk around the beds, but our children don't seem to share this concern. If they need to get from one side of the allotment to the other, they always take the most direct route and, if that means walking straight through a vegetable bed, tough luck! Perhaps my little strings will stop them!

We have been trying to stagger the sowing of seeds where possible because MJ's mum has told us that, if we stick everything in at once, we will have a problem with overwhelming quantities when it comes to harvest time. This may seem obvious, but the temptation to get everything up and running is enormous. Many gardeners find that, for three or four weeks each summer, they are literally buried under a mass of ripening fruit and vegetables and, as many gardeners are better at the growing than at the cooking end of vegetable production, they fail to keep up with the harvest.

There are two solutions to this problem: one is to buy this book for tips on using a glut – I would highly recommend this tip (and congratulations to you for having done so); the other is to stagger planting, thus extending the cropping period (but don't forget it doesn't have to be either or!).

Planting out the young plants is very satisfying. The bed is now full of small green stems all in neat rows, but there is a worry at the back of my mind. What if the temperature drops? Or there is a swarm of locusts? The plants will have to fend for themselves. I expect it is a similar experience to waving off your grown-up children at the airport as, with rucksacks on their backs, they go travelling the world. That night, as the wind whistles outside, I think of the bean and sweetcorn seedlings out in the elements, but there is nothing more I can do for them now.

I have started to daydream about succulent asparagus slowly pushing through the delicate topsoil. It's almost erotic. When I bought the crowns I was told they would show through in about a week. Each day I visit the allotment with only one thing on my mind: has the asparagus come through yet? After six days and not a single spear in sight, I am beginning to worry that nothing will happen.

The weather is still awful, especially for late May. Richie's birthday football match in the park with his friends (Brentford versus a World Eleven) is very nearly rained off. As a gardener, however, there is a small silver lining to the enormous rain cloud presently over Northfield Avenue. I can at last use the phrase 'at least it's good for the garden' and really mean it.

On the water front, I read that blueberry bushes need very soft water. The water they are currently receiving is coming from either a passing cloud or from the allotments' water butts. These butts are plumbed in and have a tap from which you can fill a watering can. At first I decide not to worry about this snippet of information, but these things play on my mind. In the end I find an Argos catalogue and look up water filters. The cheapest one looks like a big kettle and is about fourteen quid. I could fill it up at the beginning of the day and, when the water had dripped through the filter, I could pour it on to the blueberries. MJ says this is a little obsessive and she is probably right because we don't even drink filtered water ourselves, so I risk it without.

As May draws to a close the weather slowly begins to improve and I am back to watering the allotment each morning. Back home we also water our flowers and shrubs, but I can't help feel that pouring tap water on a plant that will never be eaten is completely at odds with our drive to create a greener environment. I suggest to MJ that she could use 'grey' water rather than filling the watering can straight from the tap. Since 'grey' water is used bath water and second-hand washing-up water, she cleverly points out that I have banned baths and that we use a dishwasher so I have to agree that the tap is the place for the watering can.

One evening I get a call from Andy who says our shed window has been blown out by the wind. The next morning I scrap my plans to install a water butt at home and head off to the allotment. Stuff the window – today is a great day: we have asparagus! Five beautiful, innocent, happy spears have gently nudged aside the well-limed, stone-free earth and are pointing skywards. My mind wanders back to the birth of my children –

that is the impact of this discovery. Sure, they will grow up into big bold asparagus wrapped in pancetta and smothered in hollandaise sauce, but, right now, they are the pride and joy of my short gardening career. They must not be cropped for three years but it is all I can do to stop myself dining on them there and then.

I call home and tell them the news, expecting them to drop everything and rush down to share the moment but, to be honest, their reaction is a little low-key. This could be because I have talked of nothing other than asparagus to anyone who would listen – so they may well have had their fill of the stuff before a single spear gets boiled.

The news just gets better – we also have broad beans coming through. I net them for protection, mend the window and then head off to do the family shop. Although I have been telling family and friends for some time that I will never again visit a supermarket, the truth is that I have occasionally broken that rule with a sly trip to Waitrose. This particular brand of supermarket feels slightly more in tune with the ethical shopper in my mind; they also sell a very decent version of millionaire's short-bread, which I love! Pulling up in my car, I feel like an alcoholic outside an off-licence as I lurk outside the shop, telling myself it's against the rules, but knowing I will end up going in, and hoping nobody sees me.

On the occasions that I have visited the supermarket, I have limited myself to buying only British seasonal produce that can be purchased free of packaging. I feel that this is in some way making a stand, and what could be more seasonal today than a kilo of Norfolk asparagus. In honour of our future harvest, I plan that the weekend's menus shall revolve around this little beauty: asparagus soup – both hot and chilled; asparagus wrapped in Serrano ham and roasted in olive oil; and asparagus with hollandaise sauce.

A few days on and the excitement is doubled with the appearance of yet more asparagus. However, darker times are not far away. One fine summer's evening I watch Richie playing football in the local under-eights team. He is playing up front and scores a great goal in a fine game. He is so much better at football than I ever was and I can't help feeling that, if he keeps it up, life may change for all of us just as it has for the Rooney family (we will be able to afford at least two allotments). So it is in high spirits that we stop off at the allotment to do a spot of watering before getting home.

Disaster! Three of our asparagus spears have been snapped off and lie pitifully where they fell. I am bloody gutted and furious – this is no accident. The chief suspects are:

1. a fox
2. a squirrel
3. a pigeon
4. a jealous allotment holder

Every book on the subject states clearly that irreparable damage can result from breaking the 'wait two years' rule. Now, through no fault of our own, we must wait and see if all our hard work and anticipation has been for nothing. And, in just three days, I am flying off for a business trip so there really is no time to stake out the plot and catch the perpetrator.

I decide that the following day I am going to erect the biggest damned fence ever seen on Blondin Allotments. It will make Guantanamo Bay look like a playpen. I am so pissed off – I will also consider closed circuit TV or security guards if necessary. I have slaved over that asparagus and I shan't be defeated.

Chapter 6 | Chuck Berry

The beginning of June finds me on a cruise liner from New York via the Azores to Southampton. I am there to give a couple of food lectures and cookery demonstrations en route. The ship is operated by Saga, which imposes a *minimum* age limit of 50 on all its passengers, and that guarantees that the boat is packed to bursting with expert gardeners. Each time I am on the stage I mention that I am writing a book (PR is very important!) and the obliging audience always asks what it's about. As a result I can't walk the deck without some well-meaning tip being thrown my way on growing root vegetables or pruning apple trees.

The allotment is never far from my mind, however. My intention had been to call MJ and the kids each day, but, once on board, it turns out that the satellite phones are not functioning so this is not possible. I, therefore, spend hours worrying that MJ will forget to feed the tomatoes or water the lettuce. Worse still, what if the security fence I constructed for my asparagus has been breached by the allotment saboteur? Will MJ patch it up to protect our fledgling spears? Oh, and how are the kids?

On my return home, Britain is in the middle of a heatwave and there has been little rain, but MJ reassures me that she has been watering the allotment regularly and generally keeping an eye on things. She also tells me that they have enjoyed their first strawberry of the season. I thought she was using the singular word 'strawberry' to describe many strawberries but it turns out it *was* only the *one* strawberry!

So, the following morning, I volunteer to do the watering and arrive at the allotment expecting to find things much as I had left them. I am stunned to find that, in little over a week, everything has really taken off: the broad beans are proper little plants and are beginning to form tiny pods; the Little Gem lettuce is coming through; we have a wonky line of spinach; runner beans twist around their canes; the asparagus has gone to fern; and all the soft fruit is showing signs of ripening. But, apart from the one strawberry, nothing is yet ready to eat. So near and yet so far!

While it is obvious that MJ has been watering, it is a different story where the weeds are concerned. MJ has a strange attitude to weeds: a sort of live and let live approach that simply doesn't wash with me. If a weed suddenly bursts into flower then she leaves it, saying it looks 'pretty'. What she fails to see is that even a single flowering weed disrupts the straight lines of vegetables I have been so careful to ensure and, since straight lines of vegetables are to my mind a sign of a competently managed allotment, out must come the weeds.

Weeding is a fiddly yet rewarding job as the lines of juvenile vegetables become clearer and give the whole plot a tidy, perhaps one might even say professional, appearance. Each time I visit the allotments I walk past at least a dozen other plots to get to ours. There are some people who seem to go for random planting, which, to me, just looks disorganised and lazy, but the plots I admire most are the ones with neat rows of vegetables.

This obsession with neat rows of plants is one that manifests itself in other areas of my life, all of which annoy the hell out of those around me. Right now, the spice jars in my larder cupboard are all in alphabetical order with the labels facing the front; I am forever lining up the cushions on the sofa and I tut when anyone dares sit down; and don't even start me on the lack of punctuation in phone text messages. I h8 it.

So my obsession with perfect planting comes to a head soon after my return from the cruise. Before I left we had planted a row of spinach that has grown into healthy young plants – the trouble is that, despite my use of the bamboo cane, it is a wonky line of spinach. Whenever I look at this bed it annoys me. And it has grown to annoy me so much that I set about ripping it out and plant a fresh line of spinach, guaranteed to come up in a straight row. According to my wife, this means I am a sad individual who needs to get out more, but what she has failed to notice is that, in all the gardening books we own, there is not one wavy, wonky line of anything. I rest my case. Besides, it makes for a nice early bowl of salad.

As we reach the height of summer, we are able to look back, with a fair amount of smug satisfaction, at what we have achieved thus far. We have managed to tame the inherited, barren wilderness and turn it into something that looks like a genuine allotment. Only one of our three rotational beds is left unfinished while all of our other beds are planted up and growing well.

Our original aim of self-sufficiency has not yet been achieved but it is now some time since I visited a supermarket for anything other than dry goods or cleaning products (biodegradable, naturally). I have been doing most of my shopping at local shops. The problem with this is that most of them stock only a very basic range so, if I decide that the perfect evening meal will be, say, roasted artichoke salad with a poached duck egg and Serrano ham, then I will either need to drive unnecessarily far, burning precious fossil fuel, or substitute said artichoke (and probably the duck egg and the Serrano ham …) for something available at the local store. Call me a snob, but I'm afraid that roasted celery or cucumber just don't do the same job.

However, while I have, bar the odd exception, maintained my stand against the supermarket, the same cannot be said for MJ. Our plastic bag recycling dispenser continues to be stuffed with bags from Waitrose and Tesco. I have given up trying to persuade MJ that she is sleeping with the enemy. She maintains that buying organic ingredients from a supermar-

ket is every bit as ethical as my local shop vegetables (origin unknown). Furthermore, she states (fairly forcefully) that she can park at the supermarket and get everything under one roof rather than drive around for hours like a lunatic on a treasure hunt.

The idea of 'no pain no gain' does not seem to be sinking in with my wife. If Emily Davison had taken the view that jumping under a horse was a little on the painful side so 'why don't we just sign a petition instead?', MJ wouldn't even be in a position to discuss our current dilemma as she would be too busy washing my clothes in the river. I don't actually say any of this to MJ, obviously, because I enjoy life too much (and I will very probably live to regret even writing it). Despite our differing opinions, however, food ethics is very definitely a hot topic in our house. Both MJ and I are trying, in our own way, to be more responsible and thoughtful about what we are purchasing, and our bid to expand our children's culinary appreciation and understanding continues apace. We hope that all of this will get much easier the minute the allotment really starts giving us something to eat.

Apart from the one strawberry and the pre-emptive spinach salad we haven't actually eaten anything home-grown yet. But July starts with a phenomenal potato harvest. Ellie and Richie are a bit surprised to learn that the potato bit of a potato plant is under the ground – they had expected to see the branches of the tall green bush laden with potatoes (and probably ready peeled).

The problem with growing under-soil crops is that it is really difficult to know when they are ready, but the joy of an allotment is that you are surrounded by people who are growing similar crops. Much can be learnt from just wandering around and watching them. So when, all around the allotments, people are walking out of the gate with bucketfuls of potatoes, MJ and I decide that it must be time to turn over the earth and dust off the peeler.

Because we have no idea what variety we planted, we are delighted to discover we are growing a lovely small new potato and a red potato (possibly a Desirée). We spend a morning harvesting just one row of the eight we planted and find ourselves with over four kilograms of potatoes! This is a real thrill, though also a little daunting because, if this one row indicates that all our potatoes are ready for immediate consumption, we are going to have to eat about a kilo each per day so as to avoid waste.

Several days later I phone my dad to update him on the allotment and explain our fear of suicidal potato consumption just to prevent them from going off. He tells me that they can sit in the ground for a while yet so we should just pull each of the plants as we need them. This is a big relief. I have never yet phoned my dad with a gardening query that he was unable to answer. I presume that he used to ask his father similar questions when he started to grow vegetables but I wonder how long the transition takes from being an ignorant enquirer to becoming a knowledgeable mentor. I feel a very long way off being able to give anyone advice, so perhaps it's a good thing that Ellie and Richie are still so anti-gardening.

New potatoes are, without doubt, best cooked as soon after planting as possible; to prove this point I bring out the portable camping stove I had got for Christmas. We wash some potatoes in the water butt and quickly boil them and they are one of the biggest joys of the allotment so far – and certainly the most filling, being practically the only thing we've eaten from the allotment to date.

Though we are possibly a little deficient in the growing department, we certainly make up for it in the cooking department. Every meal in July features potatoes. Gone are the pasta, polenta, couscous and rice. I spend much time with the potatoes, crushing them and mixing in olive oil and lemon, or butter and soft herbs, or baking them and filling them with smoked salmon, or (the children's favourite) boiling them until cooked, cooling them, peeling them and then roasting them in a pan.

One evening I take two very reluctant children down to the allotment to help me with the watering, which has now become a twice-daily requirement due to a very dry spell. Actually, Doug says he only waters once a day and their plot looks fine but I like to be sure. As we approach our plot the children are running through their normal list of questions, though the order can vary:

1. 'How long do we have to stay here?'
2. 'Can we have a present for coming?'
3. 'Can we go now?'
4. 'Why don't we just buy food like everyone else?'

Suddenly the interrogation stops, both of them shout, 'STRAWBERRIES', and charge off in gleeful bounds towards the plot. It can only be described as a miracle – my children are happy to be at the very place they would do almost anything to avoid. By the time I have done the watering they have eaten every strawberry we have produced. Then they discover the blueberry bush where, once again, they are only too pleased to get stuck in to picking the nine berries. I didn't get to taste one, but the sight of Ellie and Richie as they searched for each berry was more than consolation. There's hope for them yet!

As a child I can well remember the joy of picking raspberries with my grandpa. He had enormous canes reaching far above our heads, which he netted to protect them from birds. He would lift the net a little and my sister and I would crawl in and then stand up to pick literally kilos of raspberries. The bonus of doing the picking was obviously in being allowed to gorge on as many raspberries as we could eat. I wish I could remember the variety he grew because that would definitely have been the type I would have bought so that I could recall that distant pleasure of my childhood.

To harness Richie and Ellie's new-found enthusiasm for picking soft fruit, I arrange a day down at my sister's in Surrey, where we go off to the local 'pick your own' with my niece and nephew, Dominic and Roisín. My children have never seen a place like this before – entire fields bursting with fruit – and their delight is one hundred times that of their allotment berry-fest. At first Ellie and Richie try to disguise the fact that they are eating strawberries rather than putting them in the basket, thinking that I will be annoyed. However, this is absolutely de rigeur at a 'pick your own'. The cost of the fruit at these places is only competitive if you leave with serious strawberry poisoning; so on-site eating is something I encourage.

On the other hand, berry fights can lead to eviction and, in this depart-ment, I am left wanting. As I get my head down, crouched over the plants, a full-scale berry war is raging all around as Dominic and Richie start to pelt Ellie and Roisín with soft fruit. This act of violence is not ignored by the girls and soon berries are being thrown all around. We somehow manage to last the day without being chucked out, but, by the time we leave, all four children look as if they have been attacked by a particularly hungry pack of lions.

We return home with way too many raspberries and an obscene amount of strawberries, which I set about over the next week turning into sorbet, summer pudding, pavlova, trifle and jam. Shut your eyes and you would swear it was Nigella Lawson. This has to be the right way to live.

July is fast becoming the pinnacle of our fledgling careers as market gardeners. As well as potatoes and soft fruit, the rhubarb is now full of reddish stalks supporting huge leaves. I make good on my promise and give MJ a few stalks so that she can knock out her legendary crumble. Actually, I should admit that her crumble has resulted in the odd row in our house. I personally feel that a crumble topping is best made with white flour, caster sugar and butter; MJ likes to customise her crumble with brown sugar and oats. I have learnt to live with this variation because, unlike a pastry chef, you can't cheaply sack your wife.

One bed doing particularly well on the allotment is the children's own vegetable patch – they planted marrows, pumpkins, courgettes and tomatoes. What had started off as neat rows of juvenile plants is now just a huge mass of trailing leaves, extending far beyond the neat floorboard boundaries of the bed. Their pumpkins are the size of footballs and are just beginning to turn orange. In my view, the pumpkin is a vastly over-rated vegetable: it doesn't taste particularly great and it takes up a lot of space in the plot. Ellie and Richie had been insistent, though, as they felt that growing abnormally large vegetables was a lot more interesting than sowing rows of spinach. They were backed up by their mum who pointed out that, come Halloween, we would be proud to scare the local toddlers with our carved home-grown pumpkins. You can't argue with MJ sometimes.

Alongside the colossal pumpkins lie the courgette and marrow plants, which have now gone into overdrive. This would be fine if Ellie and Richie had a particular penchant for baked marrow or ratatouille, but they have just planted the things; it is apparently up to me and Mum actually to eat them.

Now, I love courgettes in moderation. They're great deep-fried, made into spicy pickles or simply sautéed with a little olive oil, basil and garlic, but they are not the vegetable I want to be eating day in, day out. The problem is that they are obscenely prolific – as soon as you pick one, another replaces it – and our children have planted seven of the damned things. In the end we become so sick of courgettes that I dig the plants up and chuck them in the compost bin to prevent them from spawning further.

As far as the marrow is concerned, I wish I had dumped this evil plant before it produced *any* fruit. The marrow is the big, ugly, hairy cousin of the cute little courgette. They grow on a similar trailing vine system, only much, much bigger, and, like the courgette, they don't know when to stop. The marrow plant just keeps on flowering and fruiting. One day you will see a little finger of a thing and, five days later, it will be replaced by a huge monster. Unlike the courgette, however, which can be consumed by one person, a marrow requires a football team to see it off.

Initially, we dutifully take them home and cook them up in a variety of ways but I eventually realise that this is one vegetable that simply fails to excite me in any way whatsoever. *I hate marrows* – there, I have said it. They are flavourless, watery and cumbersome. I have never seen a marrow served in a top restaurant and I am certain that is no fluke – any chef will admit that serving a marrow to an unidentified restaurant critic could seriously put their career on the line. In fact, I challenge any reader to send me a marrow recipe devised by any top chef.

My ultimate suggestion is not to waste your space on their culinary inadequacies, but, if you are determined to eat them, don't let your marrows grow too large. When they are small, I think what little flavour they do have is at its height. Many gardeners live out the 'big is best' fantasy when it comes to marrows; this simply means, however, that you need to find extra marrow eaters to come round for dinner. Leave the saddos to compete for the 'biggest cucumberine' prize and eat your marrow before its skin becomes as tough as old wellies and its flesh becomes disgustingly fluffy. While it is young you can serve it with the skin on, which is a small bonus because skinning a marrow renders it even more dull, and that's saying something.

The very best of a duff list of choices of what to do with a marrow in the kitchen is, I feel, Quick Marrow Ratatouille. I am including it here because I don't want it anywhere near the real recipes.

Ingredients
1 relatively interesting onion, chopped
Olive oil
4 garlic cloves, finely chopped
1 comparatively exciting red, green and yellow pepper, chopped into
   2cm pieces
1 dull, dull, dull marrow about 1 foot long
A standard-sized can of butterbeans
A tablespoon each of chopped fresh basil and marjoram
Salt and pepper

You also have a choice:
a) if you want to make a marginally interesting meal of it you'll also
   need:

4 plum tomatoes, each cut into six pieces

a little chopped chilli – 1 will be a tingle and 2 will be a kick

a few saffron strands (these are a bit expensive to waste on a marrow, but add them if you have Gordon Ramsay coming round)

b) if you just want to eat a quick meal and wouldn't dare waste your precious saffron on this revolting vegetable:

a jar of Lloyd Grossman's tomato and chilli sauce

Sauté the chopped onion in a tablespoon of olive oil on a moderate heat until it just turns golden brown, then add the garlic. Add the peppers and turn down the heat to allow the peppers to soften slightly then add the marrow (yawn).

Now, at this point, you can either add the plum tomatoes, chopped chilli and saffron or chuck in the jar of Lloyd Grossman's sauce. Cook all the ingredients together for about 5 minutes without the lid to get things going on a moderate heat, then add the lid, turn down the heat and simmer for 10 minutes.

To finish, remove the lid and add the butterbeans – stir the stew and switch off, then leave the whole thing sitting to develop for 5 minutes. Mix in chopped basil and marjoram (both available during marrow season). Season and serve.

And don't blame me if it's crap.

Chapter 7 | Freezing in August

We are a self-sufficient family. It's official. None of us has been to a supermarket or even a local store for vegetables for well over a fortnight now. So much for the doubters, including MJ, who said we didn't have the horticultural knowledge to support ourselves. How wrong they were – right now, in a small sun-baked corner of Ealing lies a small patch of land, which is solely responsible for the upkeep of a family of four. Jenny, at HarperCollins, has been emailing me asking how the project is going and I have been replying that everything is going exactly to plan. This is a huge lie, of course … until now. Game on!

Our evening menu options are now wide and varied. Lettuce, broad beans, runner beans, red baking potatoes, sweetcorn, tomatoes and spinach all vie for a spot at the dinner table. In fact, as far as vying for a place at the dinner table goes, the vegetables are doing a lot better than our children who are, rather frustratingly, still treating vegetables as objects of horror. I reckon they are now doing this precisely because there is so much 'green' choice. Their enthusiasm for newly ripening produce has waned considerably from those giddy days – not that long ago – of new berries.

August on the allotment is full on. Even though, as a chef, I have what I like to think is a fairly keen sense of seasonal eating, it is still a bit mysterious and surprising when our crops actually do as they're meant to. And, heck, they're now doing so in abundance.

Harvesting is the name of the game. The books mention things 'being ready' as if it is a happy relaxed time for the gardener, who can quietly go about in a romantic fog plucking only what they need. 'Crop in August' they casually suggest. Actually this should be announced as a screaming red alert: 'FILL YOUR BOOTS, IT'S HARVESTING TIME – HURRY, OR YOU WILL LOSE THE LOT AND *THEN* HOW WILL YOU FEEL, HUH?'

Cropping is a strain. It's a mad time of year. Think World Cup final, going one–nil down against Brazil in injury time. Panic! Suddenly each meal must involve lettuce or beans or courgettes, but which one? You can't use them all every day.

Our runner beans have been producing from late July and it soon becomes apparent that the ten rows we planted will produce a phenomenally heavy yield. Before planting I had consulted Dr Hessayon's *The Vegetable and Herb Expert*, in which he says that a 10-foot (3-metre), double row of runner beans should be expected to yield about 60 pounds (over 27 kilos) of beans. At the time, for some reason I am now quite unable to explain, that did not seem excessive, but, believe me, this is an absolute shedload, as we have been known to say in the kitchen.

It is the same with the broad beans: four rows produced a huge amount. The problem is further compounded by the fact that bean plants don't conveniently crop at a steady pace, but rather in fits and starts. We visit the allotment for days on end and don't find enough to pick, then, out of the blue, boom – we have an avalanche of the things.

We also have a full row of new spinach requesting immediate landing on our dinner table, and what seems like hundreds of lettuces crying 'eat me'. I sowed two varieties – All Year Round and Little Gem. The All Year Round seemed to get attacked by slugs and were rather wimpy in the centre. The Gem, on the other hand, got off to a flier and I soon have a straight line of really plump lettuces.

As the hot weather wears on, I notice the hearts of the Little Gem becoming thinner and the lettuces themselves becoming taller. I check this in *The Vegetable and Herb Expert* and find that the term for this is bolting and it happens because of a lack of water during very hot weather. Fearing the worst I pick the lot and we have three days of hardcore salad eating, coupled with giving lettuces to anyone who comes anywhere near the house.

I love salad; to be honest I could on the whole forgo vegetables if there was a salad offered with every meal. Crucial to a good salad is the dressing, for which there are various options. MJ is an olive oil and balsamic vinegar kind of girl, while I go for a much tangier mixture of vegetable oil, English mustard and cider vinegar sweetened with a little sugar (this is a handed-down family recipe from my granny).

Our children prove rather less enthusiastic about salad consumption. Richie decided he had an aversion to vinegar from a very early age, so, for him, dressings of any sort, including mayonnaise, are out. Ellie, on the other hand, doesn't mind the mayonnaise or vinegar bit – her problem is with the salad part of the deal. In our former existence as shop-buying vegetable eaters, this problem never arose because, if MJ and I fancied a salad, I would buy enough for us and then drop a head of broccoli in the basket for the kids. But, if they think I am 'popping' off to buy broccoli when we have a truckload of lettuces veering perilously close to the compost heap, they are very much mistaken.

In the end we have to take some hard decisions. MJ and I both agree that the only way to cope with the sudden demands of self-sufficiency is to freeze some of our harvest in order to give us time to eat the rest. After all, growing the stuff is only one half of the 'self-sufficient' ethos; the other half is eating it. There is absolutely no point in our going to extreme lengths to pronounce ourselves ethically self-sufficient if we then chuck the lot in the bin because we run out of time to eat it. Also, if we do freeze some vegetables, they will be our get-out clause when we enter the leaner months ahead when there is little to crop.

My policy at home has always been to use fresh vegetables as much as possible, but allotments bring with them a challenge – how does one eat everything that is grown during the mad harvesting months? You can eat as much as you are able to and you can give stuff away, but, to utilise the glut, you have to get practical and consider the previously unthinkable – freezing your fresh vegetables.

I would never use frozen vegetables in the restaurant. It's anathema to serve frozen vegetables to any unsuspecting customer. (There is one notable exception to this rule – frozen peas. Freezing peas at the moment of picking locks in their nutrients and preserves them in their prime. Fresh peas can often disappoint unless one is sure they were picked that day so, in the restaurant, we use frozen peas. There I've said it!)

So now here I am contemplating freezing the very stuff we have grown to eat fresh. Pickling, jams, purées and chutneys are other useful ways of giving your vegetables shelf-life but, while these are all very handy, they are no substitute for unadulterated green vegetables. Try living from December to May on pickled red cabbage and green tomato chutney – it's no fun!

Of course, we should be grateful that we have the option to freeze vegetables at all. As I recall, my granny dealt with year upon year of harvests without the benefit of refrigeration. As my grandpa merrily produced kilo upon kilo (pound upon pound to them) of assorted vege-tables, her job was to make use of it. She employed many of the aforementioned tricks (jams, chutneys, pickles) but, in order to serve greens all year round, she would finely slice the runner beans and pack them into jars, adding layers of salt as she went (the jars she used were those big sweet jars that anyone my age will remember – a quarter of cola cubes, please, Sir ...). When the time came to eat the beans she soaked them in cold water for half a day to start removing the salt. Next she boiled them for five minutes, then changed the water and reboiled them again before serving. They were always a little salty and a bit tough , and I suspect today's health gurus would frown at the high sodium content, but she lived to the age of 94 and, heck, I also feel fine. I would not actually recommend this method but I include it to demonstrate the preservation efforts of yesteryear, and because I can't see a runner bean without almost tasting the delights of salty beans out of season.

So let's get back to freezing vegetables. Freezing may not be the ideal solution for allotment holders. However, if you freeze your produce properly you can sit smugly at the lunch table and announce to your guests on a cold January lunchtime that the beans they are eating are home-grown. I've given tips on freezing over in the recipe section, so, if you want to know how to do it just skip over there, but come on back.

Now that our hard work is actually paying off, the challenge facing us is greatly increased by our decision, made back in January, to go on holiday to Italy during August. This was booked in the cold dark days when it seemed entirely appropriate to book a trip abroad, without any consideration of what actually might be growing, but our jolly holiday now threatens to disrupt our new-found self-sufficiency. Through sheer hard work we have managed to reach a point where we have more food than we can eat and, if we harvest correctly and preserve what we can, we have a great chance of holding out against the supermarkets right through the winter and into spring when we can start on next year's harvest.

I have not discussed this with the family yet but it is obvious to me that we will never be able to go on holiday in August again, or July or September for that matter; we will have to limit our fun to February when the allotment is relatively quiet. Besides, we are now trying to be responsible human beings and live a slightly greener lifestyle in general, so perhaps a foreign holiday involving air travel is something we have to forgo altogether, right? Our new-found greenness, which MJ was also so keen to encourage, demands that we consider our 'carbon footprint', correct? A green activist cannot pick and choose which aspects of planet saving appeal most. Who am I kidding? I'll be crucified.

The days leading up to our departure are spent harvesting, eating and freezing what we can. As well as lettuce and beans, we are now picking tomatoes and spinach. In my opinion, spinach really does need to be eaten as soon as it is picked, because it doesn't freeze easily. This means that we have to get a little adventurous in the kitchen to accommodate mixed salads and spinach in every meal. The joy of spinach, though, is that it can be worked into a number of recipes – quiches, gnocchi, dumplings and fishcakes all turn up on the dinner table.

Much to my relief, MJ has persuaded our friends Gill and Mal next door to water the allotment while we are away. She has also told them to help themselves to as much food as they want. We always feed their cat when they go away and they have always returned to a healthy cat very much alive – I just hope the same can be said for our allotment when we return.

The trip to Italy actually turns out to be a rather welcome break from the pressures of the allotment. We stay with MJ's mum who recently moved there; she lives in the Marche region, which is wild and rugged with lots of farms. Although we've been to plenty of local food markets in Europe before, it is still enlightening to visit them with our new-found perspective on the subject. There isn't a single kiwi fruit or bird's eye chilli on sale here. No, it's seasonal vegetables all the way: chard, endive, tomatoes, basil and fennel are all there in abundance. The market is packed with enthusiastic customers (and not just the middle class) and I am pleased to see that the vegetables are all sold loose with lots of earth still attached to the roots, and there is not a middle man in sight.

Although the break from the allotment is a welcome one, I can't put the old plot out of my mind completely. We have been in Italy for two whole days by the time I send Gill and Mal my first text message. At first I go for the softly-softly approach, 'What's the weather like over there? Is it still hot and dry?' I get no reply from Mal's phone. Mal would do this to me; he would enjoy knowing that my holiday has been disrupted by his prank of ignoring my message. I try his far more reliable wife and still I get no reply. Possibly my phone reception is a bit dodgy; I ask MJ if her phone is working and she has perfect reception. The next day I send another, 'Mal, water the damned allotment or else.' This time I get a response, 'Do it yourself.' You can choose your friends …

When we return home we find the allotment has indeed been watered but, as might be expected, things are generally in need of a bit of atten-tion. The raspberry canes are now one and a half metres tall and in need of decent support. We had initially tied the young plants up to a few bamboo canes but now they are towering above the canes and slowly toppling over with each gust of wind.

The runner beans show no sign of easing up on production and they, too, are suffering from my inadequate scaffolding knowledge; they have managed to completely outwit my bamboo construction and the weight of the plants means they are now growing at a funny angle.

One huge success is the sweetcorn. We planted twelve plants, which now have three cobs each, all ready for eating. Sweetcorn is a curious vegetable. It is rarely used in posh restaurants either on the cob or in any other form. This may just be because it gets stuck in the teeth or could in some way be due to the fact that it is held in slight scorn by the French. I have worked with French chefs who have referred to it as cattle feed and who certainly do not consider it worthy of their attention. Ellie and Richie, of course, do not live by these rules and love corn on the cob, so much so that each of the first fifteen cobs from our plants are eaten plainly boiled and slathered with dripping butter.

The pumpkins are now bloody enormous, orange spheres the size of beach balls. The kids are delighted at this development and seem to suggest that their bed is in fact more successful than all of mine put together. This inter-family rivalry is not how I had seen our allotment project developing, but I pour scorn on the pumpkins and tell them that, in terms of my book, our allotment and the project in general, they are totally worthless. Little do I know that one of those pumpkins has ambitious plans way beyond soups, tarts, pies or Halloween.

Shortly after we return, I am asked to appear regularly on a programme called *Sunday Feast* on ITV. On it, I am to cook up a Sunday treat for that week's special guest; I will be ably assisted by one of the show's presenters, Andi Peters and Anneka Rice. When we meet for pre-production, I tell them of my ongoing allotment project and, to my surprise, they are very enthusiastic about it. Thus, each week on the show I am asked by Andi or Anneka how the allotment is progressing. Naturally I tell them it is a doddle and that everyone should do it.

A few days before the final show, I get a call from a researcher who asks

me to bring in some seasonal vegetables from the allotment; they want
me to talk about them and cook them live for that morning's guest, Ronan
Keating. I agree that this is a good idea and I drive off to the plot with
Ellie and Richie to pick some vegetables. We gather beans, potatoes,
sweetcorn, tomatoes and lettuces, and, at Ellie's insistence, our largest
pumpkin for its TV début.

I have never met Mr Keating and, being more of a Paul Weller man
myself, I am not that up on his music. Ellie, however, is hugely impressed
that Dad will be hanging out with such a major star, and she proceeds
to tell all her friends at school that not only will Ronan Keating be on
the telly this coming Sunday, but so will her pumpkin. The news sweeps
around the playground like wildfire: 'Ellie Merrett's pumpkin is on TV
this week with Ronan Keating!' ... Not a word about me, of course.

On the day of the show I am a little worried that the pumpkin won't get
its starring role. It is by now a minor celebrity at Ellie's school, and I can
just see the look of utter disappointment on the faces of Ellie's friends as
I take her in to school on Monday: 'Ellie, I watched the show – it was
good to see RK, but where was your pumpkin?'

Thankfully, a member of the team places the pumpkin on the sofa and,
as we come back from the break, Anneka really has no choice but to
acknowledge that she is sitting next to Ellie's pumpkin. The pumpkin
sits on the sofa between Anneka and Ronan right the way through the
interview; every now and then either Anneka or Ronan nonchalantly
leans on the pumpkin, obligingly bringing it into frame.

After the show finishes we all mingle for a while, slapping each other on
the back, exclaiming, 'Marvellous show, darling', and generally expressing
the relief that comes at the end of a live broadcast. I donate the pumpkin
to Anneka, who faithfully promises she will cook it up. She may have
lobbed it out of the taxi window over Wandsworth Bridge for all I know,
but it isn't really important; my daughter has grown a famous vegetable
and that is all that matters.

Chapter 8 | Gentlemen of the Committee

By now, you may have gathered that my children (born to a chef) are no better at consuming vegetables than those born to a dustman, an accountant, or an astronaut. As parents, MJ and I are repeatedly challenged by them. We have tried the 'disguise the vegetable' approach and failed; we have given the 'pudding depends on you eating it' theory a go and failed again; even outright threats had little success. So, in desperation, MJ has taken to literature for an answer.

There is a theory that a particular food dislike can be overcome by exposure to the offending morsel in controlled moderate doses. It is an interesting theory, and one explained in more detail by Jeffrey Steingarten in his excellent book *The Man Who Ate Everything*, which MJ read while we were in Italy. Just imagine, then, that you are a ten-year-old girl called Ellie from west London and you particularly loathe tomatoes. Now, let's imagine your dad has grown several tomato plants that have yielded an enormous quantity of this hateful fruit. You could just refuse to eat them and suffer the consequences (no PlayStation for a week) or you could allow your mum to practise this form of aversion therapy on you that she read about on holiday ...

Ellie will eat tomato on pizzas, she loves tomato ketchup, she will tolerate tomato sauce on pasta, but she, point blank, refuses to eat the raw fruit. This is a slight problem because, as our lettuces have come to an end, it's the tomatoes that are now the glut of the moment.

We planted two varieties of tomato – a large beefsteak tomato and a smaller one called Gardener's Delight. The talk on the allotment is of a bumper year for tomatoes as growing conditions have been excellent. All over the place, plants are weighed down by ripening tomatoes and any tomato less than 100 per cent perfect is hoofed on to the compost heap as people struggle to keep up with the number of ripening tomatoes. It would be easy to imagine that, in years to come, as global warming does its bit, Blondin Allotments will become as famous as Bunyol in Spain for its annual tomato fights.

Back home I am busy knocking up tomato salads with mozzarella, or feta, or sardines, or just about anything else that goes with tomato. Alongside this, I make batches of tomato and chilli jam as well as green tomato chutney. All these are decanted into the jam jars that MJ has been saving for no particular reason, and then handed out as gifts to neighbours and friends. Tomato soup is easy to make and freezes really well, as does home-made pasta sauce. By the time the tomato season is over we have made the most of at least 40 kilograms of tomatoes and, frankly, just the thought of another tomato gives me the shivers. And I'm not the only one. Despite our efforts, Ellie hasn't changed her mind about tomatoes – and hasn't been on the PlayStation for a month.

But the talk on the allotments is not just about tomatoes. Apparently, there is someone with an allotment who has been on the telly … Ever since we took on the plot I have been doing bits on the TV, and a couple of allotmenteers have come up to me on occasion and asked one of the normal questions: 'What's Jamie really like?', 'Does Gordon really swear that much?' and 'Was that thing you did on Saturday your first time on the telly?'

I am completely realistic about my position on the scale of 'famous chefs'. I am way down at the bottom – at my level of fame, the best you can expect is people looking at you on the tube in a funny way. You can see them thinking, 'I know that bloke from somewhere. Did he go out with my sister? Or was he the plumber that came round that time the toilet wouldn't flush?' Being mobbed does not feature highly on my list of worries, to be honest. But, every now and then, someone will come up to me and hit the nail on the head: 'You're the bloke who does that food show.'

So, when I hear the whisper that we have a person 'off the TV' working at the allotments, I vainly think it is me. It puts a spring in your step to be recognised for what you do in life. I even wonder if I should come clean with the whole story and admit that, as well as a bit of telly, I am also writing a book. I decide against that on artistic grounds, but still remain quietly proud that my achievements on television have been noted.

Imagine my horror, then, when, one evening, I slump into an armchair, weary from work and, with a mug of tea in my hand, I flick on the old goggle-box to see what's on. There, smiling back at me, is my closest neighbour on the allotment and the Blondin committee Treasurer, John. John, the man who gardens in a panama hat with shorts and long socks; John, the man who told me off for having a bonfire in overly windy conditions; John, the man who knows so much more than I will ever know about vegetables is on the bloody telly. And he's not on some cheeky chappy morning cookery show; oh no, John's gone and got himself on bloody *University Challenge*, where he's sucking up to old Paxman with a string of correct answers on questions ranging from classical works of literature to Sandy Shaw's career highlights. Bugger me.

A few days later I see John down at the allotments and I congratulate him on his television debut; I also 'let slip' that I do the occasional bit of television myself. We spend a few minutes discussing the thrill and fear one feels when sitting in the green room prior to a performance and, eventually, John asks me exactly what television I have done. I proudly tell him that I have my own show that goes out on a Saturday morning. I hope this will cement our relationship and that we will now recognise each other as fellow TV personalities; it might even result in long lunches at The Ivy, but he responds, 'Oh, Saturday mornings, I don't have time for *daytime* telly.' I humbly return to weeding my asparagus bed.

Fruit has been a small bone of contention in our house for some time now. We have always kept a full fruit bowl on the sideboard and have encouraged the children to eat as much fruit as they wish. When we began this project, one of MJ's arguments against my supermarket ban was the lack of access to fresh fruit. Our local shops managed to sell us a lettuce and even the occasional cabbage, but they weren't too hot on the fruit front. Of course, initially this didn't matter because MJ simply ignored my suggestion and regular trips to the supermarket kept the fruit bowl full.

Since we have been self-sufficient for well over a month, we have enjoyed lots of soft fruit from the allotment but now the berries are behind us and the children have started to complain that there is no fruit to munch (who would have thought they would complain about not having fruit?).

Our patch on the allotments is at the far end, a few minutes' walk from the main gate. As we wander down the communal path we pass other plots and it's often hard not to poke fun at the odd plot that is clearly neglected or, on the other hand, not to gaze enviously at the ones that seem to be producing enough vegetables to support a small African nation. One of the paths leads us past a plot with two small apple trees. For some weeks these apple trees have been showing off their near perfect crop of deep red apples. I am ashamed to report that MJ, like Eve, finally succumbed and picked a forbidden apple. This is very bad form on any allotment and a better husband than I would have immediately locked her in the composting toilet and reported her to the committee chairman, who would have duly cast her out for her blatant pilferage. Instead, I decide to help myself to this forbidden fruit too, and she is right – they are amazing. It is obvious, therefore, that planting our own fruit trees on our allotment is one solution, and will go some way to alleviating the empty fruit bowl problem in future years.

One fruit that is available without fear of prosecution is the blackberry. Down by the canal there are literally thousands of blackberry bushes, which bask in the summer sun slowly ripening their fruit. Come autumn time the bushes are laden with berries just waiting for us to pick. The blackberry is surely the king of all wild foods in Britain. All over the country, you can pick blackberries throughout the autumn, and we're keen that our children experience this seasonal joy. So, one weekend, MJ takes Ellie and Richie blackberry picking. They return with over five kilos; this is a monumental effort and is most welcome, apart from the small fact that the only blackberry dish MJ knows is crumble. Actually, if you cast your mind back to the rhubarb season, you will find that MJ is a crumble bird through and through. She gamefully sets about making stewed blackberries on an industrial scale, which she then freezes. As a result, a blackberry crumble is only minutes away right the way through the following year (when I expect she'll do exactly the same again).

At home, the next phase of the gardener's year is taking place: we start to sow our brassicas in pots prior to being planted out. To the cook, brassicas are best described as leafy green vegetables; they include kale, sprouts, cabbages, broccoli and purple sprouting (I know this simply as 'purple sprouting' in the kitchen, but it will often be purple sprouting broccoli in the shops). The one blip in this 'leafy green vegetable' theory is that swede is apparently also a brassica, though it's the swollen root we eat not the leafy bit. For years I have been writing 'root vegetable purée' on menus and happily using swede – I must have been the laughing stock of every gardener who ate my food.

I have started to form a bit of a routine while sowing seeds at home. It's a routine that has sadly been overlooked by all the gardening books I have read so I feel it should be mentioned here. Firstly, it must be carried out in a warm room. Make it an evening job and make sure you have a really decent bottle of red wine open – it is important that this is consumed in full during the sowing session. Next, choose some music, preferably something uplifting (Kings of Leon played very loud is perfect) because sowing can get a little tedious. Crisps are optional, as is company, though, personally, I think this task is best done alone. Of course, if one does manage to drink the entire bottle of wine, there can be some dodgy labelling of pots towards the end of the session, but I think you will find this routine more enjoyable than standing in a freezing cold potting shed listening to the long-range weather forecast. Incidentally, shouts of 'get a life, you sad git' coming from one's wife should be expected, though not necessarily tolerated.

With all our brassicas sown, there is now a three-week gap before they need hardening off (this is one of my favourite gardening terms and we will get back to it in a minute). The three-week gap in our case is spent digging the bed that will be used to house these precious pots of winter food. We have always intended to have three rotational beds and, now our mad summer harvesting is over, we must get back and finish the third. Returning to heavy-duty digging is a bit of a shock to the system, but the thought of my plants in their little pots pushing up towards the light is all the encouragement I require.

Now, imagine you are a small plant living happily in a pot on a kitchen window sill. The room is nice and warm, and every day you are given a drop of water. Life is good. But it can't carry on like this; eventually every plant must move out into the garden where it faces the elements full on. This can be quite a shock to the pampered seedling, so the books all recommend that the plant is given little spells outside to acclimatise itself to the conditions. This is called hardening off. Well, what did you think it meant?

So, in the days prior to planting out the brassicas, we leave our fledgling seedlings outside. All is well and they cope with the autumnal weather perfectly, so, the night before planting, I decide to leave them out all night.

That night, after I have gone to bed, it pours with rain. The plants survive, but all of the labels I have made are washed clean so we no longer have any idea which plant is which. So the next day we busily plant our brassicas – pointed (or 'hispi') cabbage, savoy cabbage, purple sprouting broccoli, Brussels sprouts, broccoli and swede – but with no clue as to which one is which!

October is upon us and, as any good vegetable gardener knows, this signals the beginning of autumn, which means it's time to start clearing up the beds that have been used for summer production, and to 'batten down the hatches' on the permanent crops. The rhubarb needs to be trimmed down to the crown; the raspberries need pruning; the asparagus needs its fern cut off; and the herbs need a haircut.

October is also the month when the Blondin Allotments association holds their Annual General Meeting, which is open to everyone who has a plot at Blondin Allotments. Our allotment neighbour Andy has become a good friend and, when he asks me to attend the meeting, I feel I have little choice but to go along. Conveniently, MJ remembers that she has an appointment at the hairdresser so I am left with the kids. I decide to phone Dilly and Doug to see if I can persuade one of them to come with me to the meeting while the other looks after all the children. There is no answer from them so I presume they either have hair appointments as well or they are down at the allotment. The only option is to leave the kids 'home alone' since I expect it to be a gentle, not-too-formal get-together, which will take all of fifteen minutes.

The AGM is held in a shed close to Northfields tube station, as the facilities at the allotment itself are apparently not suitable. About thirty chairs are arranged in a wide semicircle around the 'top table'. This table is reserved for the senior members of the allotment committee: Keith (Chairman); Andy (Vice Chairman); Helen (Secretary); and John (Treasurer and TV quiz show personality).

Keith stands up and, with no more than half a glance, announces to the secretary that there are twenty-four people present. He must have noticed our admiration for his swift headcounting because he then says that, in his working days, he was a prison governor – presumably that meant headcounting came naturally – and walks over and locks the door, presumably to stop any of us escaping.

The previous year's minutes are read through; they mean little to me, being new to the group. Following this, Keith announces that the committee will now resign en masse; when this resignation process is complete, he warns the room that, for the next few minutes, Blondin Allotments association is, in effect, a loose cannon with no one in charge and, as such, we should move quickly to elect the next committee. So, with this potentially unstable situation looming, he proposes that we should elect the same people *back* to the same posts. We support this sensible proposal and, with a show of hands, security is restored to a bunch of green-fingered rebels in a shed in west London.

Next up is the Treasurer's report, which John delivers with all the aplomb of the Chancellor of the Exchequer. We hear of allotment evictions due to non-payment of rent, and about annual spending on fences, skips and the composting toilet. And how are we to pay for all this? Taxes, of course – in the form of allotment fees.

At the end of his summary, John rightly asks if there is anyone present who would like to question his obvious due diligence – all are quiet apart from one lady who questions the buying and use of ground cover tarpaulins. This lady turns out to be John's wife – he swiftly deals with her treachery by explaining that he will be publishing the accounts for all to see.

Next up is Andy, who announces that there has been an allotment inspection going on for the last couple of months for the purpose of selecting the 'New Allotmenteers of the Year'. A hush sweeps through the room as it is announced that a plaque *and* a cash prize will accompany the award. Andy does the thing that all good compères do – he looks at each eligible candidate as he speaks slowly about the tough job the judges had in reaching their decision and leaves an unbearably long gap before announcing that the winners are (you guessed it) ... Dilly, Doug, MJ and me!

Since I'm the only one of the four of us there, I stand up to receive the award and, feeling that some sort of speech is necessary, I humbly respond that we never, in a million years, expected to receive such an honour, and that this award is equivalent to at least two Michelin stars and an FA Cup.

I thought the room would break into spontaneous applause, making it easier for me to sit down and quietly revel in the glory, but it remains deathly quiet, giving me the distinct impression that there are plenty present who feel that the award should have gone elsewhere. Andy then hands over the plaque and a slightly crinkled envelope – containing £15 in used notes – which he pulls from his back pocket, and I shuffle in silence back to my seat.

After this excitement it is back to business. It is announced that we will now elect some extra, general recruits to the Blondin Allotments committee. Not too many people are forthcoming to stand for election, so, after a hard look from Andy, I duly offer my services. I am seconded (by Andy) and, within a flash, I have triumphed at my first-ever election. I now find myself as a pivotal member of the Blondin Allotments committee; it is, therefore, my duty to meet with the rest of the committee in Duffy's bar on the last Monday of every month to drink a lot of beer and run through the minutes of the previous month's meeting.

The meeting, by this stage, has already lasted two hours so it is proposed that we should break for ten minutes so Andy and Sheila can have a fag. This motion is the first to be agreed by the new committee and Keith also decides that 'any questions' should be held over a pint at the aforementioned Duffy's wine bar.

I slope off at this point because by now my children will probably have reported me to social services or, worse, MJ will have returned, found the children on their own, and it will be me requiring a social service – probably in the form of an ambulance! I also come away slightly bewildered at the turn of events. I am busy, not only working an allotment and writing a book, but also with various other projects, including trying to open a restaurant. Everything happened too quickly but, when one is voted Allotmenteer of the Year, it is a little difficult to ignore a call to service from the very body that has elevated one to such status.

At home I am working hard on next year's planting plan. Though the original plan had been to be self-sufficient within a year, next year will be our first full year's crack at the allotment. There has been so much we have *not* planted this year, simply because we have had so much clearing and preparation to do, and both MJ and I feel that some sort of plan is required if we are going to remember to plant the widest range of vegetables possible next year.

I spend a full evening busily configuring an Excel spreadsheet so that we can have a more structured approach to our allotment next year. I love spreadsheets – they deeply satisfy my Nick Hornby-esque list-writing tendencies. I have spreadsheets for our family's shopping requirements, and for our Christmas card and present-buying requirements. They are infallible – honestly – but MJ refuses to use any of them and routinely takes them down when she finds them Blu-tacked to the kitchen wall.

This is one spreadsheet she will have to use, however. If we are going to continue in our supermarket-less lifestyle and carry on eating only

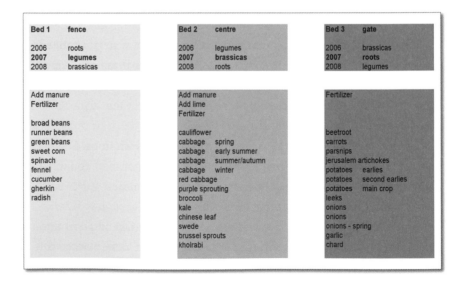

Bed 1	fence		Bed 2	centre		Bed 3	gate	
2006	roots		2006	legumes		2006	brassicas	
2007	**legumes**		**2007**	**brassicas**		**2007**	**roots**	
2008	brassicas		2008	roots		2008	legumes	
Add manure			Add manure			Fertilizer		
Fertilizer			Add lime					
			Fertilizer					
broad beans								
runner beans			cauliflower			beetroot		
green beans			cabbage	spring		carrots		
sweet corn			cabbage	early summer		parsnips		
spinach			cabbage	summer/autumn		jerusalem artichokes		
fennel			cabbage	winter		potatoes	earlies	
cucumber			red cabbage			potatoes	second earlies	
gherkin			purple sprouting			potatoes	main crop	
radish			broccoli			leeks		
			kale			onions		
			chinese leaf			onions		
			swede			onions - spring		
			brussel sprouts			garlic		
			kholrabi			chard		

produce that we grow, she is going to have to realise that this spreadsheet is our guide, our friend.

The spreadsheet is divided into three sections: yellow, green and blue, each for a different bed. Bed 1, the yellow one, will this year be planted with a full selection of legumes; the green will be brassicas; and the blue will contain root vegetables. Next growing year everything will rotate so the brassicas end up in the yellow bed, the root vegetables in the green and so on.

Having completed this spreadsheet, printed it out and stuck it to the fridge, I get slightly more adventurous. Another Excel spreadsheet is separated into twelve coloured sections and each is labelled with a month. I then go through all my books and type in the jobs that must be done for every month. This means that I now have a calendar of what needs to be planted when, meaning that we will never forget that in February, say, we need to plant our early crop potatoes or that in July we should consider pruning the strawberries.

There is a snag that comes to light, however: the gardening season does not have a neat 'first day' like the football season or the fishing season. The gardener's year is never-ending (don't I bloody know it?), and I discover that this means that, where our three rotational beds are concerned, we have an overlap. The growing season is not the same for each vegetable, which means that late in the year root vegetables need to be planted in a bed that, in practice, is still housing brassicas. I don't notice this straight away, but it all becomes obvious in October when my dad and his wife Coleen visit after one of their frequent trips to France. My dad, much impressed by the Gallic ability to grow a decent allium, has started buying his shallot and garlic bulbs when on holiday in France. So, rather than bringing me an expensive bottle of red wine from Bordeaux, he has kindly opted to bring me a hundred garlic bulbs and a similar number of shallots for the allotment.

As I consider planting them, I wonder whether they should go in this year's root bed because they are onions and they need to be planted this year, or whether they should go in next year's root bed (the next bed

January	February	March
asparagus - fertilizer basil - sow cabbage - savoy - sow cauliflower - V queen - sow garlic - sow in situ rhubarb - mulch with manure shallots - sow in situ spring onion - sow in situ	basil - sow cabbage - savoy - sow cauliflower - V queen - sow spring onion - sow in situ tomato - balconi - sow tomato - harlequin - sow potato - 1st early - accent - plant late feb carrot - amsterdam - sow	bean broad - sow in situ beans green - sow indoors blueberry - dry blood and mulch with pete cabbage - hispi - sow in situ cabbage - savoy - sow cabbage - tundra - sow in situ cucumber - sow jerusalem artichokes - plant kale - sow - plant out mid summer leeks - sow carrot - amsterdam - sow carrot - Nantes - sow lettuce - sow in situ marigold - sow melon - sow raspberries - mulch salsify - sow in situ spinach - sow in situ spring onion - sow in situ sweetcorn - sow tomato - balconi - sow tomato - harlequin - sow potato 2nd early - B queen - plant potato - late maincrop - GW - plant potato - 1st early - accent - plant potato - late maincrop - cara - plant potato - early main - picasso - plant

April	May	June
basil - sow bean broad - sow in situ beans runner - sow beetroot - sow in situ brussels - trafalgar - sow in situ and indoors cabbage - hispi - sow in situ cabbage - savoy - sow cabbage - tundra - sow in situ carrots purple - sow in situ chinese leaf - sow in situ cucumber - sow lettuce - sow in situ melon - sow parsnip - sow in situ pumpkin - sow rhubarb - harvest spinach - sow in situ spring onion - sow in situ strawberries - plant sweetcorn - sow tomato - R alert sow potato - 2nd early - B queen - plant potato - late maincrop - GW - plant potato - 1st early - accent - plant potato - early main - picasso - plant potato - late maincrop - cara - plant Sow sunflowers	bean broad - sow in situ beans green - sow in situ beetroot - sow in situ brussels - falstaff - sow indoors cabbage - hispi - sow in situ cabbage - savoy - sow cabbage - tundra - sow in situ carrot - fly away - sow in situ carrots purple - sow in situ cauliflower - pilgrim sow / harvest spring gherkin - sow lettuce - sow in situ parsnip - sow in situ potato - 1st early - accent - plant potato - 2nd early - B queen - plant potato - early main - picasso - plant potato - late maincrop - cara - plant potato - late maincrop - GW - plant radish - sow in situ spinach - sow in situ spring onion - sow in situ strawberries - mulch with straw swede - sow in situ - late in month sweetcorn - sow tomato - R alert sow	bean broad - sow in situ beans green - sow in situ beans runner - sow in situ cabbage - hispi - sow in situ cabbage - savoy - sow cabbage - tundra - sow in situ carrot - Fly away - sow in situ cauliflower - pilgrim - sow / harvest spring chinese leaf - sow in situ fennel - sow in situ khol rabi - sow lettuce - sow in situ parsnip - sow in situ radish - sow in situ spinach - sow in situ spring onion - sow in situ

July	August	September
bean broad - sow in situ beans green - sow in situ cabbage - hispi - sow in situ lettuce - sow in situ rhubarb - stop harvesting spring onion - sow in situ strawberries - prune	parsley - sow in situ	spinach - sow in situ under cloche

October	November	December
caulifower - A Y round -sow parsley - sow in situ rhubarb - fertilizer and remove dead leaves spinach - sow in situ under cloche	asparagus - trim fern - manure caulifower - A Y round -sow manure - dig in	cabbage - savoy - sow parsley - sow in situ spring onion - sow in situ

along) because they will be *picked* next year. However, the brassicas are still growing in that bed. It all proves rather daunting and I'm unsure how to progress so, in the end, I decide to put off this decision by not planting them at all and they spend October hanging in the shed. It does, however, highlight the need for careful planning.

My dad's generosity extends far beyond garlic and shallots, too – he has also brought us some radish seeds. These seeds are not your average red radish enjoyed by many people in salads; these are some obscure Japanese variety, which apparently grow into very long black vegetables. He promises me that our allotment neighbours will be hugely impressed. These are very fast-growing radishes and Dad says they need to be planted right away. Luckily, I don't have the same planning problem as with the garlic and shallots, as they will grow so fast that we can put them in this year's root bed and sleep comfortably!

During October we also manage to get into a routine of spending each Sunday at the allotment as a family. This routine is not without opposition. The kids demand ever bigger treats as payment for joining us without opposition, but we persevere and, on one happy occasion, they even admit (grudgingly) that they have enjoyed themselves.

Along with Eddie and Sylvie, Dilly and Doug's children, they build fires, dig random holes and, on one day, they find two frogs and a lizard – this final find is, I think, very exciting. Eddie and Richie hold the lizard for ages in their hands watching its every move. This is the perfect example of what I wanted the allotment to give them – a bit of nature in their urban lives.

Meanwhile MJ and I literally plough on – we spend one Sunday moving the huge pile of rubble (stones, glass and general rubbish) from the plot into a skip that has been provided by the committee as an end of season gesture in order to get the site cleared up. We also clear the beds of any plants that have done their bit, and generally have a good tidy. By the end of the day the allotment is looking like a picture from a gardening catalogue.

Later that evening MJ tells me that she reckons I am more enthusiastic in clearing beds than planting them. This hurts, but only because it is true: I really like the beds to be clean and tidy, with their wooden edgings bushed free of soil – it makes me feel in control! Somehow, when the beds are full of plants they can look a bit messy …

As our lives have become fulfilled by limitless amounts of vegetables, we have continued to pursue a greener existence elsewhere. In truth, though, it's an off-green existence – more khaki than pure green. On the plus side we are recycling absolutely everything: plastic, tin, food waste, paper and glass all mount up individually in our front yard before being driven off and dumped in the countryside under a hedge (only joking); we are brushing our teeth in minimal water; we are flushing the toilet less (Ellie still finds this horrific); and none of us has had a bath for weeks, instead opting for a shower. In fact, were we to redo the bathroom, I suggest to MJ that we could do away with the bath altogether and perhaps turn it into a novelty fish tank.

On the negative side, we have had a foreign holiday (in fact, I have used aeroplanes more than ever this year due to some foreign gigs) and we still use the car a lot. We also own – look away now, Mr Cameron – a patio heater. We bought it several years ago when the world was healthy and due to last forever; we don't use it that much but it remains on our deck like some beacon of irresponsibility. Perhaps I should put it on eBay but that would just pass on the problem to someone who might use it more than us, thereby perpetuating the problem. I suppose we could dump it or even recycle it, but the slot for metal waste at the local recycling depot is very small and we'd have a job getting it in.

We have made progress, though, despite the patio heater dilemma, and our progress is defined by our self-sufficiency. We are ex-supermarket shoppers and I am immensely proud of that. As winter approaches I sense that we have turned a corner. We have cracked this vegetable-growing lark big style. Now there is no turning back.

Chapter 9 | My Children and Other Pests

We have always known that, as beginners to this vegetable-growing game, we would make mistakes but, right now, it feels as though we have made a rather obvious one. Summer is truly over. Our bean plants are on the compost heap along with the remains of our tomatoes and sweetcorn. There is a chill in the air and the evenings are short. The happy days of salads and bumper harvests are now fast becoming a distant memory.

Just a few weeks ago we were producing so much food that we became almost complacent. We failed to look ahead and foresee the inevitable. Although we did plant some brassicas, we were slow in doing so, and now we are paying the price. On the allotment we have twelve slowly maturing cabbages, a couple of sprout plants, a few swedes, a line of purple sprouting and some broccoli. All of this looks some way off being ready, which means that we have a few weeks ahead of us with very little to eat. On the plus side we do have a freezer full of beans and tomato sauce, but this is really earmarked for January consumption when our prospects may look even bleaker than they do currently.

This all seems rather a kick in the teeth – we have worked so hard, yet still we face death from scurvy if our brassicas don't mature quickly. Life away from the allotment is no better. Three trips to watch Brentford play football result in three home defeats, and the team ends up in the relegation zone; even the car fails its MOT. I am certain all these events are linked by some strange planetary force – if only we had planted more cabbage and earlier!

As winter closes in, our meagre brassica bed is beginning to ration out the odd meal. It starts with cabbage, much to our children's dismay, and quite a lot of it. We had planted six 'hispi' cabbages – I would call these pointed cabbages in the kitchen – and six Savoy cabbages. Our cabbage yield is at least protecting our freezer stocks for the time being, but things are a little bleak. Twelve cabbages will last a family of four for about twenty days (that's nineteen too many by my children's reckoning), and, in that twenty days, we have to hope and pray that our Brussels sprouts, curly kale and purple sprouting come on leaps and bounds to the point of harvesting.

On a positive note, we continue to spend every Sunday during November as a family at the allotment clearing away and burning the skeletal remains of our summer planting. I suspect this is due mainly to Christmas being on the horizon: Ellie would do anything, including gardening, to get a hamster for Christmas; Richie is keen on a bicycle. In their view, attending the allotment with Mum and Dad seems to be a price worth paying!

To cheer us all up we decide to have a huge bonfire to celebrate 5th November. Ellie and Richie are keen to have some fireworks and the 'Dad' in me is desperate to agree, but, in the end, we decide against it. Allotments attract a lot of retired, elderly people who might take a serious turn were we to fire a rocket in the wrong direction. In our current subdued state the last thing we need is blood on our hands. Richie is left on fire-tending duties as MJ and I get some work done. His fire seems to get bigger and bigger until I realise that he is actually scavenging for bits from other allotments to burn. Later in the day I find all my bamboo canes and my wooden mallet smouldering on the fire; this is the point at which I wonder if I haven't *over* encouraged this pyromaniac tendency a little too much.

One chilly Sunday afternoon we run into Andy, who has his arms full of leeks, broccoli and cabbages ready to take home. We mention that we have nothing to harvest, in the vain hope that he might give us some of his. No chance, but he does advise us to read seed packets carefully in future. Apparently, if we had, we would have known that purple sprouting notoriously takes an age to mature. Gee, thanks, Andy.

He also has news of an opportunity. The Blondin committee has offered us an extension to our plot. This would mean that, rather than sharing our plot with our friends Dilly and Doug, we would each gain more land. We obviously look a little bemused, because he tells us to think it over.

In my view, before we can even contemplate the offer, we have to get things back on track. There is some winter planting to be done in the form of the garlic and shallots my dad brought from France. They have hung in the shed for over a month now and I absolutely have to plant them, especially the garlic, because, if we are going to be self-sufficient right through next year, a steady supply is crucial. Cooking without garlic is like swimming in the nude – you can do it, but it just doesn't feel right.

The problem with the garlic up to now has been *where* to plant it, not when. This is now an easier decision because next year's root bed (this year's brassica bed) is no longer full of plants; it is clear and awaiting a new season of root vegetables. So that is where I plant the garlic.

By the end of November things are looking serious. We have eaten a few cabbages and one swede as we wait for our purple sprouting, sprouts and broccoli to pull their finger out. We would have enjoyed more cabbage except that we experienced a problem that, up to now, has been minimal. We are being targeted: little footprints are being left across our brassica bed by what we presume must be one of the many squirrels in the area; rather large heaps of dung suggest we have a resident fox; at the same time, the pigeons and magpies have targeted the brassicas from above and, every time I arrive at the allotment, I see three or four of these birds fly off leaving behind another piece of shredded cabbage; what the birds don't finish is viewed as a cheap lunch by the slugs and snails and the few cabbages we have eaten have been full of slugs when I have started to prepare them.

All of these creatures obviously feel they have as much right to Blondin as we do, but I am ready for the battle. No comprehensive study of allotments can be viewed as complete without a look at the subject of dealing with pests. For me, the word pest means anything that deters the allotment holder from his or her gardening duty. As such, I am tempted to include children here because certainly, in my case, they have held up work on our allotment more than any other pest. Our family days at the allotment can be hugely enjoyable, but they are not hugely productive as MJ and I are forced to take turns in amusing these little people while the other one works.

Generally speaking, when dealing with pests, one has a choice of a permanent solution – which generally means the death of the pest – or a much less dramatic, ongoing campaign against the pest in question. Where children are involved, it's no surprise, that I practise the second method exclusively. I have actually failed in retrospect to deal with their 'pestiness', however. The promise of food is a good ploy and bonfires also amuse them for a period; however, there are only so many blazing fires you can have in one place before you start turning up in psychiatric studies.

The other pest you must consider carefully before extermination is the fellow allomenteer. Our experience of allotment neighbours is almost entirely positive. We have got to know some great people at Blondin who always have time for a chat (about the weather usually) and are always ready to give advice where we have needed it. However, there are occasions when you have very limited time at the allotment. Perhaps it's an hour in the evening before supper and you need to water the plot, or you have grabbed some time in a busy day to cut some broccoli or dig some potatoes; these are the times when the last thing you need is a long conversation. I have found that a radio is useful here; it forms a barrier between you and the hovering conversation-hungry allotmenteers. Rather than working in silence, it is clear you are listening to something, so it is their job to interrupt you, rather than yours to acknowledge them.

However, though human beings may cause a problem in terms of time management, they rarely attack your crops. That is the domain of the nation's wildlife. At first I felt that we could live at one with the birds and the animals but it now seems that we have reached a 'them or us' situation. I therefore bring up the subject with my gardening friend Chris, who has dealt with the odd mangy fox in his time, and I also ask a couple of people at the allotments about their approach to pests. With all this in mind, here is the Paul Merrett guide to pest control:

Foxes. I have always been fond of foxes. As a child I can remember going off with my grandparents to watch the local hunt ride out. Far from being impressed by the pomp and glory of these brave hunters, I can recall hoping that every one of them fell off their horses. But foxes in cities can be pests and I do know those who feel that a good fox is a culled one. I could never kill a fox so, when the tell-tale paw marks start appearing across my newly dug beds, I know that some other approach is required.

Foxes not only run across newly dug and planted beds, but also tend to view an allotment as a suitable toilet facility, and occasionally they may start to burrow in the ground. A friend advises me that a fox is territorial and uses scent to mark out his own territory as well as identify the territory of others. It is suggested to me that, if I were to pee randomly around my allotment, old Reynard the fox might be deterred by the scent. Not only has this manoeuvre proved successful, it also means I don't have to walk all the way up to the composting toilet. (I would like to point out that I don't actually walk the borders of my allotment peeing here and there but rather use the bucket and scatter method!)

Cats. Cats do much the same as foxes but I could never kill a cat either. Apparently, years ago you could get lion dung from London Zoo to spread around the place. Presumably Moggy the cat would get one whiff of lion dung and beat a hasty retreat, so I phone up London Zoo, but I am told that this is no longer possible. Either all their lions are constipated or health and safety are at work. I suspect, however, that the old urine trick does for them as well as the foxes.

Pigeons and magpies. These are the main two pests when it comes to birds. My brassicas are constantly harassed by both species. I am not allowed to shoot the birds because of local allotment bye-laws so netting the brassicas is really the most effective barrier. Some people also put up rows of CDs on string – they twist and shine in the sun and apparently are very good at scaring off the birds. However, I am very fond of my CD collection. One type of bird that we see regularly over the allotments is a parakeet (yes, a parakeet). I have seen flocks of 20 green birds flying overhead and settling in nearby trees. They don't appear to be a pest in any way; I just include this fact to demonstrate how glamorous our west London allotment is.

Squirrels. Squirrels are most definitely on the pest list. There are hundreds of these things all over our allotment; they live in nearby trees and come to the allotment for an easy meal. I mention this one day to Chris who tells me that what I need is a squirrel trap. For this trap, you half fill a water butt and place a disc of polystyrene floating on the surface. Scatter a few nuts on this polystyrene and eventually Mr Squirrel will leap onto the polystyrene to get the nuts. Unfortunately for him, the result is disastrous: he upends the polystyrene disc and drowns in the water below. OK, this isn't pretty but some things call for drastic measures. My children think I am horrible for even considering murdering a squirrel but they are pests and they deserve it. The squirrels not the children.

Incidentally, if you can manage to kill your squirrel by cleaner means, apparently they make a perfectly decent meal. Romany travellers have long known this fact. On a culinary level I would recommend eating only the red squirrel, which has far sweeter meat. (OK, that last bit about red squirrels was just a joke but, if your allotment has a red squirrel problem, I suggest you scrap vegetable growing and open a wildlife sanctuary; you will probably make a fortune.)

Slugs and snails. The obvious way to reduce the slug and snail population on your allotment is to scatter pellets around the place. This will help to kill off some slugs and snails but remember that these pellets are also harmful to other more-desirable animals like hedgehogs.

Slugs and snails love a drop of beer occasionally, so sinking a jar containing beer into the ground can catch a few of them. When I first did this at the allotment, we put down three different beers to see which one the slugs and snails liked best. In a 24-hour test, the super strength Special Brew came out top with nine victims, followed by Guinness with four. In third place was Heineken Export with a pitiful two drinkers at the bar.

Snails of course can be eaten. I love a plate of snails every now and then and have been very tempted to set up a snail farm at the allotments. What better way to get my revenge than by eating the culprit? Two things have stopped me: the first is called my wife – MJ made it absolutely clear that she would play no part in the allotment if I started to bring home snails to eat; the other reason is that, apparently, even a small snail farm stinks and we would probably get complaints.

Along with the pests, November is not turning out to be our most successful month, but it does herald our one-year anniversary. Twelve months ago the far end of Blondin Allotments was a barren wasteland. It is now supporting (just) a family of four. This is something to be proud of.

We had originally set out to be self-sufficient within the year but, though there have been lots of good times over the past year – picking strawberries with the children; painting the shed; our late summer harvest and, of course, winning the New Allotmenteers of the Year award – our time limit has had to be extended. Our aim for next year is obvious: we need use the experience we have gained to forge ahead. My Excel spreadsheet will make sure that we don't miss a trick and I am hopeful – confident; even certain – that this time next year we will need satellite navigation to locate our nearest Tesco.

Despite this Dunkirk spirit, however, the reality does remain somewhat bleak. Our cabbages are all used up, our other brassicas are on a 'grow slow' and we have already made a start on the beans in our freezer. We must now face up to one of two scenarios – either we return cap in hand to Willy Waitrose and ask for some fresh vegetables, or we die young.

Chapter 10 | Happy Bloody Christmas

Dear Santa

We have 24 days to grow enough Brussels sprouts for eight people on Christmas Day. That is the primary objective come December. Our brassica bed has let us down badly so far this winter. Our curly kale and purple sprouting have done neither curling nor sprouting; we have finished all our cabbages and the only hope is that our swede will come through to save the day.

Come on, Santa, we have done our planet-saving best. Please give me sprouts for Christmas.

MJ's birthday is in early December and, despite holding tight to the notion of self-sufficiency, I honestly cannot cook a 'special' swede casserole to mark the occasion and expect to live.

Nothing much has changed at Tesco since my last visit about two months ago. They still have the full range of summer berries for sale, as well as beans, courgettes and lettuce. In December – it's a joke. I creep into the store and sheepishly fill my basket with fresh fruit and vegetables, feeling like a commando behind enemy lines.

Over the last couple of months I have been writing about seasonal cooking for the BBC *Olive* magazine. In it, I am introduced as a chef who is growing all of his family's vegetables without visiting a supermarket; though it's unlikely I will be spotted at Tesco, I nonetheless keep my shoulders hunched and my head low – just in case.

On the big day MJ has a lovely bowl of stir-fried broccoli with chilli, garlic and ginger to go with her roasted scallops (from a fishmonger, incidentally) followed by a fruit salad of mango, pineapple, kiwi fruit, passion fruit and lychees – it's amazing what grows in some parts of Britain during December.

On my spring visit to Wisley Garden Centre all those months ago, I had innocently bought a copy of a book entitled *Allotted Time* by a man called Robin Shelton, who keeps a diary about growing vegetables on an allotment. When I got it home, I realised that Mr Shelton had written a book that would sit on the same bookshop shelf as mine, and I had decided not to read it in case I stole all his funny bits.

Instead I saved it until now, for MJ's birthday. It is the last present we give her to open as she sips her early morning birthday coffee and, as I hand the parcel over, I apologetically explain that it might be a rubbish present and I will understand if she takes it straight to the charity shop. Much to my dismay, MJ reads almost half the book by breakfast time and, somewhat disloyally I feel, proclaims it to be a charming, amusing and well-written book. I hope Mrs Shelton is enjoying this one as much!

With MJ's birthday behind us, the next big celebration is Christmas. I had planted my Brussels sprouts in October on the advice of *The Vegetable and Herb Expert*, who assured me that they would be ready for Christmas. However, the big occasion is only twenty days off and our sprouts are currently pathetic – the size of a pea, to be precise. Fearing the worst, I decide to go over and see Sheila and take a look at her sprouts.

My worst fears are confirmed: Sheila has row upon row of plants drooping under the weight of the sprouts. I just can't understand it so, back home, I check the book to make sure that I didn't get the date wrong. I didn't; I am completely blameless in this fiasco. I wonder whether it could be a misprint or perhaps even a sick joke.

The main task in hand up at the allotment is a new patch of land that we have been given by the allotment committee. We had been told that this was a possibility some time ago and, during last month's committee meeting, it was decided that our neighbour had fallen foul of the three-month rule and had therefore been evicted; since his plot was relatively small and ran adjacent to ours, we were offered his patch.

The biggest surprise of all is the fact that we had a neighbour on that side of our plot at all. We have never seen him there and his plot is as overgrown as ours was when we got it, which I guess explains his eviction. Although both MJ and I do not feel like starting all over again on a land-clearance project, we feel that we should accept the space and give it a go. This time we are at least armed with experience.

I spend two days pulling up the weeds and collecting the familiar bucketfuls of bottles, cans and other sundries and then I decide to speed things up. Since we haven't experienced any bad effects on our present patch, I break the golden rule where cooch grass is concerned and decide I am a born again 'rotivator-er'. A rotivator works by churning up the ground to a depth determined by the speed – if you walk quickly the blades skim the surface or, as in my case, if the land has not been maintained you walk slowly allowing the blades to dig deep as they go. Though I opt for the walk slow, deep dig version, I have the entire patch cleared and ploughed in only half an hour.

During the summer months I had noticed a few happy family gatherings taking place at the allotment. These normally took the form of a barbecue and involved very unallotment-like behaviour such as sitting on chairs in the sunshine.

While the project manager in me is horrified to spot such idle behaviour, my more human side is convinced that a patio with benches, a table and a real barbecue will make the allotment a place where we all want to spend time.

That evening I send three text messages and gather myself a work gang. Three days later I pick up Anton, Moose and Greg at the tube station, and, between us, we lay a patio over half of the new plot. OK, so it is not exactly the sun terrace at Sandringham, and admittedly some of the slabs do wobble a bit, but, nonetheless, it is a patio.

Having made quick progress with one half of the inherited patch, therefore, we now turn our attention to the other half. When we were originally approached about taking on the extra land, we immediately thought about a fruit tree – partly because we have to acknowledge that, if we are to avoid food shops, then we have to produce our own fruit. So now MJ and I agree that the most useful thing we could add to our allotment would be an orchard. Actually MJ never used the word 'orchard'; she just suggested that we plant an apple tree, but I can smell a project a mile off and I set about the research.

I immediately start swotting up on fruit trees. A recent purchase –*The Fruit Expert*, also by Dr DG Hessayon – and the *RHS Fruit and Vegetable Book* are both very useful. Once I have the basics sorted, I phone my dad to talk specifics. He recommends that we buy our trees from a specialist nursery, one that makes it its business to buy and sell fruit trees in the best condition. He goes on to suggest that there is a very good nursery near him and asks whether I will allow him to buy us the fruit trees for Christmas. This previously unknown level of generosity is too good to be true, so I agree to put together a list of five or six trees from the nursery's catalogue and email it over. My choices are:

1. Lord Lambourne apple – I have eaten this before and it's very juicy and crisp; it's also red, which is important because it means the kids will eat it
2. Red Melba apple – red again
3. Discovery apple – this is my very favourite eating apple of all time
4. Glow Red Williams pear – red skinned (I am applying the 'kids will eat red fruit' rule again)
5. Early Transparent gage – gages are part of the plum family and I actually prefer them to plums in terms of flavour; they are very good in pies (and crumble, MJ)

Not long after emailing Dad, the fruit trees arrive in a Parcelforce van. I can barely contain my excitement at the prospect of owning an orchard and rush down to the allotment; within three hours we have five fruit trees standing proud.

I try hard to find out how many trees make an orchard but to no avail. There does not seem to be a minimum requirement stipulated in the dictionary or any of my books, so I take it upon myself to classify an orchard as 'at least five trees, all planted quite close to each other'; using this explanation we definitely do have an orchard – its official.

Midway through December I am invited to a breakfast event at Roast Restaurant in London's Borough Market to publicise the Slow Food movement, an organisation that aims to 'counteract fast food and fast life' by 'preserving local food traditions and influencing opinion on how our food choices are made'. Though I have never enrolled, I have always meant to (honest!) and have long been impressed by its aims and values. So when I am asked if I would like to attend an exclusive event hosted by Slow Food *and* get a free full English breakfast into the bargain, I am only too happy to delay my digging for a few hours.

The event is hosted by Carlo Petrini, the Italian founder of Slow Food, who addresses us through an interpreter. He covers many of the vital issues surrounding food production and supply, in a speech that truly makes an impression on me. Towards the end of his speech he introduces David Cameron as the special guest speaker. With a waft of Old Spice and a smile that could confit a duck leg, in sweeps the leader of Her Majesty's Opposition.

Mr Cameron tells us that the British food industry and the bodies that govern it are doing good things ... but there is more to do. He could say, but doesn't need to, that, in his view, these achievements will happen only under a Tory government! I personally feel it is less a talk on food and more a party political broadcast, and I can't help thinking that it signifies all that is wrong with food in this country: it's all so middle class. All this talk of organic produce, food miles, regional produce; in this country it still remains too costly for too many.

Take our allotment for example – we have spent a lot of money on tools, a shed, books, seeds, plants and assorted bits and bobs and, in truth, were we to tally the money spent against the money saved by not buying vegetables, we would, I expect, be in for a shock. Having climbed off of my high horse and eaten my free breakfast, I leave Borough Market and catch the train back to Brentford.

During late December I have agreed to do some cookery demonstrations, which require various ingredients, so another covert trip to the supermarket is required. Reluctantly, we also acknowledge the need for fresh vegetables for the family, among other things, so I drive off to Waitrose with a long list of requests:

MJ – cabbage, spinach, apples, bananas
Richie – mushrooms, mango, bananas
Ellie – tinned sweetcorn, mangetout, bananas

Maybe it's just me but I reckon I can spot a theme here. We have not eaten bananas for about three months now; personally, I have not really missed them that much but, apparently, my family are suffering severe banana withdrawal symptoms and have taken the opportunity to drive the point home via a shopping list. Well, it is Christmas, almost, and there are Fairtrade bananas for sale so I shove twelve of them in my trolley and carry on shopping.

Rounding the corner from the fruit section, the supermarket ordeal gets even worse. There, in front of me, are rows and rows of Brussels sprouts. There are trimmed ones in bags (awful), loose ones in a box (slightly better), and chains of sprouts 'on the vine' for sale (these look quite good, I have to admit). All of them are British, which means that I am possibly the only gardener in the country to have mucked up their sprout-planting agenda. Very reluctantly I hide a chain of sprouts in my trolley under-neath the large plastic box I use instead of shopping bags. When I get home I am going to update my Excel spreadsheet with a stern note about sprout-planting times.

Also on the shopping list is an advent calendar (with chocolates) for Ellie and Richie. It is already late December and I have been promising to buy them an advent calendar since the beginning of the month. Feeling rather guilty about this, I decide that I won't buy them one to share; I will buy them one each.

I spend a good ten minutes searching for the calendars and, in the end, decide to ask for help. Just as the assistant is explaining where they are, I notice them out of the corner of my eye. I thank her anyway and dash to the counter, quickly shoving the calendars – a pink one for Ellie and a blue one for Richie – in en route.

Back home I give the kids a shout, 'It's your lucky day, guys. Not only do you have more bananas than you could wish for, but also your own advent calendars. One each.' They are delighted to get the calendars, and even happier when I instruct them to eat all the chocolate up to the current date. After eating a couple of chocolates they mention that they taste funny. This is typical of my ungrateful children and I give them a rerun of the 'child in Africa with no advent calendar' lecture; I insist that they carry on eating the chocolates until they get up to today's date.

Later that evening MJ sees the calendars and summons me to the kitchen; she informs me that I have bought pets' calendars – pink for a cat and blue for a dog. The chocolate, it turns out, contains fish oil and little sugar. Whoops. Acknowledging my error, I quip that I shall only worry if I find Richie on the shed roof licking his bottom. The children go to bed in tears saying they feel sick, and I go to bed hoping nobody phones ChildLine.

The last visit to the allotment of 2006 happens on Christmas Eve and, to be honest, there is absolutely no point in going. We decide to have one last check on the Brussels sprouts but they are still the size of peas. It becomes blindingly obvious that we are going to be eating supermarket vegetables on Christmas Day, which is galling, to say the least, when one is trying to have a bit of a self-sufficient celebration.

There is only one row in our house on Christmas Day, and I suspect it is the same row that happens in many other houses. We are sharing Christmas lunch with friends, and the day begins in traditional (secular) fashion with a pint at The Fox by the canal with various friends and neighbours before we walk home for lunch with Dilly and Doug. I then charge around the kitchen cooking like a madman while MJ takes on the role of kitchen porter and anger-management counsellor. Eventually, the table is set and we all sit down.

Ten minutes is spent bargaining with the four children present to get them to eat a spoonful of bread sauce and to at least try a parsnip, then we move discussions on to the green element of the meal: the Brussels sprouts. All four refuse to play ball. All of them claim immunity from parental pressure on the grounds that it's Christmas. I stand firm and demand that each child should eat at least one sprout; this will guarantee them unlimited access to sweets and chocolates for the rest of the day. Still they refuse, so, in the end, like any good parent, I put sprouts on their plate and tell them I will force them to eat them if necessary.

In my honest opinion any good wife would readily agree to endorse such a simple directive, in support of her beloved husband, but I am sadly mistaken on this front, and am told that I risk spoiling the whole day if I continue with such folly. Rising to the challenge, I gamely risk said folly and end up in the doghouse; the sprouts end up in the bin.

What is it about sprouts – why are they so loathed? It is surely a case of poor PR. In my opinion – an opinion endorsed twice by Michelin I hasten to add – it is a wonderful-tasting vegetable that rightly deserves more prominence in our national diet during the season. My children, however, are certainly not unique in their loathing of sprouts. I know many grown-ups who also share their disgust – my sister, for one, will not eat a sprout at any price.

Perhaps it's a deep-rooted genetic thing. Perhaps the vast majority of people are actually biologically programmed to throw a tantrum whenever faced with a sprout. If that's the case then I'm one of the odd ones out. I adore Brussels sprouts and always have. But this anti-sprout gene theory needs looking into because this poor vegetable does not deserve such a negative reputation.

I suspect that what most people fear is the over-cooked soggy sprout, and, in that, I am no different. You have to boil a sprout until it's cooked, but no more, at which point I would recommend plunging them into iced water to halt the cooking before draining them off. From this state it's easy to reheat them and serve them lightly buttered with a good twist of black pepper, or you can customise them with additional ingredients. They make fabulous bubble and squeak or, if you have the Ramsay family round on Christmas Day, you may wish to consider cutting the cooked sprouts in half and lightly caramelising them in a pan with duck fat, some streaky bacon, a few chestnuts and a little chopped truffle. By the way, if you really *do* have Gordon coming round for Christmas lunch then only tell him where you got your sprout recipe from if he likes it! Ta.

Chapter 11 | Johnny Depp at the Allotment

The year 2007 starts – predictably – with a hangover. Foolishly we have
invited some other hangover sufferers round for lunch, so I am up early
trying to remember how to make toad-in-the-hole. It is nearly a week
since we last visited our patch of arable joy, and we have no intention
of doing so any time soon, simply because the weather is so bad.
However, following a boozy New Year's Day lunch, MJ has the bright
idea of logging on to Google Earth and inputting the coordinates of
Blondin so we can enjoy a virtual visit.

The aim is to show our friends where we (currently don't) spend our
Sunday afternoons. It works a treat. The entire area is pictured perfectly
via satellite, with bountiful vegetable patches paying homage to the
Earth's face, though with one shocking discovery – our plot is featured
only as the barren wasteland we inherited some eighteen months ago.
I can't believe that Google Earth is so behind the times and I decide to
email Google to demand an updated image forthwith!

January is several days old by the time we take our first visit to the
allotment. I am at one with the family on this one: we have had a great
Christmas and haven't given the allotment one thought up to now; we
go only because we know we have to – rather like a post-holiday gym
membership.

It is a cold and wet Sunday afternoon – when any sensible person would fire up the heating (to hell with carbon emissions) and watch *The Great Escape* – but we are no ordinary family. We are the Ethical Crusaders Who Must Brave All Climatic Conditions in Pursuit of Self-sufficiency. Damn.

Frankly I would rather be sunbathing in Iceland but I put a brave face on it and tell MJ and the kids that it will be great fun. MJ protests and tells me I have become Clark Griswold, Chevy Chase's character in *National Lampoon's Vacation*. (She also tells me this whenever I try to strike up a sing-song in the car on holiday so I should be used to it, but still it hurts.) But, reluctantly, the guys do mount their bicycles for the short trip down Boston Road. The weather is truly foul.

Allotments really don't look their best in early January. As soon as we arrive I know that it is a bad idea. The main job at this time of year is digging over the beds in preparation for the planting season and none of us is in the mood. At times like this I honestly feel like covering the entire plot in AstroTurf and going off to the supermarket to buy strawberries from Brazil. With dissent rife among the troops, I obviously can't share this demotivating thought, however, so I commission the harvesting of the available vegetables and we beat a swift retreat home for a game of Monopoly. Unfortunately the only available vegetables that we manage to harvest are swede and Brussels sprouts. Great. I know that I will be the only one who will eat these willingly so it is inevitable that we will be making an early year visit to our local supermarket, again.

The weather does not improve either. After several nights of strong gales I visit the allotment to find what I feared – a scene of devastation. Compost bins have been blown from one plot to another; anything that had been managing to grow in January is buckled and forlorn; and sheds that once stood proud lie on their side. Smugly, I note that our shed is still standing; however, our compost bin is nowhere to be seen. I decide to head home and forget all about the place.

The trouble with allotments, though, is that they have a habit of sneaking up on your consciousness; just when you think you have managed to cast them from your mind, they rear up and yell, 'Tend me.'

I discover that one way to tend an allotment, while still staying warm and dry, is to buy seeds online for the year ahead. Computers are a necessity to the modern gardener, such as me. My Excel spreadsheet that tells me what I need to buy is now stuck to the wall in both the kitchen and in our bedroom – until MJ discovers it there that is. I spend two nights drinking too much red wine and ordering all my seeds for the coming year. In fact, after my fourth glass on day two, I realise I have probably ordered all my seeds for the following three years. But that's the problem with mixing alcohol and gardening – bravado takes over and you think, 48 cabbage seeds? That will never be enough.

Many of the seeds I buy are the same or similar to the ones we purchased last year. All types of beans, lettuce, tomatoes, brassicas and roots are in the post, as well as a couple of things we didn't grow last year like salsify, a lovely white root that I've used many times in the kitchen but never at home. I also order both Jerusalem and globe artichokes.

I am still avoiding the allotment because of the horrendous weather and a general feeling of apathy. I explain my lack of enthusiasm to MJ and she immediately tries to stir the gardener that lurks deep within me by saying, 'This time last year we felt just the same about the allotment; it was cold, it was windy, it was wet and we had buckled. We had turned our backs on the plot. This year we must toughen up and spend time at the allotment despite the weather so that we are ahead of all the other fairweather gardeners who, right now, are sitting at home by the gas-effect fire.'

Bloody hell, what a speech. I am ready to dig over and plant up half of Ealing after that. I tell her that we have to get down there this weekend. Apparently, we are off to visit her brother this weekend, however, so the results of her motivational forum are put on hold.

In the meantime, I summon up some enthusiasm by planning a herb garden. A chap at college once said to me, 'Everyone needs herbs, man.'

I am fairly sure the ones he was talking about are not sold online by the Royal Horticultural Society, and, indeed, are not the type I am recommending for everyday culinary use (though if anyone is willing to pay me to write a book about it I am ready to throw myself into the research), but the guy did have a point. We do all need herbs. I have come to realise, though, that herbs are best off at the house, rather than at the allotment. Last year I planted a small selection of herbs at Blondin, where they grew really well, but the trouble with herbs is that they are often an afterthought when cooking, so having them growing half a mile away is no help whatsoever.

For example, just imagine six good friends turn up out of the blue a mere thirty minutes before lunch. This scenario is a real favourite of food magazine editors and TV producers – they can't wait to find out what a chef would rustle up in that shocking event. Well, this chef would hide below the window sill and pretend he wasn't in; if it were ever mentioned he'd forcefully suggest they turn up only with an invite in future.

But let's pretend it did happen. You need to knock up a spot of lunch 'on the hoof' and you haven't been shopping yet. I would recommend you boil up some dried pasta; when cooked, toss it in a little unsalted butter, give it a good twist of black pepper, add some flaked sea salt and grate over lots of fresh Parmesan. There you have it: a completely satisfactory bowl of pasta. But now, go out on to the patio and pick a good handful of fresh basil, pound it in a pestle and mortar and then work it through the pasta. Now you have an Italian classic on your hands!

With this in mind I make my first journey of the year to the local garden centre to buy some herbs. MJ and I then spend a morning in our back garden potting up small specimens of permanent herbs: rosemary, thyme, marjoram, oregano, sage and mint. This selection should cope with the demands of most recipes though there are others that can be useful, among them, bay leaf.

For me, the jury is still out on bay leaves. I am not convinced that they are as vital as some chefs would have us believe. I never order them in from my restaurant suppliers, partly due to my scepticism and partly because I guarantee you that any 'tube station to restaurant' journey in London will pass a front garden or restaurant forecourt with a large potted specimen of bay from which the odd pilfered leaf will never be missed.

Annual herbs need to be replanted each year; they include parsley, tarragon, chives, coriander, basil, sorrel and dill. Unlike the permanent herbs, these are seasonal, so they are added to the Excel spreadsheet before ordering the seeds for these online.

By now I am really beginning to feel like a gardener once more. The gentle potting of herbs as well as the 'online gardening' has suckered me into assuming that a day at the allotment will be fun and fulfilling. On the last Sunday in January I drag the family down to Blondin and, once there, the gloomy reality sets in: we must dig over each bed in readiness for the coming season. MJ and I set about the task with a good deal of reluctance while Ellie and Richie huddle in the shed eating sweets.

During the course of the day Ellie wanders over to talk to me as I enthusiastically dig over last year's potato patch. The conversation predictably starts with a request to go home, but I manage to steer things back to gardening and try to encourage her to see the wonderful benefits of growing anything, be it a pretty flower or a cauliflower. I explain that, perhaps right now, gardening may not seem very cool, but I guarantee that one day she herself will give it a go. She explains that she doesn't mind so much when the weather is good – which is totally reasonable really – and then says, 'Maybe gardening *is* quite cool, Dad, because I read in my magazine that Johnny Depp loves gardening.'

Hope at last! This is the break I have needed – if I can make gardening seem *cool* then the kids will buy into the whole idea of allotments. Briefly my mind wanders as I imagine Johnny strolling down towards our plot telling a few celebrity friends that he thinks MJ and Paul are just *so* hip because they grow all their own vegetables. Suddenly I realise that Johnny is right – all this *is* so cool. I imagine that, before long, MJ and I will be hanging out at The Ivy, drinking champagne and knocking back oysters as we discuss salsify propagation with Johnny and his mates ...

And then it starts to rain – not pitter-patter rain, but serious, wet rain, unlike anything that would dare fall on a celebrity. The next half hour is spent standing in the shed with one person (me) hoping it clears up and we can work on, and three people hoping it doesn't. We retreat back home.

All my seeds arrive by post and this means more red wine and more time indoors with the central heating on as I sort through them. There are a huge amount and I need to organise them into some sort of order so that we can easily find them when their turn comes on the Excel planting plan; I decide that they will be best stored in alphabetical order. MJ, who doesn't do organisation on this level, points out my obvious sadness to anyone who will listen. I am slightly miffed at her obvious scorn and seek solace in music – I listen to an Oasis album, which I easily locate on the shelf, filed in between Nirvana and Portishead. Who says I'm obsessive?

Music, a glass of wine and a spot of cataloguing is an easy way to kill a few hours and this is a relief after our mad foray on to the winter wastelands of our allotment. The only thing that ruins a good night in is the awful smell that has been wafting around our kitchen. It is getting worse and I am eventually forced to investigate it when the kids refuse to enter the room. I start by emptying the fridge. Apart from our last swede of the season, all we have is a bottle of milk, butter, a few jars and a slab of French cheese given to me by my dad's wife, Coleen. Both MJ and I believe that it has to be the cheese so I, reluctantly, chuck the offending item in the bin and MJ empties and washes the entire fridge, then puts everything back in neatly.

Still the damned smell persists – we even take to burning scented candles when people visit lest they should flee in repulsion at the smell – and eventually MJ says she thinks it must be a blocked drain. I am commissioned to lift a manhole cover but it is obvious that the drain is flowing freely. Yet still the smell persists.

Eventually I can bear it no longer – it is now gaggingly awful. I decide to check everything once more and start with a reinvestigation of the fridge.

I start at the top and everything seems fine until I take out the swede and have a good sniff. The smell is disgusting – never in my whole life have I smelt such a rotten vegetable. And apparently it's all my fault; I should have eaten it before it went off. Never mind the fact that everyone else refused to eat any swede at all, this is my doing. Out goes the swede into the compost. No more smell.

Regrettably, MJ tells the kids the cause of the smell and it does nothing for the PR of root vegetables in general. After my incident with the swede (that sounds more interesting than it actually was!) I wonder if it is even worth planting the seeds that, right now, rest at the back of the 'S' section of my seed box. I also send MJ off to Tesco to pick up some food for the next few days.

The weather has not improved as we move into February; there are still howling gales and the temperature is just above freezing. There remain on the entire plot just three purple sprouting plants, which, after months of leafy teasing, are finally beginning to develop rich purple flowering heads. This has to be one of my all-time favourite vegetables. As well as the head, you can also eat the leaves and stalk. Even so, I estimate that we currently have about half a family's meal available – and that takes into account our children's aversion to vegetables. I decide to leave the stuff growing for now and dream of spring.

During February I am asked to appear on *Food Uncut* as a presenter along with Merrilees Parker and Jean-Christophe Novelli. On the three shows I do we have several guests come into the studio to discuss their particular area of food expertise. One is a truffle expert by the name of Dr Paul Thomas.

Most people who introduce themselves as truffle experts invariably turn out to be truffle suppliers, who are clued up on price but know little of the mushroom that earns them their living, but this guy is different – he is a mycologist who reviews truffles from a scientific angle. I explain, off camera, that I am writing a book about an allotment and jokingly mention that I, as yet, have neglected the black truffle on my planting plan.

Rather than laugh at my ignorance, Dr Thomas tells me that he runs a truffle-planting scheme. He explains that, similar to most plants, truffles enjoy fairly specific growing conditions, such as a limey soil, and they also require a 'host' tree to grow on. Their favoured trees apparently are beech, oak and hazel. Paul offers to send me a couple of hazel trees, which he will have inoculated with truffle spores from his laboratory.

This is deeply exciting. I have never heard of anyone growing truffles on an allotment before and a quick revisit of all my gardening books as soon as I arrive home reveals that none of the eminent vegetable writers has included anything on this amazing fungi. With this in mind I set about clearing a small area just large enough for three hazel trees.

Before Dr Thomas can send the trees, though, he needs to carry out tests on a soil sample from the proposed planting site. I send a small plastic bag of our allotment soil to him. I am slightly worried that he will write back saying that our London soil is simply not of the standard required for such a specialist crop. However, quite the opposite is true: our soil has a pH of 6.63, which Paul thinks is 'an excellent starting' point, though my next task is to rake in agricultural lime before planting. Paul also states that our soil is 'light and loose. Perfect for truffle cultivation'. I feel so proud that our soil has impressed someone with a scientific qualification!

What began as a whimsical chat has now really started to feel like a genuine project. Before long, the trees are in the post and, on their arrival, I unwrap them and put them in the ground. There now stands, just three metres from my shed, possibly the only truffle plantation in west London. How bloody Michelin is that?

Chapter 12 | Do the Mashed Potato

When I was learning my trade at college, I remember one lecturer
telling me that, shortly after its discovery, the potato was viewed with
some suspicion by Europeans. Legend has it that it was the then king of
France who decided to encourage its consumption by the common man.
Apparently he had a field of potatoes surrounded by armed guards, who
told enquirers that they were not under any circumstances allowed to
trespass and eat this regal vegetable, which was considered fit only for
the king himself. Obviously this whipped up quite a frenzy of interest and
soon all of France was eating the potato – a crop that could be easily and
cheaply harvested. I don't know if there is any truth in this but I like the
story, and the king's method bears out that old parenting tip – the best
way to get your kids to do something is by telling them they can't do it.

Down at our allotment we now have plenty of planting space for
potatoes. Last year our potato planting was very amateur: MJ had lost
the labels off of the bags and we knew nothing about their requirements.
In fact, we had planted them right at the beginning of our adventure
because MJ had insisted on growing something, anything. This year I
am taking full responsibility for potato planting and that starts with an
evening on the Internet.

With a simple click I am ushered into the Thompson and Morgan virtual potato shop; everywhere I look are hundreds of different varieties. At this point it helps if you have an idea of what you want. For instance, some of the waxy potatoes make excellent mash, being a little less starchy than their floury friends, which, in turn, make a great baked potato. Ultimately, you just have to sit and read the details on each before hitting the 'buy' button and proceeding to the secure online payment service. I chose four types of potato:

1. Accent – an early potato that I have used in the kitchen before. An excellent all-rounder, though you need to be careful because it does overcook rather easily. It has an excellent flavour.
2. British Queen – this second early variety is one hundred years old; apparently it is a bestseller in Ireland where, by all accounts, they know their potatoes.
3. Golden Wonder – is a main crop potato. I have heard this makes an excellent chip and you would think so with a name like this.
4. Picasso – this is, if you believe the hype, a huge cropper. It has a waxy flesh, which I reckon means decent mash.

Potatoes are cheap to buy from seed catalogues. What you buy is called a tuber rather than a potato – potato is the plant and tuber is the bit we eat. On average, twenty tubers will cost about four quid, which is extraordinary value when you consider you may get eight or ten potatoes from each tuber you plant.

Once the potatoes arrive, my suggestion (based on last year's fiasco) is to empty each type on to a tray and clearly identify them. It will be very embarrassing if you plant the wrong type at the wrong time and are spotted digging up new potatoes in August.

It turns out that identification is not the only thing we forgot to do last year. We also forgot to chit our potatoes. Now that I am in charge of a properly structured potato-planting programme, however, all sorts of information is coming to light and I set out to learn about chitting.

Chitting, Geoff Hamilton tells me, is the process by which you encourage a small shoot to grow from the side of the potato; this is done before planting and the stalky bit becomes the stem of the plant. Chitting is actually a process we all experience without even being aware of it. When you buy a big bag of potatoes and then eat rice for three days instead, you may notice that tiny stalks have appeared on the potatoes. Congratulations, you have just chitted a potato. It really is that simple.

Personally I like to chit in the kitchen(!). I unwrap, then label my four types of potatoes and put them on trays on the floor up one side of the kitchen. The kitchen now resembles a garden nursery, with chitting going on in full view of the cooker, the fridge and the dishwasher. Most gardeners might be told off by their wives for such an arrangement but, as I am also chief cook in our house, I can pull rank in the kitchen and get away with it. Once the chitting is complete, all that is left to do is plant the potatoes.

February is a hard month in terms of time management. I am filming a new series for the BBC, and MJ is away training to be a teacher. The final week of the month is very wet indeed but, in order to keep pace with the planting plan, we have to get the ground dug over. My long working hours mean there is little time to even think about digging allotments so, in the end, I decide to try working at the allotment in the early morning before my day begins. At 6.30am I get up and cycle down to the plot – my plan is to spend two hours digging before being driven to north London for the day's filming.

As soon as I arrive it starts to pour with rain, but, with potatoes merrily chitting away in my kitchen, I know I have to crack on. The soil is really heavy from recent rain and, as a result, I get just one bed dug. I do, however, manage to plant a line of carrots and spring onions.

I race back home to get dry, change clothes and head off to the studio. On arrival at the set, Dominic, the director, immediately tells me off for having dirty fingernails. Sometimes I hate bloody gardening.

The weekend is no more successful. We now seem to be really struggling to get this year's growing season underway. I had really thought that
the second year would be so much easier than the first, but life seems to
be interrupting our best efforts.

The weather is also doing all it can to put an early end to our
allotment careers. It is absolutely freezing as we cycle down to devote a
couple of hours. We are still sharing a shed with Dilly and Doug and, as
our tool collection has increased, space has become an issue, so I have
bought a large 'all weather' plastic box that we can use to store the
overspill from the shed. It has arrived flat-packed and is huge. MJ has
already made several comments, which leave me in no doubt that she
thinks it is a waste of money, but I know that, once it is up, all will be
fine.

We start by planting our early potatoes – these will be ready in June
when it will be so hot we will serve them in salads and eat them outdoors.
That's the plan, but, right now, nothing could be further from reality – it
is absolutely freezing. The kids are huddled in the shed playing on their
Game Boys – usually I would protest long and hard about such feeble
behaviour but, frankly, if my fingers weren't so numb I would go into the
shed myself and try to beat their highest score.

Our last job of the day is to assemble the box. It should be a simple task
for two mature adults but the wind is now gale force, the light is fading
and both MJ and I are cold and hungry. Just the time then to unpack a
huge pile of plastic and set about reading instructions written in very
dodgy English. It doesn't take long for tempers to fray. The flashpoint
occurs when I slot the end marked 'A' into the wrong side panel. I can't
pull the thing loose; it is stuck fast and, in the end, it snaps. MJ, through
chattering teeth, tells me how 'clever' that is. I tell her rather eloquently to
fuck off, at which she throws panel 'B' in the general direction of my head
while shouting, 'Bollocks'. Then, without a further word, she storms off up
the path and away home. Nice one.

The kids are a bit bewildered by all this – they usually only witness
scenes like this when MJ and I share map-reading/driving responsibilities

in the car. I put the unassembled box back in the shed and we walk slowly back to the gate in silence.

As we have already experienced high winds, lashing rain and sub-zero temperatures, the only climatic condition that February has yet to throw at us is snow. And we don't have long to wait. MJ wakes me one morning demanding I look out of the bedroom window. Frankly, I would only cheerfully get up and look out of my bedroom window at 6am if Keira Knightley happened to be streaking across my back garden; snow does not make such an impact.

The kids are already up and involved in a military offensive against Jake and Joe next door. Snowballs are flying back and forth over the garden fence. I start to consider how my plans for the day might have to change, since they include visiting a potential restaurant site three miles away and just half a millimetre of snow will probably mean the entire Greater London road network will be rendered useless.

When I voice this aloud, MJ seizes on the opportunity and says that I should go to the allotment and take some photos of it covered in snow. We have a 'you go, no, you go' conversation for a couple of minutes. I lose this particular match and end up walking down to the plot after breakfast.

The place does look lovely: all the shed roofs are piled high with snow and the whole site glistens under the morning sun. Fearing for the spring onions, carrots and potatoes we have so recently planted, I scrape back the snow and just hope that they will be OK. (Oh, and I put that box together, with no problem, with no wife, and in no time. So, ha ha ha.)

Underneath the snow, however, our plot remains untidy and unloved, and I am well aware of this as I traipse into the foyer of HarperCollins to have an update meeting. We sit discussing the weather, my filming, the family, but, all the while, I know the 'How's the allotment?' question is coming. After talking about a few details concerning the book, Jenny indeed hits me with this uncomfortable enquiry. 'The allotment? How's it looking?' 'Oh, great. Things are really under control. You should see it,' I respond, while desperately hoping she won't reply, 'OK, great, I will come down tomorrow.'

Chapter 13 | Frozen Vegetables

Despite the snow, the filming, MJ's teaching, some parenting, lots of restaurant searching and a smattering of book writing, there are a few things we do manage to get done as spring approaches. With the allotment covered in snow there seems little point making the trip down there so Ellie, Richie and I spend a whole afternoon sowing seeds in trays, as instructed by the Excel planting plan. The three of us formed a decent seed-sowing team this time last year so, after a short recap, we are off.

We are using plastic propagators – planting trays that contain individual modules and a plastic lid. Richie's job is to three-quarter fill each module with potting compost (peat-free, incidentally) and also to push the compost down. For this, he needs a tool because the modules are quite small. For anyone tempted to buy the tool sold by gardening shops specifically designed for this job, STOP! A bottle of Waitrose sweet chilli sauce does the same job perfectly. Maybe supermarkets do have a part to play in all this after all.

Ellie then takes the seed and pops it on top of the compost and covers it over. Her job has the added responsibility of seed identification. I sit next to the young planters with a sheet of sticky labels and some cocktail sticks (hopefully not made from unsustainable wood) and, as she calls 'carrot', I write a label, twist it around the cocktail stick and shove it into the compost.

Two hours later we have planted cabbages, cauliflowers, tomatoes and basil. With the plastic lids in place, we leave them at the lightest end of the kitchen. All we have to do now, I tell them, is to sit back and wait for Mother Nature to do the rest.

By early March all the snow has gone. It's been washed away by torrential rain, and it is still desperately cold. As the rain beats down over west London, roads come to a standstill, basements are flooded and allotments are beginning to resemble marshy swamps. I'm sure, however, that, within two months, signs will be going up in allotments all over the southeast reminding us that a hosepipe ban is in force.

The carrots and spring onions that I planted a few weeks ago have given up and died. It's a minor tragedy, but the cold weather was just too much. The only solution is to continue planting at home in a propagator and, when they are hardy enough, transfer them to the allotment. The problem is that the propagators we have bought are, frankly, crap. They were the cheapest available – thin green plastic trays with a flimsy corrugated see-through top.

My theory is this: as a seed breaks the surface of the earth it has just one thing on its mind – to reach for the light; the trouble with our 'economy' propagators is that the corrugated top distorts the light, the newly born seed is not happy about this and sets about growing as fast as it can to reach the wobbly light coming through the lid. This all means that the seed forgets about growing leaves and merely concentrates on developing a long flimsy stalk. Then along comes MJ to water it and the poor thing can't stand the weight of the water it so definitely needs. It keels over and dies.

There is only one solution – and it is going to cost money. My few bits of TV and writing have allowed me to spend time digging, but this has not made us as well off as we would like and, as a result, MJ has been delivering stirring speeches on household economics. Frankly, Gordon Brown could learn a thing or two. But we *need* new propagators

– otherwise we will fail to grow anything and then all this hardship will have been for nothing.

Canvassing MJ's opinion and getting her agreement is not an option, so off I go to the garden centre. Their selection includes: my flimsy ones; large trays with clear plastic lids in various styles; and all sorts of electric ones that regulate the temperature just to a seed's liking.

The trouble is that I still don't know much about propagation. Until last year the only thing I had ever tried to propagate was cannabis when I was a student. (For anyone who is interested, the advice I was given was to remove some seeds from one's stash and place them in compost. Ideally this should be done in an old egg box – one seed per egg 'space'. And then comes the propagation – as I now know it – part: cover said egg box with a clear plastic bag and place it near a window until the seeds start to 'hatch', at which point you should keep them near natural light and also near a light bulb for heat. Then simply await the results – probably while listening to Arlo Guthrie. But it never worked for me, Mum, I promise.)

But that was then. The question facing me now is which propagator will be best for vegetables. In the end, money makes the decision. I have to overrule the electric ones on finance grounds and the cheap version I already own are not value for money. So I end up going for two robust-looking plastic trays with lovely smooth clear plastic lids for 16 quid.

The only remaining dilemma is how to sneak the contraband past MJ, but I am not sure I'll be able to pull this off with a tactic learnt early in our relationship. When our kids were small and expensive, and my salary was all we had to live on, CDs were a serious luxury and I was a bit of a compulsive music shopper. I used to get round the CD-buying issue by stealth. I would buy three or four at a time and then sneak them home and slip them onto the CD shelf without being seen. A week or so later I would start to play them and, if questioned at length on when they were bought, I would be able to say, without deceiving anybody (much), that I had bought them some time ago.

As I arrive home I realise that two bloody great plastic boxes are tricky both to get into the house and to camouflage once in. I decide to go for the 'confident, up front, swagger in through the kitchen with my purchase in full view' method (I earn a large part of the money we spend so why should I worry? If I feel this is what we need then that's that. I wish). On seeing MJ, I back up my new-found confidence with a feeble speech generally outlining the fact that this is a necessary part of my mission and that those around me should fall in line. And then I remember I have to rush out somewhere … anywhere! Before I can get out of the house, however, MJ warms to the challenge and indicates, a little forcefully I feel, that paying the water rates and the mortgage comes just a little way before buying propagators, so now I have bought them they had better prove their worth. Still, I got my propagators and, much to my satisfaction, they work a treat.

First in are hispi cabbage, sweetcorn and broad beans. Within days they are poking through and, rather than shooting upwards, they start to form leaves. This alone justifies my purchase. Thankfully.

At last. The middle of March heralds some better weather and the allotment is once more back on the agenda. The sight of all our success-fully propagating baby vegetables is enough in itself to get us up and off to the allotment. Well, actually, that isn't true. At the moment, Wayne Rooney will have to be signing Man United shirts outside our shed before Richie goes to the allotment without a protest, and Ellie is no different, but, unfortunately for them, they are members of a happy family and their job is to tag along regardless.

We arrange to meet Dilly and Doug at the allotment so that our children can all be miserable together but, much to the annoyance of Ellie and Richie, when we arrive, there is no sign of any of them. MJ and I set about clearing the place up. This is actually the first day we have spent at the allotment together since The Plastic Box Incident, so the pressure is on.

It seems that weeds are able to endure, and even prosper, during snowy conditions. While our posh paid-for crops have withered and died during the arctic conditions, their tough-nut wild cousins have spent the time growing furiously.

MJ starts to remove the weeds while I get a bonfire going to aid their disposal, and to entertain the pyromaniacs. Eventually, some time just before lunch, a rather withered-looking Dilly and Doug turn up. They both seem a little foggy when asked how they are, and it turns out that they are the victims of excess wine. This is a serious medical condition that I have contracted once or twice myself, but there is a bright side. They have brought the dinner party leftovers for lunch so we all sit on the patio and tuck into reheated Sri Lankan curry.

Dilly had even used the chillies they had grown the previous summer on the allotment in the curry. We also grew chillies but ours fell victim to a major blunder on my part. It was Sheila who had come over one day with two chilli plants and asked if we would like to have them. We readily accepted this gift and soon had them planted up in an old sink. They grew really well and produced a number of small green chillies. By the time of our holiday the green chillies looked ready to pick, but we decided that a further ten days in the sun could do them no harm so we left them on the plant. When we returned, I was aghast to notice that every chilli had turned black. They had obviously fallen foul of some awful disease, so I lifted the plants and chucked them on a bonfire. Not long after this I read in my Royal Horticultural Society vegetable book that chillies ripen from green, through black, to red. No curry making for us!

Dilly had also brought along the remainder of a home-made Bakewell tart, which just happens to be in my top five desert island desserts. For the record, the other four are:

1. My mum's meringue cake
2. MJ's apple crumble (no pressure!) with Bird's custard *and* cream
3. Crème brûlée (must be plain vanilla not some customised version)
4. Apple tarte tatin with crème anglaise and ice cream

The sun shines down as we sit eating lunch and that raises everyone's spirits. The allotment is a different place when the sun shines; even the children start to enjoy themselves. Richie and Eddie maintain the fire while Ellie and Sylvie use some spare wooden pallets and timber to build an elaborate construction that bears no resemblance to anything in existence, but it pleases them.

As the weather seems to be looking up, we decide to take our chances and get some planting done. Four rows of potatoes, salsify, broad beans, replacement spring onions and some new strawberry plants all go in. Suddenly the allotment feels like a good place to be.

The pinnacle of our achievements, though, is the building of the compost heap. Our plastic council-issued bin had blown away in the gales and had never been found. I expect it had been claimed – based on the 'finders keepers' rule – by some allotmenteers several plots over.

The fact that it had blown away in the first place was because of the very small amount of vegetation inside it at the time of the gale. There are two reasons for this. The first is that MJ has decided to put all our home waste into a 'green bin' and leave it out for collection by the council. They take it away and compost it in a facility that traps the methane gases released; these gases are then used to make fuel. MJ's argument is that this is a 'greener' approach than having a compost heap that releases methane directly into the atmosphere. I thought compost was the very pinnacle of greenness – all this environmental stuff ties me up in knots sometimes.

The second reason for our lack of compost is that most of the weeds and vegetation that we remove from the allotment, and that could go in the bin, is burnt by our children on their regular bonfires. MJ encourages this because she knows how much they enjoy it, but I can see an inconsistency here – surely all that smoke going up into the atmosphere is at least as harmful as the methane we might have produced from the bloody compost in the first place. I give up.

This year, however, we are determined to cut the cost of the allotment and one way is to stop buying compost at £4.99 a bag and have a go at producing some ourselves. Buying a plastic compost bin seems at odds with our project and I still have a lot of timber left over from lining our beds, so we build a new compost heap from scratch with neither swearing and violence nor any mention of divorce.

During supper that night, Ellie mentions, with some justification, that the only vegetable we have eaten from the allotment this month (and last to be honest) is purple sprouting. I explain that this time of year is tough on gardeners and, unless you are really organised (and especially if you've eaten through your frozen stocks), you can find yourself with nothing to eat at all. At least we have got purple sprouting!

Ellie sees things slightly differently; she is sick of purple sprouting and wonders why we can't have some sugar snaps. MJ explains that they are not in season and we will have to wait until the summer for our sugar snaps. Ellie is not one to be fobbed off so lightly, however, and she quickly points out that you can get sugar snaps at Waitrose and Tesco whenever you want. Top marks for debating skills but, quite frankly, after all this time, our children are completely missing the point when it comes to seasonal eating, food miles and carbon footprints.

This does, however, inspire a general conversation with the kids about what food they *do* like and what food they don't. I suggest they write a list of all the stuff they hated when we first began growing our own vegetables and what they still hate now having eaten the fresh, home-grown organic versions. In the case of both Ellie and Richie the lists are the same and they are clear – what they hated then, they apparently still hate:

I tell them that I will keep their lists and show them when they are older, by which time I assure them they will love every vegetable on their lists, including purple sprouting. Maybe I am simply a bad parent, but I honestly hope both my children grow up and have super fussy children of their own. Then I am going to visit them and smirk as they beg their children to eat fresh vegetables – presuming such things exist then.

By late March it finally feels as though the winter is behind us. The good weather has continued and everywhere you look there are signs that spring has sprung. Possibly the clearest indication of this is the sight of blossoming trees. Ealing has its fair share of streets lined with cherry trees

and every year, when we walk along them, MJ remarks on how lovely the blossom looks. Personally, I don't really do the pretty flower thing; despite my conversion to the 'church of growing', I have joined a peripheral sect that deals only in edible plants.

Luckily, there is a blossom for everyone and mine is growing down at Blondin Allotments. I had added a Peregrine peach to our orchard and this, along with our gage, apple and pear trees, has started to flower. My joy at this development is harshly curtailed during a phone call to my dad, however. I excitedly tell him that the fruit trees we planted back in the winter are now in bloom, only to be told that we should remove all the blossom in this, their first year. Apparently, the initial year should be spent developing healthy roots rather than diverting the tree's attention and energy to fruit production. This is awful news – not only does this mean we won't have any fruit from our orchard this year, but it also means that I have to go from tree to tree and pick off all that beautiful blossom.

When I put the phone down I decide to check out this information. My dad has never seemed the bitter type but perhaps he has started to feel threatened by his son's progress and feels his position as head gardener in the family is under threat. If this is the case, perhaps he's handing out duff advice so that I fail in my project and turn to him for solace. Realising I am the son of such a mean-spirited man is an appalling discovery after all these years, so I decide to give him one last chance and turn to Dr DG Hessayon, our old chum *The Fruit Expert*, for confirmation on this blossom-picking issue. The Doctor agrees with Dad's advice in full. My dad is a decent friendly chap after all. Although this is a huge relief, it is only short-lived because, as a result, I have to pick all the blossom off my fruit trees – well, all but one, which I leave on the tree in the hope that we get to eat at least one apple this year.

Towards the end of the month we have been invited for dinner with some friends. It's always nice to have a meal cooked for you, but it's an even nicer experience when you are living in a house where only brassicas have been consumed for the last two months. You can fantasise about what might be served – perhaps the cook is a complete 'anti-seasons' type of cook. What joy. Perhaps, despite it only being March, we will eat asparagus, courgettes, peas and cauliflower followed by strawberries, rhubarb and blackcurrants. Thoughts like this occur to every gardener no matter how green they are, I promise you. Like everything in life, gardeners dream of what's coming, not what's arrived.

We arrive at Neil and Bec's and are immediately told to expect a meal we have never been served before. The first two courses are good but so far nothing I haven't tried before. Course three then arrives and, with the lights slightly dimmed, it looks exactly like a piece of fillet steak that has been cooked with fresh cepe mushrooms and a rather good red wine jus.

I begin to think that Neil might be under the impression that I have yet to witness the delights of fresh cepes over their inferior dried relatives, and am about to set the record straight when I have my first mouthful of fillet steak. Or is it wild boar? Ostrich then, surely? No. On a recent fishing trip to Norway Neil had managed to buy, and smuggle home, some whale meat. So here we are, sitting comfortably in a house in Acton, consuming a bloody protected animal – and the biggest shock is how good it tastes. MJ is clearly suffering pangs of guilt as she munches her way through her bit of a minke whale, while I, on the other hand, am enjoying it so much I would pop out and harpoon another were we anywhere near the coast. (Just for the sake of interest, if any reader should stumble across a dead whale, my advice would be to cook it nice and rare, much the same as you would a piece of beef, and serve it very simply – with cepes and a jus, come to think of it.)

The point is that, here we are, three-quarters of our way through an allotment project – a project that has embraced all the hot food topics of the day including ethical shopping – and now I find out that I am a huge fan of roasted whale. The following morning I feel no less guilty for having enjoyed supper so much but I can begin to see that life is full of contradictions when it comes to food.

In Norway, minke whale is considered plentiful enough to catch and, if this is the case, then why the fuss. I have sat next to fish-eating vegetarians (itself a complete nonsense) who have explained to me that they don't eat meat on moral grounds. They feel rearing an animal for slaughter is wrong. They then turn to the waiter and order the pan-fried cod – one of the fish that tops the 'to avoid' list on the Marine Conservation Society's website.

I am guilty to some degree of a similar inconsistency. I have been known to enjoy the odd kilo or two of pâté de foie gras even though I know that there are justifiable claims that its method of production is cruel and unwarranted. I have, through all this, pursued my foie gras consuming habits regardless. Yet, recently, I met a Korean chef who told me that he had seen dogs bought and sold at market for food, which I immediately denounced as wholly unacceptable.

I guess that, to some extent, we choose our causes, but that doesn't mean that our allotment project is devalued. Whatever our particular food whim may be, the fact remains that, as an omnivorous animal, we humans also need a reasonable amount of vegetation in our diet (despite my daughter's best efforts to disprove this theory) so allotments and their produce will always play their part in the national diet.

Chapter 14 | A Load of Shit

According to my Excel spreadsheet, April is one very busy month. By now
the land should be dug, fertilised, manured, free of weeds, and
generally ready for a big push on the planting front. Our plot is clear of
weeds and, after a decent end to last month, it is also dug over. However,
I have still got to work manure into the relevant beds and this should
have been done a while back.

Last year MJ and I spent a small fortune on bags of manure from our
local garden centre. All the books had advised us that most plants will
thrive in a bed that has had manure added, so we had seen paying for it
as a necessary expense. This year, though, things are looking up. My sister,
Ali, has bought a horse and keeps it in a field with other horses – which
means that we now have unlimited access to all the horse shit we could
ever need.

As our plots are joined, it seems fair to let Dilly and Doug benefit from
our horse manure windfall, so, one Saturday morning in early April, Doug
and I set off for Milford in Surrey armed with shovels and bin liners.
Apparently, when selecting manure, it is advisable to go for stuff that is
well rotted. Ali points to a huge pile of manure that she says is at least
five years old. I am not sure if 2002 was a vintage year for horse shit but

it certainly looks and smells good. Well, obviously it doesn't *actually* look and smell *good* – it is a pile of crap – but, in manure terms, there is a look about the stuff that says to me that it will do the job. We fill up ten bin liners, load them into the car (Doug's car, thankfully) and, with the windows wound down, we drive back to the allotments and immediately work it into the beds.

I have found it very difficult to actually pin down how much manure is needed for any given area. Most books give less than helpful guidelines by suggesting a 'liberal amount of manure per bed'. If I were to write a recipe for puff pastry and just direct people to use 'a liberal amount of butter per liberal handful of flour' there would be complaints from dissatisfied puff pastry makers everywhere. Finally, however, I manage to get one of my books to commit to a slightly more scientific formula of 'one barrowload per ten square yards [nine square metres]'. If we were to buy this sort of amount it would cost us a fortune so it's good that we've found a free supply source.

Digging in manure is not an easy task. Firstly Doug and I have to carry flimsy dustbin bags full of the stuff all the way down to our plot, and then it has to be thoroughly incorporated into the earth. This done, we both struggle home to clean up.

Back at the house the propagators continue to prove their worth. We now have cucumbers, tomatoes, sweetcorn, and even melons beginning to grow leaves. These little plants are like pets that need love and attention. Each morning I carry them out and leave them where they get the most of the day's sun then, at night, I bring them in to the house where they will be nice and warm. I do know how sad this sounds.

The weather is really starting to look up now. The sun is a permanent feature from the beginning of April and it's obvious to me that we are in for a terrific summer this year. I visit the plot nearly every day for about a week and carry on digging and weeding, all the while stripped to the waist. This is not a pretty sight for the houses overlooking Blondin, but I now realise any suntan worn by a gardener has to be a home-grown one because only the most cocky of allotmenteers would go on holiday in April with such a big 'to do' list hanging over them.

Saturday 7 April is a bittersweet day. In the morning I spot the first asparagus spear poking through a bed that has seemed redundant for many months. This is our second year of asparagus growing so we are still unable to eat any; they will still need another year's growth after this season before cropping can begin. All the same it is good to know that, under the ground, my asparagus crowns are still working hard towards their goal of an appearance at my dinner table. In stark contrast to this happy event, Richie and I then head off to Griffin Park, Brentford FC's home ground, where we witness them get relegated to League Two in the afternoon. Asparagus comes back each year – I fear the same might not be true for the mighty Bees!

Ellie and Richie have by now started their Easter holidays and I am looking after them full time while MJ continues her spell at university for her teacher training. We go for bike rides, visit Granny, go to the cinema and take daily trips to the park.

In exchange for all this, I suggest a day on the allotment. Both consider this as some sort of violation of their human rights and start to protest. Apparently, in their view, the role of a parent during holiday times is split between generous bank manager and tour operator. Any deviation from full-on entertainment, such as suggestions concerning allotments, is treated as a dereliction of duty.

I am reduced (as usual) to bribery. If they come to the allotment then I will organise an Easter egg hunt for them there, while I do an hour's potato planting. This is a deal they agree to – after confirming that it was 'one' hour I mentioned and not several.

This constant battle with my children is wearing me down; surely not all children can be so anti-gardening. They have recently been coming home from school and telling me about projects they are doing concerning the environment. They have even started to pick holes in the genuine efforts MJ and I have been making in regard to living a more environmentally aware lifestyle.

'Are all our bulbs energy efficient?'
'Where did the wood come from for our kitchen floor?'
'Did you plant a tree after you used an aeroplane?'

Questions like these show that they are at last becoming aware of the world they live in, but there seems to be no connection between these factors and our allotment commitment in their minds.

During April there is an article in the paper that catches my eye. At last, I think I might have received some support, from none other than the Secretary of State for Education, the Right Honorable Alan Johnson MP. ALLOTMENT IDEA TO CULTIVATE FATHER-CHILD BONDING is the headline on page eleven of the *Guardian*, with the text, 'Fathers should be encouraged to bond with their young children by working together on an allotment ...' Nice one, Alan. But surely, in my case, your advice is arse about face. It is not the father who needs encouraging to bond at the allotment, it's the pesky kids.

I am not sure if Mr Johnson's idea of allotment bonding includes bribing one's children before locking them in the shed while hiding Easter eggs, but this works for me, and finally our potatoes are in the ground.

The sun continues to shine and there are small signs that spring has arrived. Plants are beginning to come back to life and insects are buzzing about. There are not many dangers involved in allotmenteering, as far as I can see. I guess you might drive a fork through your boot if you are a bit absentminded, but it's not exactly up there alongside swimming with great white sharks. The main dangers I have noted to date are sunstroke (if you're lucky) and alcoholism. But there is one danger I have overlooked ... wasps.

One morning I am at the allotment early to do a spot of watering. As I open the shed door a wasp flies straight at me and off out into the open air. This in itself is nothing to worry about, but then I notice a strange conical thing about the size of a walnut hanging from the inside of the shed roof. Crawling around inside this is a second wasp. It is all too obvious to me that a gang of wasps has selected our shed in which to construct a home where they can rear their child wasps. That thing hanging on the inside of our shed roof, I realise, must be the initial stages of a nest.

We have a very small shed and, while there is always room to cram in another trowel or ball of string, there certainly isn't enough room for a family of squatting wasps, so eviction is the only option. I remember reading once that wasps are particularly aggressive when defending their home (entirely understandable really) so I carefully back out of the shed and look for a weapon. Once tooled-up with a plank of wood, I creep back in and splatter the foundations of the wasps' nest as well as the architect, and think nothing more of it.

I had only popped down to the allotment to do the watering, tie up the raspberries and pick some purple sprouting. All of this should only have taken twenty minutes, yet I have already wasted fifteen in destroying the wasps' nest. When I come to tying up the raspberries, I go back into the shed to fetch the string, where I immediately notice two more wasps flying around as if they are looking for something. Neither looks very happy.

I don't like wasps – they make me nervous. This is based on an incident that took place a couple of years ago in our shed at home. At the time I wasn't bothered by wasps at all so, when I was in the shed one day looking for something, I casually palmed away a wasp that was buzzing around. The problem was that I palmed it straight down the neck of my shirt, where it got extremely pissed off and stung me about 20 times. It sent me flying out of the shed and careering up the garden waving my arms and screaming like someone who has just had a limb bitten off by a large grizzly bear. MJ calmed me down, removed my shirt and, sure enough, I was covered in stings. My poor body couldn't deal with the amount of poison I had been injected with and soon I had swollen lips and was starting to shiver. Several hits of antihistamine were prescribed by Gill next door – she is a senior nurse, so I trust her – and, fortunately, I lived through this harrowing ordeal but, to this day, I get twitchy at the slightest mention of a wasp.

So the thought of having two wasps intent on revenge is too much for me to bear. I abandon the gardening and drive up to the garden centre for a can of the most lethal wasp spray. When I return, two wasps have become four. It is very obvious that they realise that their new home has just been destroyed, and I have the feeling they know by whom. But by then I am armed and determined to eradicate any wasp problem before it begins. One spray: they fall from the sky, and I get back to work.

I plan not to mention this ordeal at home, simply because it's hard enough getting my children to the allotment without the addition of vicious stinging insects, but, forgetting this, I mention the episode, and it turns out that killing wasps is exactly what Richie wants to be doing. Before bedtime he makes me promise to take him to the allotment soon so that he too can spray a wasp. This sort of violence should obviously not be encouraged, but I am only too happy for him to be on wasp patrol.

April continues to warm the country with lots of sunshine. Traditionally, you might expect showers but these never materialise; instead the country is warm and vaguely Continental. Nevertheless, I am still the only member of the family who visits the allotment on a regular basis, and this hurts just a bit. I can really see no choice but to plough on alone and hope that the rest of my family eventually decides to visit me.

In the spring sunshine even tedious tasks like weeding are made far more pleasant, however. The allotment is once more a great place to be and jobs that I have been postponing during the cold winter days can now be completed. At last the soft fruit bushes get pruned and the gutter that I bought six months ago is attached to the shed. Spurred on by this progress, with the allotment up to date and a gap in my work schedule, I decide to have a go at a bit of DIY.

I have time to consider ambitious projects – ambitious because I am completely inept at any sort of DIY. Shelves, light bulbs and plastering have all beaten me in the past. But here, in the April sun, I am inspired to build something, anything.

MJ has said she will look on eBay for a cheap pub bench to go on the patio on the allotment but, as yet, one has not turned up. The answer is obvious: I will have to make one. Woodwork had never been my strong point – to be honest I am far more likely to get a job in a Chippendale's dancing troupe than a Chippendale's carpentry shop – but I am undeterred. Over two days I saw through old scaffolding planks and get busy with a hammer; as a result we finally have seating for six with a table to match. The table even has a hole in the middle to support an umbrella. We'll ignore the fact that the table is only 18 inches high and that you're liable to poke your eye out with your knee when you sit on the even smaller bench.

As I sit alone on my seating for six I honestly wonder if any of my family will ever see it. My solo gardening is by now really getting me down. It occurs to me that, perhaps right at the beginning of this project, MJ had secretly met with the children and suggested to them that they should all encourage Dad to get an allotment in order to get him out of the way. Solitude breeds paranoia. This paranoia eventually leads me to demand a house meeting where I tell MJ, Ellie and Richie the bare facts: I am presently carrying this entire allotment project single-handed; everything that is happening down at Blondin at the moment is happening because of me. I warn them in no uncertain terms that, unless I get help – willing help – I will write the book with no reference to any of them and people will read it thinking it to be the work of a single man.

I have saved this threat for emergency use only and feel that now is that moment, so I have been anticipating a reaction. Just not the one I get.

MJ asks if I have finished and then says that she feels I have taken this whole project way too seriously. Instead of being a fun addition to our lives, I have made it into a millstone around our necks. She says I have become obsessed with perfect lines of vegetables and Excel spreadsheets; she tells me the kids are scared to run around at the allotment in case I explode when they nudge a spring onion; and, to cap it all, she says that my supermarket ban is silly and should be lifted immediately.

MJ then asks Ellie and Richie for their views (the damned modern parent approach) and they say they would love to go to the allotment if it was just for a while but, apparently, I always make them stay all day. Richie says we never have nice food when we go there because I am always too busy to help with a barbecue. Ellie says she wants to eat bananas and cherries and drink tropical fruit juice, adding that Dilly and Doug's children Eddie and Sylvie also have an allotment but their Mum and Dad still go shopping for nice things.

This is all a bit of a blow to me, to be honest. I know I do become wrapped up in little missions, but I had honestly felt that, without the challenges before us, we would have nothing to strive for. MJ responds that this is precisely the point – we don't have to spend our weekends *striving* but rather just enjoying. MJ then tries to cut a deal with me: if I let the family go to the supermarket during the months when the allotment is not producing all that much, without becoming morose and moody, then they will come down to the allotment and help me get things moving. I really have no choice but to agree and, having waved them off on a shopping expedition, I do the grown-up thing: I phone my friend Moose and go and get very drunk.

Having said her bit, MJ is suddenly very enthusiastic about the allotment. I suppose she feels a burden has been lifted – either that or she is worried that I really will write them out of the book! The weather is still glorious so trips to Blondin are made in shorts and T-shirts and, just to show willing, I organise a barbecue for the kids; I also invite my sister and her children. Nothing gets done in the way of work, which secretly frustrates me beyond belief, but I flip the burgers with a smile on my face.

Despite relaxing the rules about supermarket shopping, I am still keen to go as little as possible. However, with the kale coming to an end, we are in a kind of no man's land until the next crops reach harvesting point. We have Swiss chard, spring onions, radishes and carrots all pushing through, while, at home, our propagators are full of fledgling plants not quite ready to leave the nest.

Although our allotment is not fulfilling our culinary requirements, it is clear that other more experienced gardeners are well ahead of the game. Our closest allotment neighbours, John and his wife Susan, are already harvesting broad beans and their chard is well ahead of ours. I have no intention of begging, but there are other ways to get a vegetable handout. The most successful ploy is flattery: during a conversation with an allotmenteer you need to quickly identify a vegetable that you are not growing and then proceed to tell the owner of said vegetable that you wish you had thought of planting such a wonderful specimen; if you carry on like this for long enough, you may well be offered a sample.

Susan is kind enough to give MJ a huge bag of New Zealand spinach one afternoon. This might have been because they simply have too much to eat themselves, or because they noticed our children's bandy legs, or perhaps it was MJ's ten-minute talk on how, next year, we will plant some ourselves, and didn't it look delicious.

New Zealand spinach is a curious plant. I have never come across it in a professional kitchen and, indeed, have not seen it mentioned in any culinary books, but I did find it in the RHS's book of *Fruit and Vegetable Gardening*. It says that it is a half hardy perennial – if left, it comes back each year – that is often grown in hanging baskets. John and Susan didn't have theirs growing in hanging baskets; in fact, I got the distinct impression that what they were giving us was actually, in their eyes, an invading vegetable they didn't plant, and that they were fast reclassifying it as a weed. I expect it grows elsewhere on the allotments and has sown itself on their plot.

Incidentally, New Zealand spinach is *very* tasty. We took ours home and had a salad with croutons, bacon lardons and a poached egg one night, followed by a chicken and mushroom risotto with wilted New Zealand spinach the next.

Thanks to the handouts we have received, our supermarket shopping is limited to emergency provisions only. I have decided that, if we are going to buy food to eat, then I am prepared to spend time buying it from small shops rather than unleash MJ on the supermarket full time. I travel to Chiswick where there is an excellent greengrocer close to the excellent butcher and not far from the excellent fishmonger. Chiswick still has a typical high street feel to it; sure there are lots of mobile phone shops and the supermarkets are represented but, in between these, are real food shops selling real food – a baker, a chocolate specialist, several delis and a great wine shop can all be found within easy walking distance of each other.

I fully understand MJ's argument about convenience when it comes to supermarkets, but shopping in them is so bland and sterile, with row upon row of characterless aisles, each one full of shoppers. In a supermarket you are never served by someone who understands what they are selling. You simply pick it off the shelf and throw it in the trolley. Contrast this with going to a shop where you are served by the owner who is selling you something they are passionate about. Talking to shopkeepers is also a great way of learning about ingredients. I have often gone to the fruit and veg shop on Chiswick High Road for a few tomatoes and come out with an aubergine, a kilo of wild mushrooms and a bag of fresh figs.

The end of April means it's time for the monthly meeting of the Blondin Allotments committee. We all arrive on time at Duffy's wine bar and, having ordered our drinks, we settle down to business. Keith, the Chairman, as normal runs through the agenda – fencing, paths, vacant plots, one incident of vandalism and the locking of the main gate are the first few items up. As each item is discussed, all is calm; the committee listens intently, drinks furiously and nods enthusiastically in agreement with all that is being said. Then Keith mentions hosepipes and, all of a sudden, nine vegetable gardeners slam their drinks on the table and request a chance to speak. What passion.

Currently there is no hosepipe ban in place by Thames Water. However, the allotments are owned and let by Ealing Council, and *they* have imposed their own restriction in view of April's uncharacteristically warm and dry weather. Sheila (committee member) and Helen (committee secretary) both admit they are unlikely to comply with the council's policy on the grounds that they pay water rates to Thames Water; when *that* authority declares a hosepipe ban then they will comply, but not before. Helen adds that she simply is not fit enough to carry countless heavy watering cans about unless absolutely necessary.

Chris to my left and Joe to my right both denounce this attitude as irresponsible. By the look on Sheila's face you would have thought she had been accused of personally melting an iceberg with a blowtorch. The first obscenity is thrown as Sheila reminds everyone that, although we are using water, we are actually part of the global solution rather than the problem, because our watering discrepancies are helping us to grow our own food, thus reducing food miles.

Chris says that he actually thinks watering by hand is all part of the spirit of allotmenteering – with which I agree (though not out loud). Someone says 'bollocks', at which point Andy attempts to quell the riot by explaining that he has discovered a legal loophole. Apparently, watering a plant directly by hosepipe has been banned by Ealing Council. However, if one turns on the hose and places the running hose in a watering can before using that, then *technically* one is watering by hand.

This encouraging news is lost on the baying masses. Keith attempts to reconcile the situation by calmly assuring Sheila and the watering rebels that, until Thames Water enforce their own ban, he, as Chairman, will simply turn a blind eye to what goes on, and then says he's off to the bar. The mêlée continues in his absence.

Moments later Keith sits back down with a fresh pint of beer and amazes everyone by completely contradicting what he's just said; he announces that, as chairman of the allotment committee, he will personally evict anyone caught using a hosepipe. Sheila immediately stands up, says she has had enough and, as of now, is resigning from the

committee (at least that's what we all think 'bugger you' probably means);
she does, though, agree to have 'one for the road', which I offer to fetch
from the bar. My reason for offering is actually because I am keen to see
if there is anything between us and the bar that would have forced Keith
into such an amazing political U-turn. I am expecting to find a female
member of Ealing Council 'watering division' lying naked on the bar
offering favours to anyone who can contribute to water conservation;
I quickly think up a few contributions myself just in case my hunch is
correct, but the bar is quiet so I can only imagine Keith must have
bumped his head or something.

The issue is not really settled but the committee, now officially minus
Sheila, all agree that we should have an allotment clear-up day when all
plot owners will be encouraged to come down, strim paths and turn over
the communal compost. I agree to run the barbecue. I am surprised when
Sheila offers to help but am grateful for the offer, so we discuss issues
before going our separate ways.

Chapter 15 | Sodden, Sodding, Sod

April, as it turns out, was just a tiny joke, weatherwise, on God's part. The sunny days have now gone, replaced by torrential rain and flooding throughout the country. Rain features more than any other subject on the *News at Ten*. England is in the grip of the worst wet weather for decades. Parts of the country are entirely submerged, lives have been lost and the transport system is in chaos. Summer 2007 will forever be remembered as 'the wettest summer ever', and it's still only May!

Our visits to the allotment are now preceded by a study of the sky, as we search for a break in the weather. Some of our late spring crops such as carrots, radishes and spring onions are ready for eating and we would also be anticipating a few beans shortly had it not been for a serious lapse of judgement on my part. We had sown the full array of bean varieties, as well as sweetcorn and tomatoes, in biodegradable pots in our propagators and, not wishing to ignore good advice, I decided to leave our plants uncovered, outside, for a weekend while we went away. We returned to the devastating site of soggy broken pots and drowned seedlings; they had been battered into submission by torrential rain.

With my Excel planting plan 2007 now in complete disarray, we replant all of the seeds again, but realise we will now be at least two weeks behind schedule, which, in a gardener's life, can be make or break. All the more annoying is the fact that we seem to be the only people on the allotments to have blundered in such a way because, all around us, is the sight of happy couples erecting bean poles and planting fledgling tomatoes.

In order to retain a little pride MJ and I sow broad beans directly into the bed, as well as lines of spinach and lettuce, in the hope that these will survive the forecasted continual bad weather. Our root vegetable bed has so far only been planted up with potatoes and carrots so we make the most of a dry afternoon and get some parsnips, salsify and beetroot seeds into the ground.

Root vegetables are not particularly sexy. If any reader finds themselves in need of a romantic meal, I can suggest asparagus and truffle butter, or oysters in a light creamy broth with herbs from the garden (a dead cert), but don't go anywhere near root vegetables. They're too heavy – and, let's be honest, they can leave you a bit windy – so far as first dates go, turnip purée is a no-go zone. That doesn't mean you can't enjoy root vegetables. Once married, a little flatulence is the least of your worries, so root vegetables are back on the menu.

By the way, post-root vegetable wind is not the only way these vegetables can affect a marriage. My wife says she is Scottish. She grew up and went to school there, though her Scottish accent is about as convincing as Gordon Ramsay's. I am sure Mr Ramsay is well up on his root vegetable identification but MJ, along with other Scots I know, insists on saying swede when she means turnip. This all seems to arise from that fabulous Scottish dish called neeps and tatties. She argues that 'neeps' are in fact turnips but, when she cooks the dish, it's actually swede that she uses and not turnip at all. Swedes are large, round and yellow; turnips are smaller and white with a pinkish hue. I don't care what you put into your neeps and tatties – the same applies.

The rain continues to disrupt all our plans. Weekends come and go with no chance of family visits to the allotment. During the week I brave the conditions as best I can but the entire plot is a mudbath and digging is twice as hard in the wet because of the weight of the soil. The seeds that were sown at the beginning of the month are starting to push through the soil only to find themselves buckling under the weight of the water or being attacked by the slugs and snails, which seem to love this wet weather. We are not alone, though. My allotment radio carries reports on farmers who fear losing entire fields of vegetables and we are all being warned about vegetable price rises.

Our re-sown seeds back home are now young plants ready for the transition to the allotment. The question is whether they are ready for the weather that will greet them. In the end we take our chances and plant the lot.

One crop that seems to be doing OK either despite, or because of, the weather is our potatoes. Our early new potatoes are ready for digging; I know this because Andy is digging his up and we planted ours in the same week, so I grab a dry afternoon and gather as many as I can. Last year we left potatoes in the ground and just dug them up as we needed them, but Andy suggests lifting them as soon as they are ready this year in order to avoid them rotting in the wet ground. I return home with over two hundred new potatoes in a bin bag and wonder what we are going to do with them. MJ calls her mum, who suggests putting them in a large bucket, re-covering them with earth and then keeping the bucket in the shed. There's no substitute for experience.

Weeds, it turns out, love the wet weather. They were bad last year but this year they seem to be growing at an incredible rate. One of the extra problems with having an infestation of weeds at this time of year is that they cover up the fledgling plants and block out the light. This constant struggle against weeds makes me wonder why Neanderthal man did not bother trying to live off weeds alone. In my view, if the early hunter-gatherers in the borough of Ealing had worried less about sautéed potatoes and had rather explored the delights of lightly buttered cooch grass then we would now be gardeners supreme and streets ahead of the game!

There was no way we could have foreseen that this year's summer would get off to such a slow start. But, by the middle of the month, we have at last started our harvesting season. MJ and I had sown several lines of Little Gem lettuce, which we are starting to enjoy, and spinach and chard are also turning up at the table.

Chard is a lovely vegetable, similar to spinach but with slightly more texture. Any chef will tell you that having spinach on the menu is a pain, simply because it takes so much spinach to make a portion. As soon as spinach starts to cook, it wilts down considerably, so a decent portion requires a large amount of leaf. Chard doesn't react quite so drastically to heat so it goes that bit further. You can also eat juvenile chard leaves in a salad, as you can spinach.

While we feast once more on home-grown vegetables, we keep a wary eye on the slowly maturing plants that we have transferred to the allotment. It's good to see that they have survived the wet weather so far; with a bit of sun they might just make it.

As well as maintaining our own plot, I need to organise the 'allotment clear-up day', where all plot holders are invited to contribute to the general maintenance of the entire site by neatening all of the pathways, spraying weeds and turning over the communal compost heap. The plan is to entice plot holders into helping with the lure of a barbecue.

Sheila and I are organising the food for the barbecue and we are given a budget of £40 to cater for the 30 people expected to attend. Though £40 is not very much money to put aside for 30 hungry people, cash-poor allotment committees are not made of money so they have to budget accordingly. I am, however, a little surprised to learn that a further budget of £60 has been set aside for the purchase of strong beer. This seems a bit unbalanced to me, but the committee seems adamant so I don't argue.

On the day, despite it being nearly the end of May, the weather is predictably foul. It rains solidly until midday, when Sheila and I take our chances with a break in the rain and fire up the barbie. The money does

not go far but we have done our best. I have bought sausages and burgers and Sheila has come along with spare ribs and marinated chicken legs.

The workers start eating at about 2pm and there is a feeling of genuine camaraderie. Many of us have never said more than a nodded hello, so it is nice to get to know the allotmenteers who spend their time at the other end of the site.

The work is clearly considered to be over as all present, predictably led by the committee, wade into the beer. By about 4pm the sun is shining, the food is finished and the barbecue is reduced to dying embers. More worryingly, the beer is also fast running out so, after an emergency committee meeting, more funds are released and someone shoots off to the shop.

Andy also disappears and I assume he has gone home to avoid the clearing up, but, after a few minutes, he returns on his motorbike and offers all the children a go around the allotment. The last I see of Richie is him on the back of the bike doing a wheelie through a puddle and holding onto a pickled allotmenteer.

A few days after the allotment clear-up, the committee meets for its monthly meeting at the pub and everyone declares the day a huge success. The food went down well and all of the work got done so we agree that we should try another work-day soon. This is where the good news ends, though.

All the wet weather is taking its toll and Keith has bad news: Blondin has succumbed to tomato blight.

I have never heard of this before but, as I am surrounded by seasoned gardeners gravely nodding their heads at the mere mention of the words, I decide to keep quiet and look it up when I get home.

Blight is a serious problem that infects potatoes and tomatoes. One of my books even claims that local radio stations in rural areas sometimes give out a 'blight warning'; this is no help to us in London, but does show how grave a problem it is. The book goes on to give me detailed information on the causes of blight in order to prepare me fully in the event of an emergency.

Blight is apparently a fussy fungus called *Phytophthora infestans*, which becomes active only after two consecutive 24-hour periods in which there is a minimum temperature of ten degrees and a relative humidity of 89 per cent. Rainwater then splashes infected leaves and washes down the plant to the root to infect the plant fully.

I have been having a regular moan about 'this crap summer' to anyone who would listen. However, like the ignorant novice I am, I have forgotten to regularly record either the temperature or the relative humidity. This oversight on my part turns out to have been a serious one, but luckily Keith has spotted the invading mushroom. At the meeting, therefore, he discusses the implications: apparently, if one tomato plant gets blighted, then all other tomato plants on the site will go the same way.

Keith suggests spraying as the best way to counteract the disease. Andy offers to get hold of something called Bordeaux mixture, which he says will do the job; spraying is scheduled to take place as soon as possible. Keith then moves the agenda forwards by mentioning the related topic of 'safe spraying'. Some folk apparently like to spray all sorts of chemicals over their plots and it is agreed that we should remind the *non*-organic contingent at Blondin Allotments about spraying chemicals responsibly and well within the boundaries of their own patch. Keith then asks Andy how his cat is. Andy replies that he thinks the animal is fine; he looks a little surprised until Keith kindly explains that he sprayed weedkiller in the direction of the unsuspecting feline recently to stop it peeing on his chard.

This, in my opinion, seems somewhat contrary to the initial 'responsible spraying' advice, but Keith is the chairman and history shows us that leaders do not always practise what they preach.

June is just around the corner but there is still no sign of a big hot yellow thing in the sky. Farmers, allotmenteers and fair-weather gardeners are all desperately trying to contend with this climatic challenge. The good news is that nothing needs watering, but the flip side is that some things are simply rotting in the ground. All of the onions, shallots and garlic that we planted at the beginning of the year are now in grave danger, and both MJ and I have depressing conversations with people who have lost their entire crop of alliums due to the weather.

This would mean no garlic bread, no white onion soup with chorizo and none of my beautiful roasted shallots – it would be a tragedy, so, at the first opportunity, MJ and I whiz down to the allotment and pull up our entire crop. We are lucky allium growers indeed. Every red onion sown has come up trumps and our garlic and shallots yield about 75 per cent of the original number planted.

The normal course of action is to dig up onions and garlic and leave them to dry on the bed where they grew, before stringing them up and hanging them in the kitchen. This is simply not an option with the forecast as appalling as it is, so we take home our red onions (148), shallots (212), and heads of garlic (73), and leave them for a week, drying on the kitchen table.

We are almost back on course with our self-suffiency plan, albeit a little overdue. We now have a regular supply of French beans as well as chard, lettuce, beetroot, potatoes and carrots. The tomatoes, sweetcorn and runner beans are all behind schedule but then so is summer itself, so perhaps our timing may coincide with nature. Our soft fruit is also well on the way despite the lack of sun, and our three rhubarb plants are several stalks bigger than they were last year, which means MJ dusts off the old crumble recipe once more.

Last year we had not planted our brassicas in time to coincide with the end of our summer vegetables. This year we are determined to do better, and I have flagged this point up in bright green for June on my Excel planting plan, 2007 version. The other event flagged up for June is my 40th birthday.

Chapter 16 | Here Comes the Sun

To me, strawberries mean June. For my kids, strawberries mean we have just been to Tesco. That is what is meant by a generation gap! Perhaps the strawberry season has taught my children more than any other plant on the allotment, however. Because the strawberry is a permanent plant, it stays where it is planted initially and its progress through the year is there for all to see.

As June progresses, the weather seems to be improving. We still have lots of rain but the sun does muscle in for the odd appearance. The family once more start to visit the allotment and Ellie spots the first red strawberry early on in the month. 'Dad, the strawberries are back,' is all she says, but just to hear that is fabulous. My socially de-seasoned daughter is on the mend – she understands that excitement at finding the first fruit of the season.

This particular June is not just about berries. It is also my birthday and the day kicks off with coffee, croissants and presents. Among my many gifts is a gardener's penknife. This may sound a touch dull if you are someone who had a set of alloy wheels or a PlayStation on your birthday list, but, for me, it's a vital tool. We have bought just about every available tool for our allotment, but the one thing I have regularly needed but never had was a decent penknife. This is no ordinary knife either – it's a Swiss Army specialist gardening knife. I am not sure how much pruning and twine cutting the Swiss Army does while out on active duty, but, with a specialist knife available, it's obviously a bit more than 'our boys'.

It also dawns on me that I am now old enough to carry a knife without it being considered a dangerous weapon and that, from this birthday onwards, gardening is something I can talk about in mixed company without embarrassment; before the age of 40, it is considered prematurely geriatric, if not plain weird.

After breakfast we all go down to visit my mum so that she can see her little boy on his birthday (I wish I could write that I spent the day drinking champagne with six Brazilian lap dancers, but there is really no point in deceiving myself). First, we stop in at Blondin and pick all the available berries, because my mum has promised to make her prize-winning meringue cake (the one on my desert island desserts list) for pudding, and the only accompaniment that can do it justice is fresh summer berries.

My mum is the only culinary legend in our family. When I was awarded a Michelin star a few years ago, my relatives smiled sweetly as they congratulated me, but it was obvious that they were thinking that, if it had been my mum, she would have been awarded at least two!

I can remember seeing a comedy sketch once where the unions were negotiating with the employers around a small table in a smoky room. The militant union rep has secured the pay rise and the extra day's holiday and several other worker benefits, but he insists that, to conclude negotiations, he must also secure the boss's wife's recipe for lemon ice cream. The point here is that every home cook likes to think that they have one recipe that is their speciality. They are known among their friends for a particular dish and no dinner party is complete without it. It would be wrong for me to suggest that my mum's culinary reputation is built on just one pudding but, like all the great chefs, she has her signature dish – her meringue cake. And it goes without saying that a son turning 40 is reason enough to start whisking egg whites. Step aside Nigella, Delphine Merrett is in the house.

By now the summer has officially arrived. Up go the beanpoles and out
come the watering cans. Our root vegetable bed is proving a real success.
We have plenty of spring onions, the chard is being put to good use,
the Jerusalem artichokes are over a metre tall and the potatoes that we
planted back in February and March are now being given away to friends
in order to keep up with the harvest.

Back at home we have chillies and aubergines beginning to flower –
we've kept them at home as they prefer the heat of a greenhouse or
glass-roofed room to the outdoor allotment – as well as a vast amount
of flat-leafed parsley and basil. After a lengthy period with very little of
our own food to eat, all this is a huge relief.

Of course, no gardening year is perfect, however, and my blunder
this year turns out to be in the tomato department. The seed catalogue
recommends planting marigolds next to tomatoes. The theory here
is that the marigolds are an even tastier treat to the bugs that would
normally eat a tomato, meaning that one's tomatoes are more likely
to remain in perfect condition. This is obviously a tried and tested
theory because all over the allotments I can see the burnt orange flower
blossoming alongside ripening tomatoes (those that escaped the blight,
that is).

My tomatoes were planted back in April before the monsoon season
but there are only a few tomatoes that have limped up to the finishing
line. Oddly, it does not seem to be the blight or the heavy rains that
have reduced my crop of tomatoes to such a meagre level, but rather
suffocation. My marigolds, which I had planted out at the same time as
the tomatoes to protect them, are a huge mass of tangled branches with
a profusion of bright orange flowers that any passing satellite could easily
mistake for a small nuclear explosion, and these marigolds have crawled
all over my tomatoes and smothered them.

At least we now have a full brassica bed planted up with Brussels

sprouts, broccoli, purple sprouting, pointed and Savoy cabbage. This is a real improvement on last year when we forgot to plant any brassicas until September. All of these are covered with netting to deter the pigeons and magpies, which enjoyed so much of last year's crop. Alongside this is our legume bed, which has sweetcorn, spinach, lettuce, and green, broad and runner beans all coming along nicely.

Just as the gardening party is about to begin, I am called to New York to give some cooking demonstrations at a large food fair. I am going with another chef and we have been invited to some fabulous restaurants while we are there. It's a tough job, but someone's got to do it, so I leave a long list of jobs for MJ and head off to New York City.

On my return MJ updates me on the allotment – much of our belated crops are yet to reach maturity but they are all OK and on the way. Our asparagus bed has produced double the amount of spears this year (we still can't eat any until next year though) and all the brassicas are growing undisturbed by magpies under the netting. All this and … we have an apple. The one blossom that I left on one of our trees has apparently become a big red apple. This is fantastic news. Actually, this is half the good news: we have *two* apples, well you can't go to New York and come back without an iPod.

MJ also tells me that she has booked a last-minute holiday to Italy to see her mum. This is not such great news. Last year the allotment went off course specifically because we went on a summer holiday. We returned to find overripe fruit and under-watered plants. At the time I decided to pull the plug on summer holidays, opting instead for a couple of weekend breaks in the horticulturally less demanding month of February. I didn't share this decision with the family at the time because I knew the right thing to do was to wait until an opportune moment arose. Eleven months and several, not quite opportune enough, moments later, MJ has booked flights to Rome in July (and yes she *has* offset our air miles).

I calmly explain that I have a duty as an author and market gardener to stay in the UK during the summer months to tend the crop and write the book. MJ – quite unfairly – mentions that I didn't say this before jetting off for New York, and that the flights to Italy are paid for so I really have no choice but to tag along.

And that is how I come to find out that the Pope has an allotment. We arrive in Rome with a few days to spare before heading off to MJ's mum's up in the mountains, so we decide to give the children a spot of culture. We go to all the places one must go when in Rome and, among these, are St Peter's Square and the Vatican.

I am not really a religious sort – being the son of a biologist I have one foot firmly planted in the camp that is evolutionary science – but one cannot fail to be impressed by the splendour of the Vatican. Having done the churchy bit at ground level, the kids and I persuade MJ to go all the way to the top, from where, apparently, the view of the city is amazing. Several hundred stairs later we emerge and look down on this beautiful city. From high up, it is also possible to get a good idea of the scale of the Vatican buildings that lie in the grounds. We can see beautifully manicured lawns and fabulous old stone buildings and there, among all the splendour, is the unmistakeable sight of an allotment. I scream to MJ to look, and point down towards it. People close by presume that the excited British tourist must have spotted the Pope out rollerblading because every head turns in the direction of my pointing finger.

There is no mistake: it is an allotment. Not a whole series of plots – that would be ridiculous. The Pope has just one perfect walled plot and I can clearly see lines of vegetables basking in the sun. I suspect the previous pope dug in many of the vegetables because some of the plants looked more established than the two years of the present pope's tenure. It will be interesting to return next year and see if the plot is covered with weeds, which will obviously happen if this pope is not the market gardening type.

On our return to our own allotment, I am shocked, and a little disappointed, to find that things appear to have managed very well without me. We have cucumbers ripe and ready to eat, beans of every variety, pumpkins the size of beach balls and rows of spinach, carrots, chard and lettuce in peak condition. Last year we went away during the same week and returned to find that we had lost a lot of our crop; this year everything was that bit slower after the vast amounts of rain, so we have actually missed very little.

Back home the summer barbecue season is in full swing in our bit of west London. Barbecuing is strangely a male-dominated sport. Women and children are pushed to one side as the chaps all grab a beer and give advice on precisely the right point to start the cooking. Personally I am not a keen barbecuer – I prefer a slightly more controlled method of cookery – but a chargrilled steak is still always a treat.

Some of the barbecues never happen at all – bad weather forces us indoors while the coals lie wet under the summer sky. One such event is being organised by friends, who clearly have the foresight to check the weather forecast and then phone around to issue a storm warning. Rather than give up, it is suggested that everyone brings a dish of something and the event goes ahead as planned.

I am shocked to see that, despite the lack of a barbecue, it still seems to be the men who have spent the afternoon cooking. As each couple arrives and places their offering alongside the others, it is usually him not her who humbly says, 'I hope it's OK – it's a bit last minute.'

MJ had offered to make a crumble (no surprise there) but now, seeing the array of dishes turn up in male hands, I am glad I put her off and decided to cook myself. Being a chilly summer evening, I opted to make a beef bourguignon and a dish of dauphinoise potatoes, which seem to be very well received. However, I am knocked into second place by Doug, who pitches up with a perfect moussaka. In fact, it is so good that I have to ask him for the recipe so that I can put it in the recipe section here.

As the wine begins to flow, I get into conversation with a fellow member of the much-feared Ealing 'Hit and Hope' football team. Graham asks me how the book is coming along and I explain that the project is all but over and that the book is not too far off. We start talking about book sales and Graham asks me if I have included any sex or violence. I reply that I haven't, though only through lack of opportunity. He says this is a shame and probably won't bother buying it.

A conversation like that is just what you don't need as you sit down to write the last chapter in a book. It has been some months since I visited a supermarket but I can well remember standing at the checkout as my ethically purchased products roll down the conveyor, and turning around to see the books for sale section across the way. There, smiling back at me, are Gordon, Gary, Jamie and Hugh. How I long to join them on that shelf of literary success. How I wish I had written a simple collection of recipes, rather than plodding down the road of book writing with a heavy load of stories to tell.

Chapter 17 | The End is Nigh

The problem with this story is that there is no real ending. It would
be neat and amusing to end the story by tarmacking over the allotment
and selling it off as a Tesco Metro, but I didn't think of this in time.
And, anyway, MJ and I are now committed gardeners and that is a
commitment for life.

If we could have made one change to the last eighteen months, it would
have been to have more time to spend on the allotment. Our busy lives
kept on interfering with progress, which is I suspect the reason so many
people give up their allotments. But now we have the opportunity to hang
up our wellington boots, we realise we can't. We are hooked.

Our family's mission is over if not accomplished. We set off to prove
nothing to the world but everything to ourselves. As a family our achievements have been worth all the effort. We have never truly realised our
dream of sustainable self-sufficiency, but we have challenged our former
consumerist lifestyle and made some lasting changes. We have eaten with
the seasons for well over a year and our diet has been surprisingly varied.
What I now realise, however, is that the truly seasonal eater is under the
spell of the seasons, not in control of them.

Despite my affection for Geoff Hamilton and his sensible footwear, and my complete trust in the *Vegetable and Herb Expert*, my true gardening mentor will always be my grandpa. I see now that my grandparents lived their life by the seasons, whatever the cost. As kids we used to joke about their autumn holidays, but now I realise that the autumn was the only time they could leave their garden once the harvesting was done and without fear of falling behind.

We used to gently rib Grandpa for never going out to a restaurant but, really, if one works so hard to produce one's own food, then why go out and eat someone else's. I also used to tire of his lectures on food waste as I pushed a sprout to the edge of my plate, but now I can see that the effort involved in food production limits one's tolerance of food waste. Perhaps food is all a bit too easy these days. Perhaps a spot of hunger is no bad thing. Perhaps we all need to plough a field once a year just to help us appreciate food that bit more.

An allotment can be a valuable member of any family, whatever their income. Native Americans used to express surprise at the white man's assertion that they 'owned' the land. Their philosophy stated that the land owned them. A tree or a rock would be around long after they had hopped off the mortal coil. An allotmenteer understands this. We dig and plant and dig some more but, in the end, we are just brief custodians sowing parsnips in a patch of land that will support many more families.

Soon after I accepted the job of apprentice chef at The Ritz all those years ago I knew I would never stop cooking. I feel the same about running an allotment. It's part of our lives now and always will be, and I truly hope that one day my phone rings and one of my children asks, 'Dad, when should I plant my potatoes?'

In twenty years as a professional chef I have learned to cook. In eighteen months on an allotment I have learned about food. Those lessons have not always been easy, but they have been worthwhile.

soups, starters and salads

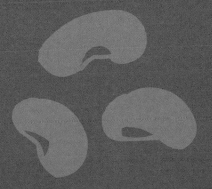

Creamy Potato and Parsley Soup

serves 4

Potatoes and parsley work well together in this soup. The trick is to cook the parsley enough to add flavour but not so much that it discolours the soup. A jug blender is the best way to purée soup, although a stick blender will also get the job done. Bear in mind that the parsley will carry on cooking even when removed from the heat, so have a blender to hand, and blend as fast as possible.

1 tbsp butter
4 shallots, roughly chopped
1 garlic clove, roughly chopped
1.2 litres (2 pints) chicken stock
   (vegetable stock is also fine)

900g (2lb) white potatoes, peeled and
   cut into 5cm (2in) dice
300ml (1/2 pint) double cream
1 large handful of parsley, coarsely
   chopped (use the stalks)
salt and pepper

1. Melt the butter in a large, heavy-based saucepan, over a medium heat. Sweat the shallots and garlic so that they soften without colouring.
2. Pour in the chicken stock and add the potatoes, then bring to the boil. When the potatoes are just cooked, add the cream and return the pan to a simmer.
3. At this point, taste the mixture and season to taste. Then add the parsley to the soup and stir in. Allow to simmer in the soup for 1 minute.
4. Remove the pan from the heat and immediately blend it to a very fine creamy consistency. Depending on the capacity of your blender, you may need to do this in stages. This is not a problem, but do make sure that you complete the blending process as quickly as you can (ignore the phone if it goes!). I like to pass the soup through a strainer, but if it is well blended this isn't essential.
5. If you are preparing this soup in advance, leave to cool and then refrigerate. It will also freeze well. Otherwise serve immediately with a sprig of parsley to garnish.

Hot and Chilled Tomato Soup

serves 4

A really quick and basic tomato soup recipe, this can be knocked up whenever the glut strikes. You can use plum, beef or cherry tomatoes but do feel free to embellish the recipe with the addition of roasted peppers, chillies or cream.

2 tbsp olive oil
1kg (2lb 4oz) very ripe tomatoes
3 shallots, roughly chopped
1 garlic clove, chopped
400ml (14fl oz) tomato juice
350ml (12fl oz) water
salt and pepper

To serve
1 ciabatta loaf
olive oil
a little freshly grated Parmesan
some fresh basil

1. Heat the olive oil in a pan over a low heat and chuck in the tomato, shallots and garlic. Cover this with a lid and allow to cook gently for 15 minutes.
2. By now, the tomato should be well cooked down and there will be liquid in the pan. Add the tomato juice and water, then season.
3. Blend everything in a liquidiser and pass through a sieve.

Hot version with croûtons

1. Preheat the oven to 180°C/350°F/Gas Mark 4.
2. Break up a ciabatta loaf into irregular bite-sized chunks. Place these in a bowl and sprinkle over olive oil and a little grated Parmesan.
3. Spread the croûtons out on a baking sheet and bake in a hot oven for 4 minutes, or until they begin to colour.
4. Re-boil the soup and serve with the warm croûtons.

Chilled version with basil

1. Cool the soup in the fridge. Check the seasoning because it may need more once cold.
2. Chop some fresh basil, stir into the soup and serve.

French Onion Soup

serves 4

This is simple French cooking at its best. Don't skimp on the onions because they will cook right down and become deliciously caramelised. The big cheesy croûton on top adds to this hearty soup, which is ideal for a warming lunch.

This soup relies on a good-quality, strongly flavoured stock, so here's my recipe for a rich stock in just 2 hours. You can buy fresh beef stock and beef trimmings from a good butcher. This stock recipe will make about 1 litre (1³/4 pints) and you need 600ml (1 pint) for the soup.

The best vessel for cooking the soup in is a high-sided casserole pan.

For the rich beef stock
1 tbsp vegetable oil
1kg (2lb 4oz) beef trimmings
¹/2 onion, coarsely chopped
¹/2 head of garlic
1 star anise
1.5 litres (2¹/2 pints) beef stock, (from a cube or fresh from the butcher)

For the soup
50g (2oz) butter
1kg (2lb 4oz) onions, sliced finely into rings
200ml (7fl oz) white wine
600ml (1 pint) beef stock (see left)
1 day-old French stick
400g (14oz) Emmental, grated
splash of Madeira

To make the stock

1. Heat a casserole pan over a gentle heat and add the oil. Add the beef trimmings and onion and cook slowly for about 15 minutes until they are well browned and beginning to caramelise. Throw in the garlic and the star anise and then pour in the beef stock.
2. Allow to simmer for up to 2 hours and then pass through a muslin-lined sieve or strainer. Save the liquid and discard the rest.
3. The stock can be made in advance and stored in the fridge or freezer.

To make the soup

1. Melt the butter in a high-sided casserole pan over a low heat, then chuck in all the onions. The onions will fill the pan but don't worry, they will cook down and slowly caramelise. Cook the onions for about 1 hour, stirring occasionally, until they are deep brown.

continued overleaf

2. Now add the white wine and allow it to reduce completely, then pour in the rich beef stock. Preheat the oven to 160°C/325°F/Gas Mark 3.

3. Simmer the soup for about 40 minutes whilst you prepare the cheesy croutons. Cut four generously thick slices of French stick on an angle and place on a baking tray. Dry in the oven for about 5 minutes. Remove and top each slice with the grated cheese, then return to the oven so that the cheese starts to melt.

4. Finish the soup by adding a splash of Madeira, then pour into bowls making sure each bowl has a good balance of onions to liquid. Float a crouton on each soup and serve.

Asparagus Soup

serves 4

In this delicious soup, the asparagus is added towards the end of the cooking ensuring that its delicate flavour and colour are unspoiled.

900ml (1½ pints) chicken stock (a cube is fine)
300ml (½ pint) milk
100g (3½oz) butter
40g (1¾oz) plain flour

300ml (½ pint) double cream (optional extra!)
15 asparagus spears, very finely sliced
salt and pepper

1. First, warm the chicken stock over a low heat. Add the milk and then bring to the boil.

2. Melt the butter in a heavy-based saucepan and add the flour. Stir together over a gentle heat for about 2 minutes.

3. Using a ladle, gradually pour the hot milk and stock mixture into the saucepan. Allow the soup to come to a simmer in between ladlefuls.

4. Once all the stock is added, let the soup simmer for 15 minutes. By this time, the soup will have thickened, but should be no thicker than double cream.

5. Pour in the cream, if using, and warm through. Add the asparagus and simmer for about 3 minutes.

6. Blend in a liquidiser. Check the seasoning, then serve.

White Onion Soup with Chorizo and Herb Oil
serves 4

This is a fabulous soup and easy to make. The chorizo and herb oil aren't essential but I recommend both. They turn a tasty soup into a stunning one.

100g (3½oz) butter
5 large onions, finely sliced
900ml (1½ pints) hot chicken stock
   (a cube is fine)
300ml (½ pint) double cream

125g (4½oz) chorizo sausage
100ml (3½fl oz) herb oil (see
   page 284)
salt and pepper

1. Melt the butter in a saucepan and add the onions. Allow these to sweat very gently for up to 30 minutes. They will cook down and produce liquid. Stir occasionally and don't allow them to colour at all – a lid on the pan and a low heat will help here.
2. Add the hot chicken stock and the cream, then allow the mixture to simmer gently for 15 minutes.
3. Blend the soup well in a liquidiser, then pass through a fine sieve.
4. Season the soup to taste and serve at once. Alternatively, leave to cool before putting in the fridge to keep for up to 2 days.

To serve with the chorizo and herb oil
1. Simply break the sausage into bite-sized chunks and cook gently in a frying pan. Allow the sausage to colour very slightly. A little coloured oil will bleed from the chorizo into the pan, which is good news.
2. Warm the soup and serve in wide soup bowls. Drop the chorizo on top of the soup and use a teaspoon to drizzle a little of the chorizo oil over the surface of the soup. Do the same with a little herb oil.

Sweetcorn Soup

serves 4–6

Sweetcorn is best eaten fresh and simple. We ate most of our crop boiled and served with a little butter (well, okay, quite a lot of butter) and milled black pepper. A few cobs did, however, get used for soup. We froze this and ate it in the winter months with various additions.

6 fresh corn cobs
several thyme leaves
1/2 garlic clove
2 small shallots, cut in four

900ml (1½ pints) chicken stock
900ml (1½ pints) milk
150ml (¼ pint) double cream
salt and pepper

1. Place all the ingredients apart from the cream and seasoning into a saucepan. Over a high heat, bring to a simmer. After about 5 minutes, remove from the heat and take out the cobs. Set them aside to cool slightly so that you can safely handle them. Don't chuck away the cooking liquor, though.
2. One at a time, stand the cobs up on end and shave the sweetcorn off in a downward stroke with a sharp knife.
3. Return the shaved-off corn kernels to the cooking liquor. Add the cream, then season to taste. Return the pan to the heat and bring to a simmer, then cook for 5 minutes.
4. Blend the contents of the saucepan in a liquidiser. The soup can be frozen or used in a variety of ways; the following are my favourite combinations.

With roasted scallops and liquorice
1. Bring the soup to a boil with the addition of a 15cm (6in) piece of liquorice root. Once hot, allow the soup to sit for about 20 minutes, to absorb the liquorice flavour. Remove the root and discard.
2. Serve the soup in wide, flat soup plates with a roasted scallop placed in the centre of each bowl.

With smoked haddock

1. Add 1 teaspoon of mild curry powder per portion of soup; this quantity makes about four large portions. Simmer for 8 minutes. Whisk the soup well to disperse the powder.

2. Finely dice 85g (3oz) of smoked haddock per portion. Stir into the soup, then serve.

Jerusalem Artichoke Soup with Oyster Mushrooms and Truffle Oil serves 4

I can't claim this soup as my own creation; I owe it to one of my former chefs, James Mclean. Jerusalem artichokes are not a widely used vegetable, which is a shame because they really are good. They need to be peeled and stored in water to prevent them discolouring, but once peeled they can be pan-fried, mashed or turned into soup.

400g (14oz) Jerusalem artichokes, peeled
900ml (1½ pints) water
50g (2oz) butter
pinch of fresh thyme leaves
900ml (1½ pints) double cream

To garnish
200g (7oz) sliced oyster mushrooms
white truffle oil

1. Keep the peelings from the artichokes and cover with the water. Simmer for 15 minutes to produce a flavoured stock. Set aside to use later.

2. Cut the Jerusalem artichokes into even dice. Melt the butter in a pan, then add the artichokes and thyme. Cook this over a gentle heat for 5 minutes, then add the stock and the cream.

3. Simmer for a further 10 minutes, then blend in a liquidiser. Meanwhile, sauté the oyster mushrooms until they caramelise lightly.

4. Finish the soup by pouring into shallow soup bowls, then scatter over the mushrooms. Drizzle over a little white truffle oil and serve.

Toasted Goat's Cheese Salad

serves 4

This is an easy and delicious way of cooking goat's cheese.

4 medium slices of white bread
4 slices of goat's cheese
1 tbsp olive oil
8 small cooked beetroot (see page 217)

200g (7oz) cooked green beans
1/2 red onion, very finely sliced
2 tomatoes
handful of salad leaves, such as Little Gem, rocket or baby spinach

1. Take a sharp knife and slice each piece of bread through the middle horizontally to produce two extra-thin slices. This may seem like a tall order but actually it's not as difficult as it looks. My suggestion would be to start with the crusts removed and, using a long knife, just 'fillet' the bread in two.
2. Using a pastry cutter just slightly bigger than the goat's cheese, cut out a disc from each of the eight slices of bread that you now have.
3. Place a disc either side of the goat's cheese and press down so that they stick.
4. Heat the olive oil in a frying pan. The oil should be hot but not so hot that it smokes. Pan-fry the goat's cheese 'sandwiches' until the bread is golden and crunchy. This will only take a couple of minutes either side.
5. Assemble your chosen salad ingredients on a plate and place the goat's cheese on top. Serve straight away.

Warm Tomato Tart with Rocket Salad

serves 4

Try this tart with a slab of grilled goat's cheese on top or with roasted scallops and a herb vinaigrette.

500g (1lb 2oz) quality, shop-bought puff pastry
flour, for dusting
8 ripe plum tomatoes

1 tbsp freshly grated Parmesan
good handful of rocket leaves
1½ tbsp olive oil
4 tsp balsamic vinegar

1. First make the pastry discs for the tarts. Cut a small slab of the puff pastry and roll it out until it's about 3mm (⅛in) thick and big enough to yield a disc of pastry about 14cm (5½in) in diameter. Repeat this until you have four discs. Prick the discs all over with a fork; this will help keep the pastry flat during cooking. Put the discs on a plate and leave to stand in the fridge for 20 minutes.

2. Preheat the oven to 180°C/350°F/Gas Mark 4.

3. Find two baking trays of even size and cut two sheets of silicone baking paper the same size as the trays. Lay a sheet of paper on one tray and arrange the four discs on the paper, taking care to spread them out. Place a second piece of baking paper on top of the discs and then place the second tray on top of the paper. Place a weight on top of the top tray – I use a brick covered in tin foil for this job!

4. Cook the discs for about 8 minutes, then check them. They should be golden brown, round and flat.

5. Meanwhile, slice the tomatoes crosswise with a sharp knife into slices about 3mm (⅛in) thick.

6. When the discs are cooked, remove from the oven. Lay them out and sprinkle each with a little grated Parmesan, then carefully lay slices of tomato on top of the cheese. Set aside for up to 30 minutes.

7. Before serving, put the made-up tarts back in the oven for a further 6–8 minutes. Remove from the oven, top with rocket leaves dressed with olive oil and balsamic, and serve.

Asparagus Wrapped in Parma Ham with Toasted Brie serves 4

This is a great way of eating asparagus; serve it with a roasted breast of chicken or, for a light lunch, simply as is.

Asparagus loses some of its flavour when boiled in water. By cooking it dry in a pan, you retain the full flavour. I like to serve this dish with a butter sauce called *beurre blanc* (see page 286).

12 asparagus spears
4 slices of Parma ham (you could use Serrano or Bayonne instead)
1 ciabatta loaf

1 small Brie
olive oil
salt and pepper
4 tbsp *beurre blanc*, to serve

1. Along the length of the asparagus you will notice a few scaly leaves. Use a small knife to pick these off at the point where the 'spear' starts.
2. Lay a slice of cured ham on a board and then lay three pieces of asparagus across it – each end of the asparagus should extend past the ham. Roll the asparagus up in the ham tightly; put to one side.
3. Cut two slices of ciabatta about 1cm (1/2in) thick. Place a slice of Brie on top of a slice of ciabatta and cover with a second slice of bread. Press down to firmly secure. Make 4 of these 'sandwiches' altogether.
4. Place a large frying pan over a high heat. When hot (but not too hot), add some olive oil and place the wrapped asparagus in the pan. Turn the asparagus every 2 minutes so that it cooks evenly all the way around. You should expect the ham to crisp up and contract around the asparagus, securing it nicely. The exposed bits of asparagus will colour very slightly but don't allow them to overcolour. After 5–6 minutes, the asparagus should be ready – test this by prodding the stems with the point of your small knife. Set aside.
5. Add a bit more olive oil and increase the heat in the pan slightly. Drop your Brie sandwiches in and pan-fry on either side until golden. This will take about 3 minutes on each side.
6. Place the asparagus and Brie on individual plates and serve with the *beurre blanc* drizzled over the top.

Pan-fried Goat's Cheese with Serrano Ham, Fig and New Zealand Spinach serves 4

I love this! There is a perfect harmony between the goat's cheese, the fig and the honey. One of our allotment neighbours gave us a pile of New Zealand spinach to use, and this was one of the many ways that we ate it. Equally good, though, would be rocket or watercress.

4 slices *chèvre bouche* (goat's
   cheese log)
4 tbsp plain flour
2 eggs
50ml (1³/₄fl oz) milk
8 tbsp white breadcrumbs

8 slices of Serrano ham
4 ripe figs, each cut into quarters
generous handful of New Zealand
   spinach
2 tsp honey
1 tsp truffle oil

1. The goat's cheese must first be 'paned' before cooking. This is a kitchen term to describe coating an ingredient in breadcrumbs. You will need three bowls. Put the flour in the first bowl. In the second bowl, beat together the eggs and milk. In the third, put the breadcrumbs. Dust the slices of goat's cheese in the flour, then douse the slices in the egg and milk mixture, and finally pass them through the breadcrumbs, making sure they are evenly coated.
2. Heat a non-stick frying pan and fry the cheese until golden brown on both sides. Now place one slice each on four plates.
3. On top of each goat's cheese lay a couple of slices of Serrano ham, then the fig quarters.
4. Top the fig with a ball of New Zealand spinach, then drizzle over some honey and truffle oil and serve.

Chorizo and Goat's Cheese Puff Pastry Slice with Broccoli, Mushroom and Tomato serves 4

These are dead simple and a bit of a favourite in our house. I usually knock them up for lunch, but mini ones can make a decent nibble with drinks if that's your bag.

500g (1lb 2oz) quality, shop-bought puff pastry

4 really good chorizo or kabanas sausages (standard sausage size)

16 small broccoli florets

8 button mushrooms, sliced thickly

4 slices *chèvre bouche* (goat's cheese log), skinned and each broken into 6–8 pieces

8 cherry tomatoes, halved

4 tsp grated Cheddar

1. First roll out the puff pastry. It should be about 5mm (¼in) thick and about 30 x 30 cm (12 x 12in) in size.

2. Cut this large square into four smaller ones, then crimp the edges with your fingers. Using a fork, make a few holes across each puff pastry square. Place them on greaseproof paper on a baking sheet, then pop them in the fridge to rest for about 20 minutes, and in the meantime make the topping.

3. Preheat the oven to 180°C/350°F/Gas Mark 4.

4. Skin the sausages and break into bite-sized chunks. Fry these in a hot pan for about 2 minutes, then set aside.

5. Meanwhile, blanch the broccoli in hot water for 30 seconds, then refresh in cold water.

6. Take out the pastry bases and arrange the chorizo, broccoli, mushrooms, goat's cheese and tomatoes on top. Make sure that the entire base is evenly covered. Sprinkle over a little grated Cheddar. This will melt and hold everything in place during cooking.

7. Bake in the oven for 8 minutes, or until the pastry is golden brown around the edges. Serve warm.

Pan-fried Sardines with a Parsley, Lemon, Chilli and Red Onion Vinaigrette serves 4

The trick with this dish is to open up the fish so that the two fillets lie flat in the pan. (If you don't feel confident about doing this, ask your fishmonger to prepare the sardines for you.) Cook the sardines quickly over a high heat, preparing the vinaigrette at the same time.

To serve, all you need is sunshine, crusty bread, cold beer and friends.

3 or 4 good-sized sardines per person	2 red onions, finely diced
6 tbsp olive oil	1 tbsp coarsely chopped flat parsley
juice and zest of 1 lemon	4 tbsp plain flour
2 hot red chillies, finely chopped	4 tsp paprika
1 garlic clove, finely chopped	salt and pepper

1. Start by preparing the sardines. Place a fish on a board with the head pointing away from you. Gently run a dessertspoon from tail to head to remove the scales. Next, snip off the fins and tail of the sardine, then cut off the head. Now open up the stomach and remove the innards, leaving the cavity open. Repeat with the remaining sardines. Rinse the fish and the board before continuing.

2. Lay each fish on the board sideways on and cut along the stomach from head to tail almost all the way through. This will allow you to open the fish flat so the two fillets lie flat on the board, joined only in the middle. The backbone should pull away easily at this point and can be discarded.

3. Now make a start on the dressing. Place the olive oil in a bowl and add the lemon juice and zest. Add the chopped chilli, garlic, red onion and parsley, and season to taste.

4. Mix the flour with the paprika and dust all over the open fish. Heat some oil in a frying pan and lay the fish skin-side down in the pan. Give them about 3 minutes either side. Don't pack the fish into the pan. Instead, cook the fish in batches, and keep them warm in the oven while you cook the rest.

5. Finally, lay all the fish skin-side up on a platter and spread some of the vinaigrette over. Serve with the remainder of the vinaigrette in a bowl on the side.

Crispy Squid with Fennel, Tomato and Lemon Coleslaw serves 4

Crispy squid was always destined to be in this book because it is Richie's favourite food. Given the choice of visiting a sweet shop or a fishmonger, he would always choose the latter.

The secret to cooking decent crispy squid is in the temperature. You need good hot oil – at least 175°C/350°F. The squid should cook quickly because the aim is to crisp up the batter without overheating the squid flesh. If the flesh gets too hot for too long you will have very chewy squid! To save work, ask your fishmonger for squid tubes. This will mean that he prepares and cleans the body of the squid.

The coleslaw is a light and tangy mixture of vegetables mixed with a lemon dressing. The acidity of the lemon balances well with deep-fried food, thus allowing you to eat much more squid than you probably should!

8 medium-sized squid tubes (roughly 20cm/8in long)	**For the coleslaw**
	1/4 Savoy cabbage
600ml (1 pint) milk	1 head of fennel
200g (7oz) plain flour	1 carrot
1 teaspoon cayenne pepper	1 red onion
1.5 litres (2½ pints) sunflower or corn oil	6 basil leaves
	2 plum tomatoes
	1 tsp cracked black pepper
	1 tbsp extra virgin olive oil
	½ tsp sherry vinegar
	1 lemon

To make the coleslaw

1. Remove the core from the cabbage, and finely shred the leaves. Put into a large bowl.
2. Cut the fennel into quarters, remove the core and finely shred it – a mandolin is great for this, but be careful and always use the guard. Add to the bowl.
3. Peel and grate the carrot, halve and finely slice the red onion, chop up the basil leaves and finely dice the tomatoes. Add all of these to the bowl.

continued overleaf

4. Separately mix the pepper, olive oil, sherry vinegar and the zest and juice of the lemon. Pour this over the vegetables and leave to stand for 10 minutes.

To cook the squid

1. Cut the squid into rings about 5mm (¼in) wide. Place the rings in a bowl and cover with milk.
2. In a deep, heavy-based saucepan, heat the vegetable oil to 175°C/350°F (see page 215 for how to test the oil without a thermometer).
3. Mix the flour and the cayenne pepper in a bowl. Take some of the squid rings and shake off the milk. Toss the rings in the flour and then add to the pan, to deep-fry. Do this in small batches to maintain the oil at the correct temperature. Each batch of squid should take no more than 3–4 minutes to fry.
5. Serve the squid rings straight away, with the coleslaw on the side.

Couscous with Red Onion, Parsley, Courgette and Mint serves 4

Couscous has an interesting texture and is a great vehicle for other flavours. I often serve this with a roasted rump of lamb or a grilled breast of chicken.

200g (7oz) couscous	2 plum tomatoes, finely chopped
4 tsp olive oil – or 1 tsp per person	1 red onion, finely chopped
1 chicken stock cube.	20 mint leaves, finely chopped
1 courgette, finely diced	1 heaped tbsp parsley, finely chopped

1. Put all the couscous in a bowl, then drizzle on the olive oil and mix in well. Meanwhile, prepare the chicken stock in a measuring jug according to the packet instructions.
2. Pour the stock onto the couscous whilst it's still hot – you will need about 1 tablespoon per person. Mix in the stock, then push all the couscous flat in the bowl and cover with a sheet of clingfilm.
3. After 10 minutes, return to the couscous and fluff it up with a fork.
4. Add the finely chopped vegetables and serve.

Salmon Skewers with Marjoram and Red Peppercorns makes 4 skewers

When I planted my herb garden, I knew some herbs would be used less than others, and so it was with marjoram. I've tried to find uses for it and have put it with both roasted lamb and rabbit to good effect, and in this dish I've matched it to fish. The red peppercorns add a zing to the overall taste, which contrasts well with the floweriness of the marjoram. (Do not use white or black peppercorns. I suspect that they would overpower the delicate flavour of the fish.)

These skewers are easy to make and I generally do them as part of a selection of light bites in place of a starter.

250g (9oz) piece of salmon
2 tsp fresh marjoram leaves
1 tsp dried red peppercorns

Neil's Sweet Chilli Dipping Sauce,
to serve (see page 287)

4 long wooden satay sticks

1. Cut the salmon up into even-sized dice, about 2cm (3/4in).
2. Thread the cubes onto the sticks, leaving a section to hold at the blunt end. Push the cubes up tightly together and set aside.
3. Crush the marjoram leaves and the peppercorns in a pestle and mortar, until granular but not too fine.
4. Sprinkle the herb and pepper mix over each skewer and make sure the salmon is evenly covered.
5. Cook the skewers on a hot grill, a barbecue or in a large pan. Don't overcook them; they will need only 1 minute on each side.
6. Serve warm with the dipping sauce.

MJ's Warm Salad of Spinach, Chicken and Blue Cheese serves 4

When I first met MJ, she invited me round to meet some of her friends and she chose this dish for supper. It was absolutely fabulous, and I thought I'd met someone who could really cook. Little did I know that I would see this dish many, many times over the coming years, as it's her standard recipe when entertaining. In fact, there are probably friends of MJ's all over the country reading this and thinking, 'Yeah, I had that'. Despite this, it gets in the book due to the great combination of flavours and the fact that I honestly do love it.

Incidentally, on that first night round at her flat she also made a treacle tart – but forgot to put in the breadcrumbs. Worse still, she served it pretending it was just as she had intended!

4 generous handfuls of baby spinach
4 handfuls of rocket leaves
handful of green beans, blanched
250g (9oz) blue cheese – Dolcelatte or Roquefort work well
2 tbsp plain flour
1 egg
splash of milk

200g (7oz) white breadcrumbs
4 chicken breasts, weighing about 160g (5½oz) each
olive oil
150g (5oz) wild mushrooms
a few splashes of Worcestershire sauce
good-quality balsamic vinegar

1. Wash all the leaves and put them in a large bowl along with the beans. Break the blue cheese into small chunks and add to the bowl.
2. Next, take three bowls. In the first, place the flour. In the second, mix together the egg and the milk. In the third, put the breadcrumbs. Cut the chicken breasts into strips and coat them in flour. Place the floured chicken strips into the egg and milk mixture, then finally dip in the breadcrumbs, turning over until evenly coated.
3. Heat a large pan with a little olive oil and fry the chicken until it is golden brown and cooked through. Set to one side.
4. Put the pan back on the heat and sauté the mushrooms until they are caramelised. Before removing the mushrooms, add a few splashes of Worcestershire sauce to the pan and then empty the mushrooms and the reserved chicken into the bowl with the leaves.
5. Drizzle some olive oil and some good-quality balsamic vinegar, mix everything together and serve.

Panzanella-style Salad with Tomato and Little Gem Lettuce serves 4

This is a fabulous salad, simple and tasty. It is best made when tomatoes are at the height of their season, because they give the salad its magic.

4 heads of Little Gem lettuce, separated into leaves
6 very red plum tomatoes
1 garlic clove

10 basil leaves
2 tbsp olive oil, plus more for frying
1 ciabatta loaf
some Parmesan flakes

1. Wash the Little Gem leaves and put them in a bowl.
2. Bring a pan of water to the boil and blanch the tomatoes. To do this, first remove the eye of the tomato (where the stalk meets the tomato). Lower each tomato into the boiling water for 10 seconds, and then transfer to a bowl of iced water. Finally, peel off the skin and cut the tomatoes in half. Using your hands, squeeze out all the tomato juice into a bowl and set this to one side.
3. The tomatoes themselves will now look a bit ragged, but don't worry, this is fine. Cut the tomato halves into large chunks and add to the lettuce leaves.
4. In a pestle and mortar, pound the garlic clove and the basil leaves and add them to the tomato juice. Then whisk in the olive oil.
5. Tear the ciabatta loaf into irregular bite-sized chunks. Heat some olive oil in a non-stick frying pan, and pan-fry the ciabatta pieces until just turning golden brown.
6. Add these, whilst still hot, to the leaves and tomato, then pour on the tomato dressing. Scatter Parmesan flakes over the salad and serve immediately.

Warm Chorizo Salad with Rocket, Little Gem, Oven-dried Tomato and Parmesan serves 4

I always have chorizo in the fridge because it is such a great addition to pasta dishes, salads and spicy stews. When pan-fried, it yields a lot of oil, which is infused with flavour. In this salad, I use that oil as the base for the dressing.

I recommend using a vegetable peeler to grate the Parmesan as this produces large shavings.

2 hearts of Little Gem lettuce	1/2 ciabatta loaf
2 handfuls of rocket leaves	2 tbsp olive oil
8 cherry tomatoes, halved	260g (9¹/4oz) chorizo sausage, broken
1/4 head fennel	into chunks
handful of large Parmesan shavings.	1 tbsp balsamic vinegar

1. First prepare all the cold ingredients. Break the lettuce into individual leaves and mix it with the rocket in a bowl. Next, throw in the cherry tomatoes. Shred the fennel very finely and chuck this into the bowl as well. Finally, add most of the parmesan, keeping a few shavings to one side.

2. Now take the ciabatta and tear it into irregular pieces. Heat the oil in a frying pan and fry the ciabatta pieces for about 5 minutes, or until they are golden brown, and add these croûtons to the bowl.

3. In the same pan, cook the chorizo for about 2 minutes, or until hot and slightly browned. The pan will now contain chorizo oil and the pieces of sausage. Chuck the meat into the bowl with the other ingredients and then add some balsamic vinegar to the chorizo oil still in the pan. Mix together, then pour into the salad bowl and sprinkle over the remaining Parmesan.

Thai-style Beef Salad

serves 4

This is an easy salad to make and conveniently uses a wide variety of salad items that grow well during the summer months.

2 x 150g (5oz) sirloin steaks
3/4 cucumber, seeded and finely
    sliced
2 tomatoes, cut into wedges
2 banana shallots, finely sliced
    lengthways
4 spring onions, finely sliced
1/4 Chinese leaf, finely sliced
handful of coriander leaves
handful of torn basil leaves

For the dressing
juice of 3 limes
4 tbsp fish sauce
as much chopped green and red
    chilli as you want – depends on
    heat required
2 tsp grated palm sugar

1. First make up the dressing: mix the lime juice, fish sauce, chillies and palm sugar in a bowl; this can be done well in advance.
2. Prepare the cucumber, tomatoes, shallots, spring onions, Chinese leaf, coriander and basil as above and place in a large bowl.
3. Cook the steaks as you wish. My recommendation here is to keep them rare and juicy: 2 minutes on either side in a hot pan should suffice, then leave them to rest for 5 minutes.
4. Pour the dressing over the salad ingredients, then slice up the steak into thin strips before adding to the bowl.
5. Mix everything thoroughly and garnish with chilli if you want a little more heat. Serve in shallow bowls.

A Few Words on Fish

Writing about fish is a problem for me. On the one hand, as a chef, I love fish because of its flavour and variety, but, on the other hand, we should be aware of the implications of a fish supper, and how the word 'sustainable' should now be synonymous with the word 'fish'.

This book was always going to discuss fish – it was inevitable. My dad is a marine biologist (and a Pisces). When my sister and I were young, he would be gone for weeks and return with tales of storms, waves and all the fish he had caught that had never been caught before.

To the experienced cook, fish are a joy. Any chef will tell you that one of the most skilful sections in a professional kitchen is the fish section. There is such a huge range – from shellfish to shark – and it can take many years to really understand how to prepare and cook the many varieties. (Generally, fish should be cooked 'just enough' and no more.) Fish not only tastes great, however, it is also good for us. Oily fish such as salmon, mackerel, trout, sardines and tuna are rich in omega 3 fats, which reduce the risk of heart disease and stroke. White fish is good for us, too: cod, haddock and plaice are all good sources of low fat protein, and are rich in vitamins, iron and zinc. However, there is a huge sinister irony contained within this advice.

When it came to compiling recipes for this book, I began to realise that I might have a responsibility that extends beyond teaching the reader how to cook a decent fish pie. I felt it would be useful to get the view of a marine biologist before I put pen to paper, so I had a long chat with my dad about fish consumption and, by the time we finished, I was ready to vow never to cook any fish again.

Believing it couldn't be as bad as his gloomy opinion, however, I decided to talk to some friends. Martin Hickman is a journalist, who, at the time we spoke, was pondering an article on fish consumption in restaurants; Jay Raynor is a respected food critic who I know has enjoyed many a fish supper; Neil Freeman is one of the country's leading anglers. With this enviable collection of know-it-alls I felt I would get the whole picture. I spoke to each one about their views on fish both from the scary 'should we eat it at all?' point of view and also from the 'lovely, isn't it – which is your favourite?' angle. We all seemed to share very similar thoughts on fish as food.

If you're thinking of cooking fish tonight there are a few things to consider. Firstly, the species. If in any doubt you should keep a copy of the *Good Fish Guide* handy. This is a booklet written by the Marine Conservation Society, which bills itself as 'the ultimate consumer guide to eating "eco-friendly" fish', and it is just that. Look up skate, for example, and it will tell you that this menu choice is very vulnerable to over-exploitation due to its low fecundity. You can't cook that then. What about monkfish? Well, monkfish are apparently from a single stock that spawns to the west of Scotland – this area is heavily over-fished and mature females are very rare. OK, what about some swordfish? 'No way,' scream the Marine Conservation Society. 'Are you mad? You may as well roast a panda.' Actually, they didn't say that, but you get my point.

I picked the above fish because they are very popular on restaurant menus. As Martin pointed out, it's not just the home cook who needs to wake up and tune in, it's the restaurateurs as well. We are all contributing, it seems, to an environmental disaster. Yes, another one. But this disaster is one we have known about for a while. Man has been aware of over-fishing since before 1900. The only time stocks have recovered was during World War II.

Despite all this, should we worry if we over-fish a particular species? Well, yes actually. As one eminent marine biologist – okay, it was my dad – pointed out to me, each species is interconnected and over-fishing one can affect not only the species being fished but also others around it.

There are, of course, some methods of fishing that are clearly better than others. Trawling catches indiscriminately and, at the same time, greatly and adversely disturbs the ground over which a net is dragged. Line-caught fish, on the other hand, while contributing to the over-fishing problem, only do so to the tune of one per hook, and the bait used can target the larger individuals particularly, with little or no damage to their habitat. For the cook, the condition of line-caught fish is also usually superior to that of trawled fish.

And then there's fish farming. As Jay pointed out, restaurant diners seem to split into two groups here: there are those who say that everything should be wild because it has a superior flavour; and there are those who recognise that fish farming has a part to play in the overall solution. Even here, though, there is a word of warning from our resident marine biologist: 'Herbivorous fish farmed in tropical waters are the only truly ethically farmed fish'. Apparently this is because they feed off plant plankton which is naturally produced by year-round sun. These aside, all other farmed fish require feeding. And that food is made up of wild fish (e.g. sand eels) taken from lower down the food chain.

Okay, so we can eat as much farmed tilapia as we like but what about the odd portion of farmed salmon?

There is some very good farmed salmon available. I have always used Loch Duart farmed salmon and decided to take a trip to see exactly how responsible they were. I found that, despite my dad's cynicism, these guys do care; every conceivable business decision is based on the environment, not profit. Fish are farmed in low-density pens, the food they are fed is from sustainable sources, and disease is low. So, in my opinion, salmon sashimi is back on the menu.

But, as a foody, I can't go the rest of my life without eating halibut, sea bass, brill and, perhaps, even the odd cod or three. So I reckon we should ban all large trawlers and concentrate on small fleets of smaller fishing boats. We should make use of line-caught fish where possible and eat a wide variety of fish including those less-fashionable specimens such as sardines, mackerel and pollock. Oh, and we should ban all processed fish – including fish fingers. Sorry Ellie and Rich, but there you go!

Get to know a real live local fishmonger who is sympathetic to your fish-stock-preserving ways and ask his advice on what is seasonally plentiful and what has been caught in the most sustainable fashion. By doing this you can serve up your home-grown cabbage with brill wrapped in bacon without feeling as though you have to pray for forgiveness.

vegetable dishes

Broad Beans with Fried Potatoes, Garlic and Pancetta serves 4

Every plot holder grows broad beans. In our first year, we planted them all at once and suffered a glut. I had to be very creative in the kitchen to make full use of the harvest!

I first ate a dish like this in northern Spain, where it was served with bread. I also serve these beans with grilled fish and grilled chicken.

I keep the outer husk on the bean, and if they're very young and tender I skip the blanching stage and just use them raw.

4 handfuls of broad beans – about
  50g (2oz) per person
2 average-sized potatoes
2 tbsp virgin olive oil

150g (5oz) bacon lardons or pancetta
2 garlic cloves, chopped
2 tsp chopped marjoram
salt and pepper

1. Bring a large pan of water to the boil. Blanch the beans for 30 seconds, then remove with a spoon. (The boiling water will be used again for the potatoes.) Plunge the beans into cold water to stop the cooking process. Drain them and set aside.
2. Next, peel the potatoes and cut them into large dice – about 2cm (½in). Put these potato pieces into the pan of water you used for the beans and gently simmer them until they are cooked through. Drain the potatoes and set to aside.
3. Pour the olive oil into a large, non-stick frying pan and place over a high heat. When the oil is hot, add the bacon lardons and fry for a couple of minutes.
4. Next, add the potatoes to the pan and cook them until they are really crispy and the bacon is golden brown.
5. Add the chopped garlic to the pan, then throw in the blanched beans. Toss the ingredients together and season. Finally, sprinkle over the marjoram and serve immediately.

Courgettes à la Francaise

serves 4

Despite the posh name, these are really just nice n' easy, crispy, deep-fried courgettes. Choose nice firm courgettes and remember that, as with all deep-fried food, they do need to be eaten as soon as they are cooked.

4 courgettes
500ml (18fl oz) vegetable oil
300ml (1/2 pint) milk
4 tablespoons plain flour

pinch of cayenne pepper
Neil's Sweet Chilli Dipping Sauce,
   to serve (see page 287)

1. Cut the courgettes into 5cm (2in) lengths, and cut each length into regular-sized wedges. I cut about 6–8 wedges from each chunk of courgette.
2. When this is done, put the oil in a saucepan and slowly heat to 160°C/325°F. A temperature probe is very useful to determine the heat of the oil. If you don't have one, add it to your Christmas list, and use this method: throw a small piece of bread into the hot oil. If it sizzles immediately and gently turns golden brown, then the temperature is correct.
3. Meanwhile, pour the milk into one bowl and put the flour and cayenne into another bowl. Make sure you have some kitchen paper to hand for draining the courgettes when they are done.
4. Dip the courgettes in the milk, then toss in the flour. (If preparing a large number, do this in batches.)
5. Carefully lower the courgettes into the oil and deep-fry until crispy and lightly golden in colour, about 2 minutes. Remove the cooked courgettes with a slotted spoon and drain briefly on kitchen paper. Serve immediately with a bowl of the dipping sauce.

Stir-fried Purple Sprouting Broccoli with Garlic, Ginger and Chilli serves 4

This particular take on purple sprouting broccoli gives it an exciting Asian twist and is perfect for serving with seafood such as bass, scallops or larger prawns. Try to get hold of young purple sprouting broccoli with long thin stalks – this is ideal for stir-frying.

1 garlic clove, finely chopped
1cm (1/2in) piece of fresh root ginger, finely chopped
1 red chilli, cut into thin strips

650g (1lb 6oz) purple sprouting broccoli, leaves still attached
about 1 tbsp sunflower or corn oil
1 tbsp teriyaki sauce

1. Heat a wok over a high flame and add the oil. Throw in the broccoli and allow it to sizzle briefly before tossing it over. This should take only about 2 minutes – the idea is to soften the broccoli without colouring it too much.
2. Throw in the garlic, ginger and chilli and stir-fry for a further 2 minutes. Finish by adding the teriyaki sauce.

Fried Green Tomaytos (not tomaaahtoes)
serves 4

My dad's wife, Coleen, is American and when I asked her to let me use this recipe she insisted that we all pronounce the title correctly. So, in the interest of family harmony, I have played ball. Whatever you call the dish, it is without doubt a great way of serving green tomatoes.

4 green tomatoes
2 garlic cloves
4 tbsp fresh white breadcrumbs

extra virgin olive oil
salt and black pepper

1. Slice the tomatoes into 5mm (¼in) thick slices.
2. Finely chop the garlic and mix it together with the breadcrumbs, salt and pepper.
3. Place a slice of tomato in the crumb mix and press onto the tomato so that it is well covered.
4. Pan-fry the tomatoes in olive oil until golden brown and tender. Serve straight away.

Pea Purée with Chervil and Tarragon

makes 8 generous tablespoons (enough for 4 people)

This purée is the perfect accompaniment to roasted lamb or grilled fish such as bass or salmon. It works equally well with either fresh or frozen peas. See picture on page 215.

450ml (3/4 pint) water
100g (3½oz) butter
½ chicken stock cube
400g (14oz) fresh or frozen peas

1 tbsp coarsely chopped chervil
1 tbsp coarsely chopped tarragon
salt and pepper

1. Bring the water to the boil and add both the butter and the stock cube. Allow the butter to melt and the stock cube to dissolve.
2. Throw in the peas and cook for 3 minutes, then stir in the herbs. Remove the pan from the heat straight away, then drain off and reserve half the liquid.
3. Using a stick blender, purée the contents of the pan to a coarse purée. Season, and if it's very dry add a little of the reserved cooking liquor. Serve straight away or leave to cool and then reheat in the microwave.

Stir-fried Brussels Sprouts with Bacon, Carrot, Parsnip and Chestnuts serves 4

Let's face it. Boiled sprouts can be less than appealing to some people, so this is a neat way of giving them a makeover.

Serve this side dish with a roast, whether game, lamb or turkey.

about 30 Brussels sprouts
1 parsnip, peeled
1 carrot, peeled
1 garlic clove

6 rashers streaky bacon
8 roasted chestnuts
2 tsp duck or goose fat

1. Bring a large pan of water to the boil whilst you prepare the sprouts by removing the outside leaves. Keep a little stalk intact, or else the sprout will fall apart whilst cooking.
2. Empty the sprouts into the water and boil them for about 3 minutes, or until just cooked. Then take them out of the boiling water and plunge them into cold water to stop the cooking process. When they are cold, drain and then cut the larger sprouts in half. Set aside until needed.
3. Cut the parsnip into 1cm (^{1}/$_2$in) dice, then cut the carrot into matchsticks. Chop the garlic, cut the bacon into small strips and break up the chestnuts a little.
4. Heat a saucepan on the stove and add the duck or goose fat (you could use corn or sunflower oil, if you prefer.) Add the bacon to the pan and allow it to start colouring, about 2 minutes, and then add the parsnip cubes. Once the parsnip turns golden brown, add the garlic and the carrot sticks. Mix everything around in the pan, then add the sprouts and the chestnuts.
5. Heat through, then serve straight away.

Creamy Leeks Baked with Rosemary and Goat's Cheese serves 4

This is a great dish to serve at home with roast chicken or roast lamb. It can be made an hour or so in advance and then just flashed through the oven to reheat it.

I think the goat's cheese is perfect with the leeks, but feel free to prove me wrong and try out other cheeses.

6 medium leeks
900ml (1½ pints) double cream
2 garlic cloves, chopped

200g (7oz) soft goat's cheese
4 slices of white bread, blitzed into crumbs

1. Place a pan of water over a high heat and bring to the boil. Preheat the oven to 180°C/350°F/Gas Mark 4.
2. Meanwhile, prepare the leeks. First slice off the root end. Then trim back the other end, but don't cut off all the dark green bit; just cut it back slightly. Now cut the leek into slices about 2cm (3/4in) thick.
3. Carefully lower these slices into the boiling water and blanch them for about 30 seconds. Try to keep them in complete slices, but if they fall apart into rings don't worry too much.
4. Lift them out of the water with a slotted spoon and let them drain for a moment. Place them evenly across the base of a 20x24cm (8x10in) shallow baking dish. An even layer is important, but you don't need to be too fussy.
5. Pour the cream into a pan and add the chopped garlic. Over a gentle heat, bring the cream to simmering point. Simmer until the volume is reduced by about a third, season, then pour this over the leeks, being sure to cover the entire surface area. Allow the cream to seep through the leeks.
6. Crumble up the goat's cheese and sprinkle over the leeks, then place the uncovered dish in the oven for about 20 minutes, or until the goat's cheese has started to melt.
7. Remove the dish and sprinkle over the breadcrumbs. Turn the heat up to 200°C/400°F/Gas Mark 6 and put the dish back in for a further 5–10 minutes, or until the crumbs are crisp and golden.

Beetroot Baked in Foil

serves 4

I love beetroot, but sadly I am the only person who eats it in our house.
I am not too keen on pickled beetroot, so I normally bake it in foil, which
concentrates the flavour.

  You can keep baked beetroot in the fridge for a few days. Serve it with roasted
meats, or use it in salads or even as a sorbet (see page 218).

10–15 walnut-sized beetroot
olive oil
handful of thyme leaves

about 2 tsp water per beetroot.
salt

1. Heat the oven to 170°C/340°F/Gas Mark 3½.
2. Choose equal-sized beetroots and wash. I leave some of the stalk, but
   remove any trailing root.
3. Lay a large piece of foil on the work surface and brush it with a little
   olive oil. Place the beetroot in the centre of the foil and sprinkle over
   a little salt and a few thyme leaves. Add the water and then wrap up
   the foil so the beetroot is well contained.
4. Place this on a baking tray and bake in the oven. The cooking time
   depends on the size of the beetroot, so you may need to open your
   foil package to test the beetroot from time to time. A walnut-sized
   beetroot will take at least 45 minutes to cook. When the beetroot is
   cooked you should be able to slide a knife in with little resistance.
5. Remove the cooked beetroot from the oven. Open the foil packages
   and allow to cool slightly. It should then be very easy to pop the
   beetroot out of their skins. Serve warm with a roast or allow to
   cool and add to a salad.

Beetroot Sorbet

serves 4

This unusual sorbet goes well with smoked salmon or salmon gravadlax, or sweet dishes such as apple pie.

300g (10oz) cooked beetroot (see
    page 217)
250g (9oz) stock syrup (equal
    quantities of sugar and water
    simmered for 5 minutes)

100ml (3¹/₂fl oz) water
2 tsp lemon juice

1. First purée the beetroot. Then mix in all the other ingredients. Chill it in the fridge, and then churn this mixture in an ice-cream machine until it's a smooth sorbet.
2. If you don't have an ice cream machine, pour the mixture into a tray and slide the tray into the freezer. After 15 minutes, take out of the freezer and fork through the mixture. Keep doing this every 15 minutes for at least 1¹/₂ hours, or until the mixture is frozen.

Root Vegetable Mash

serves 4

a mixture of carrots, parsnips, swede
    and turnip (about 150g/5oz per
    person)

100g (3¹/₂oz) butter
salt and pepper

1. Peel the vegetables and cut into even-sized pieces, then throw the lot into a saucepan. Add just enough water to cover the vegetables and place a lid on the pan.
2. Bring the pan to a boil over a high heat, then reduce the heat to a gentle simmer. When the vegetables feel just cooked, drain off two-thirds of the water. Add a generous knob of butter and some salt and pepper, then mash the vegetables up.
3. Serve immediately. Alternatively, leave to cool and then reheat in a microwave when required.

Onion Purée

makes about 1 litre (1³/₄ pints), enough for 6–8 people

This is a creamy white purée made from onions. With a little water added, it becomes a white onion sauce. It works really well with lamb and chicken.

250g (9oz) butter
8 onions, coarsely chopped

200ml (7fl oz) double cream

1. Gently melt the butter in a casserole pan over a low heat, then add the onions. Place a lid on the pan and cook over the lowest possible heat for about 25 minutes.
2. After 25 minutes, add the cream and a splash of water to the pan. Continue cooking for a further 10 minutes, then blend everything together in a food processor.

Root Vegetables Roasted with Garlic, Duck Fat and Thyme serves 4

First things first – one thing I have learnt during my allotment mission is that swede is actually a brassica and not, as I had always thought, a root vegetable. However, once I get my home-grown vegetables into the kitchen they do as they're told, so for this dish swede is a root vegetable!

¹/₂ swede
4 carrots
2 parsnips
2 tbsp duck fat

sprigs of fresh thyme
8 garlic cloves, unpeeled
1–2 tsp honey
salt and pepper

1. Firstly peel the three types of root vegetables and then cut into large chunks each about the size of the next. The shapes are not important; in fact a little irregularity is quite pleasing.
2. Preheat the oven to 180°C/350°F/Gas Mark 4.

continued overleaf

3. Heat a heavy-based frying pan on the stove, add the duck fat and allow it to melt. Now add the vegetables and allow them to colour on the side that hits the pan first and then roll them over until all sides are evenly coloured a gentle brown.
4. If your pan is ovenproof then the next stage can happen straight away; if not, then first transfer your vegetables to a roasting tray or shallow baking dish.
5. Throw in your sprigs of thyme and the unpeeled cloves of garlic, then drizzle over no more than 2 teaspoons of honey. Finally, season the mixture and roast in the oven for about 40 minutes or until all the vegetables are cooked through.

Caramelised Shallots

This is a great way of serving shallots. Not only do they taste great when roasted, they also look good on the plate.

as many shallots as you choose   olive oil

1. The shallots don't need any peeling or advance preparation. Simply place as many shallots as you wish to serve in a pan and cover with cold water. Bring to a boil and cook the shallots for at least 1 hour.
2. By this time, the shallots should be very soft to the touch. Remove from the water and allow them to dry and cool. At this point, you can either store them for use the next day or proceed with the recipe.
3. Cut each shallot in half lengthways straight through the root. Carefully peel off the outside skin, but leave the root intact.
4. Place each half cut-side down on a tray until ready to continue.
5. When the shallots are all prepared, place a frying pan over a moderate heat. Heat a little olive oil, then fry the cut surface of the shallot for about 5–6 minutes, until it is deeply caramelised. Turn the shallot over, and cook for a further 5–6 minutes, to caramelise the outside. Serve warm.

Roast Potatoes

For really good roast potatoes, I would suggest growing Charlotte, Queen Victoria or Golden Wonder. I have grown all of these varieties, and was impressed by the results.

In my view, you can never have too many roast potatoes. If, by chance, there are any left, you can eat them cold the following day with a dollop of mayonnaise.

potatoes, 350g (12oz) per person
duck or goose fat, melted

several heads of garlic, cut in half

1. Peel a generous amount of potatoes and cut them into regular-sized pieces – as a guide, I cut a 200g (7oz) potato into two pieces.
2. Rinse the potatoes in cold water to rid them of starch and then put them in a large saucepan, then fill the pan with cold water.
3. Over a low heat, slowly bring the pan to a gentle simmer to cook the potatoes – this may take up to 40 minutes.
4. Meanwhile, preheat the oven to 180°C/350°F/Gas Mark 4. Find a suitably large roasting tray and pour in enough melted fat to form a 5mm (¼in) thick layer. Warm this tray in the oven for at least 10 minutes.
5. When the potatoes are cooked through, drain in a colander. Give the colander a little shake just to 'rough' up the edges of the potatoes.
6. Remove the hot tray with the fat from the oven and carefully place the potatoes on the tray. Add the garlic.
7. Place the tray back in the oven and roast the potatoes for up to 1 hour, turning them every so often, until crisp and golden brown.

Vegetable Samosas
makes 20 samosas

I love Indian food and often go shopping in Southall, west London, where the shops are packed with unusual ingredients you'd never find in a supermarket. I also love to cook Indian food and samosas are one of my favourite snacks. These crunchy treats are cheap to make and not as difficult as they might seem. They freeze really well, so make plenty! Try serving with Tomato and Chilli Jam (see page 277) or Cucumber, Green Tomato and Mint Raita (see page 281).

For the filling
1 onion
1 tsp cumin seeds
1/2 tsp yellow mustard seeds
1/4 tsp fenugreek seeds
1/2 tsp turmeric
1 tsp ground coriander
1 tbsp corn or sunflower oil
1 garlic clove, chopped
1 fresh red chilli, chopped
1 fresh green chilli, chopped

800g (1lb 12oz) baking potatoes
2 tbsp frozen or fresh peas
1 tbsp coarsely chopped coriander
salt and pepper

For the samosas
225g (8oz) self-raising flour
50g (2oz) butter
75ml (2 1/2 fl oz) water
corn or sunflower oil, for frying

To make the filling

1. Chop the onion very finely and crush all the dry spices in a pestle and mortar.

2. Place a pan over a medium heat and add the oil. When this is hot, add the onion and lightly brown for about 4 minutes. Add the garlic, chillies and all the crushed dry spices.

3. Meanwhile, peel and cut the potatoes into 1cm (1/2 in) dice. Add the potatoes to the spice mix along with the peas. Stir the potatoes and peas into the hot oil and spice mixture, then add 1 tablespoon of water. This will cause the pan to steam, so cover the pan and allow the potatoes to cook in this steam. Add a little more water if necessary, but it is important not to add too much water, as this will make the mixture too wet to fry later.

4. Turn the heat off when the potatoes are soft, then mix in the chopped coriander and allow to cool. Store in the fridge until needed.

To make the samosas

1. Place the flour in a bowl and rub in the butter. Gradually add the water until you have a silky dough. Be careful not to overwork the dough, and do let it rest in the fridge for 30 minutes.

2. Dust a work surface with flour, divide the dough into ten even-sized pieces, then roll all of them into balls. Take one ball and roll it out to a disc about 10cm (4in) in diameter and 1mm (1/16in) thick. Cut the disc in two – each semicircular disc will make one samosa. Dab a little water along the straight edge of the semicircle and fold in two to make a triangular pocket.

3. Put some of the the filling inside the pocket and seal the remaining open edge with a little water. These can now be frozen or fried straight away.

4. To cook, pour the oil into a heavy-based saucepan. The oil should be about 8cm (3¼in) deep. Heat to a temperature of 175°C/ 350°F (see page 211), then fry the samosas in batches, for about 4 minutes each.

5. Drain on kitchen paper and then serve with the jam and raita.

Crushed New Potatoes

serves 4

Many years ago, when I was working for Gary Rhodes, the nation's chefs were going through their crushed new potato period. Every decent chef had something on their menu which sat upon a pile of crushed new potatoes. Not satisfied with this, we then started adding various ingredients to the crushed potatoes to customise them.

Well, I still like the crushed new potato idea. It's very easy to prepare and the variations are indeed endless. Here are a few ideas that I think worth trying. Personally, I leave the skins on my crushed new potatoes, but all of these would work just as well with the skins removed.

250–300g (9–10oz) new potatoes

Olive oil, lemon juice, shallots and basil
5 tbsp olive oil
juice of 1/2 lemon
2 shallots, chopped
8 basil leaves, chopped

Parsley and red onion
100g (3¹/₂oz) butter
1 tbsp chopped flat parsley
1/2 red onion, chopped

Crumbled goat's cheese and chive
100g (3¹/₂oz) goat's cheese
20 chives, finely chopped

Chorizo, basil and black olive
150g (5oz) chorizo, finely diced and fried
10 black olives, chopped
10 basil leaves, chopped

Mustard and horseradish
100g (3¹/₂oz) butter
2 tsp horseradish
1 tsp English mustard

1. Boil the potatoes in a large saucepan until just done. Drain, then crush with a fork whilst still warm. Add olive oil or butter, depending on your taste.
2. In this state they can be left until needed. Just before serving, add the remaining ingredients.

Garlic Flat Bread

makes 1 flat loaf, serves 4–6

This is a really simple bread recipe that works fabulously well every time.
Serve it as you would normal garlic bread, or add toppings to make a pizza.
  The garlic butter can be made in large quantities and frozen, like the
Flavoured Butter on page 285.

For the garlic butter
250g (9oz) unsalted butter
6 garlic cloves, finely chopped
salt and cracked black pepper
chopped herbs (optional)

For the bread
250g (9oz) strong flour
35g yeast
1 tbsp soft brown sugar
150ml (1/4 pint) water
2 tbsp olive oil

To make the garlic butter
1. Leave the butter to soften at room temperature – it should be very
   soft but not starting to look oily. Mix in the chopped garlic and some
   salt and pepper. You could also add a herb if you want; basil, parsley
   or oregano will all work well. Set aside until needed.

To make the bread
1. I use a mixer with a dough hook attachment for all my bread making.
   However, hands do the job just as well. Put all the ingredients in
   a bowl or mixer and combine well to form a dough. Allow the mixer
   to run for 5 minutes at a slow speed to knead the bread. Alternatively,
   you can go for the calorie-busting 'by hand' method and knead for
   about 20 minutes.
2. Cover the bowl with a damp cloth and leave in a warm place to
   'prove'. This term means that the dough is allowed to develop as the
   yeast activates and releases carbon dioxide. Expect the dough to
   double in size. As a guide, 26°C/79°F is a perfect temperature, but a
   slow proving at a cool temperature gives better results than a quick
   prove at a higher temperature.
3. After about 30 minutes, the dough should have risen. Now, you need
   to 'knock it back': gently punch the dough a couple of times.

continued overleaf

4. Now lightly flour a work surface and roll out the dough to the thickness of a pizza base – about 4mm (1/8 in). Transfer this to a baking sheet, then spread with the garlic butter. Put it in the fridge to rest for at least 30 minutes.

5. Meanwhile, preheat the oven to 180°C/350°F/Gas Mark 4 and heat a baking tray in the oven – this will give the bread a crispy base.

6. Slide the chilled bread from the tray in the fridge onto the hot tray in the oven. Bake for about 8–10 minutes.

7. Remove from the oven and immediately paint over more garlic butter before serving.

Oven-dried Tomatoes
makes 20

This is a great way of using tomatoes. The low oven slowly dries out the tomato, which has the effect of concentrating the flavour. Choose your ripest tomatoes, of any variety, because this will mean you end up with a really sweet dried tomato.

10 tomatoes   flaked sea salt
chopped garlic   a little olive oil
fresh thyme leaves

1. Preheat the oven to about 50°C/120°F/Gas Mark 1/4. If your oven won't go this low, wedge it open slightly with a wooden spoon.

2. Cut your tomatoes in half through the 'eye' (the point where they were joined to the stalk). Lay the halves of tomato cut-side up on a tray covered with tin foil. Sprinkle over a little chopped garlic, a few thyme leaves and some salt, then drizzle olive oil over each tomato.

3. There is no real 'ready' moment to look out for, but you will notice the tomatoes looking slightly withered after 2 hours (don't be tempted to increase the heat to speed up the process). Squeeze one of them to see how moist it is. I like to leave a little moisture in them.

4. The best way to check them is to take one out and slice off a little bit to try. If you are happy with the taste and texture, then they are ready.

Freezing Vegetables: A step-by-step guide

Step 1: Choose your vegetable carefully
It may seem obvious, but only certain vegetables freeze successfully.
Go for the more fibrous stuff over the leafy ones or anything with a high
water content. Peas, sweetcorn, runner beans, French beans and broad
beans work well; salad leaves don't! Choose only the best quality for
freezing; eat the seconds fresh.

Step 2: Pick and freeze
Don't leave your picked vegetables to mount up; freeze the same day
as harvesting. Remember that famous pea advert.

Step 3: Wash and prepare
Washing should be pretty obvious but, in case you are tempted to take
the casual approach, it's worth remembering that soil harbours a large
number of microbes and should be removed. Prepare the vegetables as
you would if you were serving them. To use a couple of examples:

   Broad beans – remove from the pod (I like to leave the white husk on
as I think the husk protects them slightly during freezing, but it's up to
you. It can always be removed prior to cooking if fibre isn't your thing).

   Sweetcorn – shave the corn off the cob before freezing. However,
I recommend doing this after blanching the whole cob.

   Runner beans – slice finely. Many restaurants serve these beans in a silly
diamond shape, which I hate. They're so much better when finely sliced.

Step 4: Boil and blanch
This is a crucial stage. Correct blanching locks in the colour. To do so, boil
plenty of water (for a coffee cup of beans use at least $2^1/_2$ litres/4 pints of
water). Don't add salt – it makes no difference. Blanch bit by bit. Adding
too many beans to your boiling water causes the water to take too long to
re-boil, thus discolouring the vegetables. Boil for about 30 seconds then
immediately plunge into cold water to which you have added ice cubes.
At this point the idea is to stop the cooking process abruptly. Repeat until
all the veg is blanched. You can then drain the lot.

Step 5: Freeze, bag and freeze again

Having stood there all afternoon juggling beans between hot and cold water, the temptation is to bung the lot in a freezer bag, open the freezer and stuff them on top of the breaded haddock. Hold on. When you come to use your vegetables, the plan is to go from freezer to hot water as quickly as possible. If you simply bung the beans into a bag they will freeze in a huge clump, which will take an age to separate and boil. This will result in discoloured beans. Instead, take the time to line a roasting tray or similar flat dish with kitchen paper, scatter the blanched beans over the surface in a single layer and then pop it into the freezer. Freeze for a couple of hours until they are individually frozen. Then put them in a freezer bag and they will remain 'loose' in the freezer. It is also important to wrap vegetables as tightly as possible to avoid freezer burn, which will leave a stale flavour.

main courses

Pumpkin and Ricotta Ravioli with Sage Butter
serves 4

Pumpkin seems to be more widely used in other parts of the world than here in Britain. It's certainly not because they don't grow here. We planted one plant and grew at least six fabulous pumpkins, all bigger than a football! Most ended up on the doorstep with scary faces carved into them and a candle in the centre. However, one specimen was saved for the house chef!

If you get a large pumpkin, you need to be armed with a few recipes to make the most of it. Pumpkin soup and pumpkin tart are two obvious recipes, or you could try this ravioli. I had this dish in Italy last year and thought that the sweetness of the pumpkin was perfectly balanced by the earthy flavour of the mushrooms and the creamy cheese.

If making ravioli seems like too much hassle, buy some fresh egg lasagne sheets. Roll up the same filling in the sheets and bake it in a cheese sauce.

For the pasta dough
160g (5½oz) flour
120g (scant 4oz) semolina
6 egg yolks
2 whole eggs

up to 3 tbsp ricotta cheese
1 tbsp grated fresh Parmesan,
   plus extra to serve
1 egg, beaten
salt and pepper

For the ravioli filling
about 2 tbsp olive oil
350g (12oz) pumpkin slice, with skin
12 button mushrooms

For the sage butter
250g (9oz) butter
1 garlic clove, chopped
16 sage leaves, chopped
black pepper

To make the pasta dough
1. Put the flour, semolina and egg yolks into a mixer. Add the whole eggs and, using the dough hook attachment, combine them to form a dough. Allow the machine to run at half speed for at least 5 minutes to stretch the dough. Alternatively, mix together in a bowl using your hands.
2. The result should be a firm dough – if it is a bit too sticky to handle, add a little more flour, but don't add so much that the dough becomes very dry.
3. Wrap the dough in clingfilm and leave it in the fridge whilst you prepare the filling.

continued overleaf

To make the ravioli filling

1. Preheat the oven to 170°C/340°F/Gas Mark 3½.

2. Heat a non-stick frying pan over a medium heat and add
   1 tablespoon of olive oil. Pan-fry both sides of the pumpkin wedge
   for 5 minutes, or until nicely browned. Transfer the pumpkin to the
   oven and bake for about 15 minutes. It is cooked when it starts to feel
   soft to the touch. At this point, remove the pumpkin from the oven
   and transfer it to a chopping board.

3. Remove the skin of the pumpkin with a knife and mash the flesh
   with a potato masher. I think it's nice to leave a bit of texture to the
   pumpkin. Place your mashed pumpkin in a bowl and set aside.

4. Slice the button mushrooms very finely. Heat 1 tablespoon of olive
   oil in a frying pan over a medium heat, then cook the mushrooms
   with the chopped garlic. When cooked, mix into the pumpkin mash.

5. Add the ricotta and the Parmesan to the mix and taste it, adjusting
   the seasoning as necessary.

To assemble the ravioli

1. Roll out your pasta dough. If you have a pasta machine, roll it to at
   least the second thinnest setting. This will mean you have a very long
   length of pasta going through the machine, so do it in batches if that
   is easier. If you don't have a pasta machine, use a rolling pin.

2. Cut small pieces of pasta and roll them out to about 1-2mm (¹/₁₆in)
   thick. You need 8 rectangles about 12cm (4½in) long by 8cm (3¼in)
   wide and 1–2mm (about ¹/₁₆in) thick.

3. Place about 2 teaspoons of filling on one half of each rectangle. Paint
   around the edges with the beaten egg and fold over the pasta securing the edges firmly with your fingers or back of a fork.

4. Bring a large saucepan of water to the simmer, then cook the ravioli
   for 5 minutes.

5. Meanwhile, make the sage butter. Melt the butter in a small saucepan
   until it foams, then add the sage leaves and some black pepper.

6. Spoon this over the cooked ravioli and serve some Parmesan flakes
   on the side.

Roasted Pepper Stew with Red Onion, Sausage, Tomato and Courgette serves 4

Tomatoes and courgettes were both at their peak when I first made this dish. If you are growing peppers, you should find that they also ripen at a similar time, so this is a really good seasonal stew.

There is no need to chargrill some of the vegetables as I do here, but I find it adds another layer of flavour.

about 3 tbsp olive oil
1 orange pepper, sliced into thick rings
1 red pepper, sliced into thick rings
2 garlic cloves, finely sliced
250g (9oz) chorizo, torn into chunks

8 plum tomatoes, each cut into eight slices
3 red onions
2 courgettes, cut into thick slices
1 leek, very finely sliced
20 basil leaves, torn
1 stick of French bread

1. In a heavy-based casserole pan, heat 2 tablespoons of olive oil over a medium heat. Add the peppers and allow them to caramelise slightly.
2. Now add the garlic, shortly followed by the chorizo. Gently fry these together for 1 minute, then add the tomatoes. Place a lid over the pan and let it simmer very gently whilst you prepare the next stage.
3. Peel the red onions and leave the root end intact. Cut the onions in half through the root, then cut each half into six wedges. Ensure that each wedge has a piece of root to hold the wedge together.
4. Brush a griddle pan with about 1 tablespoon of olive oil and place over a high heat. Grill the red onion wedges so that they take on charred stripes from the griddle pan. Add the chargrilled wedges to the stew.
5. Grill the courgettes, again allowing them to char slightly. Add these to the stew.
6. Meanwhile, make the croûtons. Cut the French bread at an angle into thick slices, then grill until golden brown.
7. Finally, add the sliced leeks and the basil leaves and cook for 2–3 more minutes. Season to taste and serve with the grilled croûtons.

Mushroom Risotto with Parsnip Purée and Parsnip Crisps serves 4

At college, I was taught that risotto was made by cooking normal Uncle Ben's-style rice for a long time and then adding bits. (It was a long time ago.)

As we all now know, risotto needs proper risotto rice, which is grown in Northern Italy. There are various kinds available, such as Carnaroli, Arborio or Baldi; I prefer Carnaroli.

Mushroom risotto is one of my favourites (possibly equalled by a saffron, clam and basil version). However, before the vegetarians get excited I must admit that I think a chicken stock is the best stock to use. I also use butter rather than olive oil, but all these points are preferences not rules.

There are, however, some rules that must be followed. Don't use too much rice in proportion to the mushrooms, stir your risotto constantly, don't overcook the rice – a little bite at the centre of the rice grain is a good thing. You can choose how to plate the up but I like the mohican look.

200g (7oz) unsalted butter
2 medium onions
3 garlic cloves
sprig of thyme (optional)
500g (1lb 2oz) mushrooms, sliced
(a mix of wild mushrooms and button mushrooms works very well)
4 handfuls of risotto rice, about 350g (12oz)

up to 1.2 litres (2 pints) hot chicken stock
salt and pepper
85g (3oz) Parmesan, grated

For the parsnip purée and crisps
4 parsnips
200ml (7fl oz) vegetable oil, for frying
15g (1/2oz) butter

First make the parsnip crisps
1. They can be made up to 2 hours in advance. First peel one parsnip. Then use the peeler in long downward strokes to cut slivers of parsnip. They should be fairly broad once you are halfway through the parsnip.
2. Heat the frying oil up to 170°C/340°F (see page 211) and drop the parsnip slices in. Allow them to sizzle until golden, about 2 minutes.
3. Remove and drain them on kitchen paper. Set aside until needed.

continued overleaf

To prepare the parsnip purée

1. Peel and cut the remaining parsnips. Place in a pan and barely cover with water. Add the butter and simmer until the parsnips are cooked.
2. Using an old-fashioned potato masher, break up the parsnips to a coarse purée and season. The consistency should be firm but creamy, so add a little extra butter if it is too stiff. Set aside until needed.

To make the risotto

1. Put 150g/5oz of butter in a saucepan, then melt very slowly over a low heat.
2. Meanwhile, chop the onions and garlic very finely and add to the butter; you can also add a few thyme leaves. They need to soften but must not colour; a lid on the pan may be useful at this stage.
3. Add the sliced mushrooms to the pan. Again, let them soften without colouring. Now add the rice and let it cook for a while, about 2 minutes, without adding any stock.
4. Add the stock a ladle at a time and keep stirring as you do – stirring will cause the rice to rub and release starch, which will give a good creamy consistency. Allow the stock to come back to the boil after each ladleful.
5. Meanwhile, reheat the purée for a few minutes in the microwave or on the hob.
6. Keep testing the rice and stop adding stock when you are happy with the texture. At this point it is ready to serve, so add the remaining butter and the Parmesan. Give it a quick stir and spoon into bowls or onto plates.
7. Serve the parsnip purée in a neat quenelle or a casual dollop in the middle of the risotto. Stick the parsnip crisps into the purée and serve immediately.

Smoked Haddock Risotto with Sweetcorn and Spring Onions serves 4

Smoked haddock may not seem like a very Italian addition to risotto, but I promise it works very well indeed. Use corn on the cob instead of the awful tinned stuff, and use naturally dyed smoked haddock.

4 corn on the cob, husks removed
1kg (2lb 4oz) smoked haddock
up to 1.2 litres (2 pints) hot chicken stock
150g (5oz) butter, plus 1 tbsp extra
2 onions, finely chopped
1 garlic clove
4 handfuls of Carnaroli or Arborio risotto rice (about 350g/12oz in total)
6 spring onions, finely sliced
100g (3½oz) Cheddar, grated

1. First cook the sweetcorn. Bring a pan of water to the boil and drop in the corn cobs. Simmer for about 4–6 minutes, then remove the corn from the water and allow them to cool. Stand each corn on one end and shave off the corn with a knife. Place to one side.

2. Now prepare the haddock. Remove all the skin and bones, then cut the fish into large chunks. Place the pieces in a pan with the stock, then simmer for 4 minutes. After this time, turn off the heat and cool the fish in the stock. Remove the haddock with a slotted spoon and break it into flakes. Set aside.

3. Return the stock to the heat, and warm through.

4. Melt the butter in a large pan over a medium heat, then sweat the chopped onions and garlic for 5 minutes, or until soft. Add the risotto rice, and stir for a couple of minutes.

5. Add the stock to the rice one ladle at a time, allowing the stock to come to the boil after each addition. It's really important to keep stirring the rice, as this will bring out the starch and make the risotto creamy. The rice will take about 25 minutes to cook, from start to finish.

6. As the rice nears completion, add the haddock, the corn and the spring onions. Mix these into the rice and cook for another minute. To finish, add the tablespoon of butter along with the grated Cheddar. Serve immediately in warm bowls.

Smoked Haddock Fishcakes with Parsley Sauce and Fried Egg serves 4

This is Sunday brunch food. Do the work the day before, because poaching and flaking smoked haddock first thing in the morning is not all that appealing!

When buying your smoked haddock, look for the naturally dyed stuff, which will be pale yellow in colour. The more vibrant yellow fish is synthetically dyed. Also, make sure that you get haddock with the skin on because this can be used in the sauce.

The fishcakes and sauce can be made in advance and kept in the fridge overnight.

For the fishcakes
500g (1lb 2oz) smoked haddock fillets
600ml (1 pint) milk
4 average-sized potatoes
1 tbsp chopped parsley
4 tbsp plain flour
1 egg
200ml (7fl oz) milk
300g (10oz) white breadcrumbs

For the sauce
milk left over from poaching
    the haddock
25g (1oz) butter
20g (3/4oz) plain flour
4 tbsp chopped parsley

4 fried eggs, to serve

To make the fishcakes

1. Remove all the skin and any bones from the haddock fillets. Place these in a pan and cover with the milk. Over a gentle heat, bring this to a simmer, then immediately remove from the heat and allow the fish and milk to cool.

2. Meanwhile, peel the potatoes and cut into quarters. Rinse these under cold water and then place them in a pan of water. Bring to a boil, then simmer for about 20 minutes, or until cooked. Drain the potatoes, then mash them. I think this is best done with a potato ricer, but you could press them through a sieve instead.

3. Now remove the fish from the milk, retaining the milk to use for the sauce. Flake the fish into a bowl. Add the parsley, then add enough mashed potato to just bring all the fish together. Season to taste.

continued overleaf

4. Divide the mixture up into balls slightly bigger than a golf ball. Place each ball on the table and pat down into a cake shape, then firm up the edges with the palm of your hand.

5. Next take three bowls. In the first one, place the flour. In the second, beat together the egg and the milk. In the third, place the breadcrumbs. Coat each fishcake in flour, then place the floured cakes into the egg and milk mixture. Finally, dip each cake in the breadcrumbs and coat evenly. These will happily sit in a fridge overnight.

To make the sauce

1. Put the milk used for poaching the fish in a pan, over a high heat. You can boost the haddock flavour at this point by adding the haddock skins to it. Bring to a boil, then simmer for 5 minutes. Remove and chuck the haddock skins.

2. Meanwhile, you need to make something we chefs call *beurre manié*. This is a paste of flour and butter, used to thicken sauces. Take the butter and soften it slightly and then mix in the flour so that you have a paste.

3. Drop small pellets of this paste into the boiling haddock milk and watch it thicken. Remember that you cannot know the true consistency of the sauce until it reaches boiling point, so keep whisking the sauce and keep it boiling. You are looking to create a sauce about the thickness of double cream. Then add the chopped parsley.

4. This sauce can be made up to 24 hours in advance, but don't add the parsley until just before serving.

To assemble the dish

1. In a non-stick frying pan over a medium heat, pan-fry the fishcakes until golden brown all over.

2. At the same time, fry the eggs in a separate non-stick frying pan.

3. Place a fishcake on each plate, pour some sauce around and place a fried egg on top of each fishcake. Follow this with several cups of tea, two hours reading the Sunday papers and perhaps a quick nap.

Scallops Baked in the Shell with Carrot, Leek and Shallot   serves 4

I usually serve these as a starter. They may appear a little tricky because it involves a few stages, but are well worth the effort. The idea is to allow your guests to open their own scallop shell at the table and enjoy the delicate aroma that will rise up.

Ask your fishmonger for large, diver-caught scallops and, if you wish, ask him to prepare them for you. These will be in far better condition than dredged scallops and are caught without any damage to the sea bed.

12 scallops (3 per person)
1 leek
2 shallots
1 carrot
60g (2¼oz) butter
60ml (2fl oz) sweet white wine, such
   as Sauternes

1 tbsp chopped chervil
½ tbsp chopped tarragon
250g (9oz) quality, shop-bought puff
   pastry
1 egg, beaten
beurre blanc (see page 286),
   to serve

1. Open the scallops using an oyster knife or a pallet knife. Push the blade between the shells and twist slightly. Once partially open, cut down the inside of the flat half of the shell. This will release the top flat shell and leave the scallop meat attached to the more concave bottom shell.

2. Flip out the scallop by cutting through the muscle attaching it to the base of the shell. Remove the orange coral (you could pan-fry this in butter for lunch) and discard any sinew. What you should be left with is a pure white piece of scallop meat. Rinse these in cold water and keep in the fridge until you are ready to use them.

3. Clean the four nicest scallop shells (top and bottom shells) in cold water and keep to one side. (Use the other shells as ashtrays, soap dishes or anything; we don't need them for this recipe).

4. Now it's time to test your knife skills. We need to cut a 'julienne' of carrot, leek and shallot. Start with the leek because it's the easiest. Cut the leek into sections about 6cm (2½in) long. Then cut a section in half lengthways. Remove the centre so that you can press the leek

continued overleaf

flat on the board. Cut this into very fine strands using a sharp knife. Peel the shallots and cut each in half. Shred the shallot from one side to the other, again producing fine strands of shallot. The best way to tackle the carrot is to peel and slice it into strips using a mandolin or even a peeler. Then layer the strips up and slice them into julienne.

5. In a pan over a moderate heat, sweat the vegetables in the butter for about 2 minutes, or until they just start to soften. Then add the wine – just enough to create some steam. This steam will cook the vegetables.

6. Remove the pan from the heat and allow the mixture to cool. As it cools, add the chopped herbs and season the mixture. The vegetables should be moist with wine and butter.

7. Spoon a generous amount of the vegetables into the base of each concave shell half, .

8. Slice three scallops per person in half so that you have 6 scallop discs. Lay these discs on top of the vegetables and put a little more vegetable mix on top. Add a few extra drops of wine. Lightly butter the inside of each top shell and place back in position.

9. Preheat the oven to 180°C/350°F/Gas Mark 4.

10. Roll out the puff pastry and cut a long strip about the width of your middle finger. Brush this strip of pastry with beaten egg and wrap it right around each shell, effectively sealing the gap where the shells meet all the way around. Place the scallops in the oven for about 8 minutes, or until the pastry is golden brown.

11. Open the scallop at the table and serve with a little *beurre blanc* on the side.

Grilled Cider-cured Salmon with Potato Salad

serves 4

For all these years, MJ and I have not grown a thing apart from a few miserably inedible daffodils. And yet, now we have discovered that we are expert growers of new potatoes.

There's nothing worse than a new potato that's been undercooked, then dropped into a bowl of mayonnaise. I think a great potato salad is one in which the potato and mayonnaise blend together harmoniously. It's all in the method. Trust me.

The potato salad goes equally well with ham, roasted chicken or simply a tossed salad. The mayonnaise really should be home-made. However, I have been known to slip a jar of shop-bought mayo into the house and it does work.

750g (1lb 10oz) piece of salmon with
   the skin attached
1 heaped tbsp freshly chopped dill
olive oil

For the marinade
150ml (5fl oz) white wine vinegar
375ml (13fl oz) white wine
375ml (13fl oz) cider
150g (5oz) honey
200g (7oz) demerara sugar
handful of pickling spice
2 large gherkins, finely chopped

For the potato salad
30 average-sized new potatoes
about 2 tbsp light olive oil
4 tsp balsamic vinegar
1 tbsp chopped rocket leaves
3 hard-boiled eggs, roughly chopped
2 tsp capers, rinsed under a cold tap
6 tbsp mayonnaise
salt and pepper

To marinate the salmon

1. Put all the ingredients for the marinade into a large saucepan and bring to the boil. Simmer for about 5 minutes and then taste. It should be acidic from the wine and vinegar, yet the acidity should be balanced by the cider, sugar and honey.
2. Leave to cool, then chill the marinade overnight in the fridge.

3. The following day, add the chopped dill and pour the marinade into a roasting tray. Place the salmon in the roasting tray so that it is submerged in the marinade and allow to stand for 12 hours in the fridge.

To make the potato salad

1. Boil the potatoes in water until they are soft. I test this by using a spoon to crush one against the inside of the pan. If it breaks up nicely, then they are ready. Pour the potatoes into a colander.
2. Now here's a crucial point: *don't* cool them with water, but instead cut all the potatoes in half (yes, I know they are hot). Place them in a bowl, then douse with a slug of olive oil and a dribble of balsamic. Stir this in and then cover the bowl with clingfilm.
3. Every now and then, give the bowl a shake to make sure all the potatoes absorb some moisture and fur up at the edges. After 10 minutes, uncover the bowl and add all the remaining ingredients. Mix well, making sure that the potatoes break up slightly.
4. The final tip is to eat the lot; it simply won't taste as good tomorrow.

To cook the salmon

1. Remove the salmon from the marinade and pat dry with a cloth. Cut the fish into four portions and pull off the skin. Cut each portion in half almost right through, stopping 3–4mm (about 1/8in) short. Fold back each half so that the marinated bit is now around the edges – this is called 'butterflied' salmon.
2. Heat a ribbed griddle and brush it with the olive oil. Season the salmon with a little salt, place it in the pan and grill each side for about 2 minutes until just done. The outside should be beautifully caramelised whilst the inside should be medium rare.
3. Serve warm with what's left of the potato salad on the side.

Whole Roasted Trout with Chard, Bacon and Mushrooms   serves 4

This dish tastes far better if you catch your own trout. Happily, since that's not always possible, it does work with fish bought from the fishmonger. Most trout sold (and, sadly, all the trout I seem to catch) are enough for one portion only, but if you land a whopper, simply multiply the ingredients and proceed as directed in the method.

4 trout (or 2 if they're large)
60g (2¼oz) butter
150g (5oz) oyster mushrooms, torn into thin strips
1 garlic clove, finely chopped

200g (7oz) Swiss chard
a little tarragon
16 very thin slices of cured bacon

beurre blanc, to serve (see page 286)

1. Fish preparation is a messy business, so you may wish to ask your fishmonger to do it for you. But if you have caught your own, here's what to do. Carefully snip all the fins off of the fish and trim the tail. Lay the fish on a board with the belly facing you. Using a sharp knife, cut open the stomach and remove the innards and discard. Extend that cut, slicing all the way up to a point between the gills and all the way down almost to the tail. The fish should now have a large cavity and the backbone should be in sight. Run the knife along the underside of the backbone and remove it completely – you may need to snip it at the tail and gills to release it. Place the fish in the fridge

2. Put half the butter in a heavy-based casserole pan, add the oyster mushrooms and caramelise in the pan; this will take only about 2 minutes. Towards the end of this process, add the garlic.

3. Meanwhile, remove and discard the stalks from the chard and roughly chop the leaves down a little. Throw the chard in on top of the mushrooms and garlic and add the remaining butter.

4. Allow the chard to cook down slightly; this will take 2–3 minutes. Remove the pan from the heat. Add the tarragon, then allow the chard and mushroom mix to cool completely.

5. Preheat the oven to 180°F/350°F/Gas Mark 4.

continued overleaf

6. Take the trout from the fridge and fill the cavity you made earlier with enough of the chard and mushroom stuffing to make each trout its original un-butchered shape.
7. Secure each trout by putting bands of bacon around the fish.
8. Heat an ovenproof frying pan over a medium heat, then lay the trout in to colour. When it is brown on one side, turn it over and then slide the pan into the oven and cook for about 10 minutes.
9. Serve at once, with *beurre blanc* poured over.

Fish Pie

serves 4

This is my idea of comfort food. Creamy fish pie is best served in front of the telly on a cold winter evening! You can prepare the fish a day in advance and keep in the fridge. The next day, just add mash and bake, whilst you go off to pick up a DVD.

2 smoked haddock fillets, 250g (9oz) total weight
125g (4¹/₂oz) fillet of fresh pollock
1 lemon sole, filleted, 140g (scant 5oz) total weight
500g (1lb 2oz) raw king prawns, left in their shells
about 1.5 litres (2¹/₂ pints) milk
1kg (2lb 4oz) mussels

300ml (¹/₂ pint) white wine
150g (5oz) butter
125g (4¹/₂oz) plain flour
1 tbsp chopped parsley
10 button mushrooms, finely sliced
2 hard-boiled eggs, chopped
mashed potato, made from 900g (2lb) raw potato
75g (3oz) Cheddar, grated

1. First prepare the fish. Remove the skin and all the bones from both the haddock and the pollock. Then cut the fillets into large chunks and place in a wide, heavy-based pan. Cut the lemon sole fillets into chunks and add these and the king prawns (complete with shells) to the pan.

2. Cover the fish with milk and bring the pan slowly to a simmer. As soon as it simmers, remove the pan from the heat and carefully spoon out all the chunks of fish (reserving the milk for later). The flesh will be very delicate, so handle carfeully to avoid it breaking. Remove the prawns and peel. Discard the shells. Add the prawns to the rest of the cooked fish and put everything in a pie dish.

3. Place a saucepan over a medium heat, allow to heat up and then chuck in the mussels. Immediately add the wine and put a lid on the pan. Let the mussels cook for 1 minute in the wine and then pass them through a sieve, reserving the wine. Make certain to discard any mussels that haven't opened.

4. Pick the mussel meat from the shells and add this to the cooked fish and prawns in the pie dish.

5. To make the sauce, melt the butter in a pan over a low heat and add the flour. Cook these together for 2 minutes, ensuring that they don't catch on the base of the pan. Add the wine to the reserved milk and bit by bit, add to the pan. Each time you add some, allow the sauce to return to a boil. When you have a fairly thick sauce, turn off the heat and pass through a sieve.

6. Preheat the oven to 180°C/350°F/Gas Mark 4.

7. Now take the pie dish with the fish in it and add the parsley, the sliced mushrooms and the chopped egg. Gently mix these bits in with everything else, still taking care not to break up the fish. Pour over enough sauce to cover the fish and give the dish a shake to allow the sauce to spread out and coat evenly.

8. Add a decent knob of butter to the prepared mash. Pipe or spoon the mash over the fish mixture and sprinkle on the grated cheese.

9. Bake in the preheated oven for about 20 minutes, or until the mash is golden brown.

Grilled Sea Bass on Stir-fried Lettuce with a Coconut and Basil Broth serves 4

4 sea bass fillets, weighing about
  175g (6oz) each

2 shallots
2 tbsp corn or sunflower oil
2 green chillies, finely chopped
1 tsp cumin seeds
1 tsp coriander seeds
1 tsp ground turmeric

400ml (14fl oz) coconut milk
300ml (1/2 pint) chicken stock
4 heads of Little Gem lettuce
1 tsp chopped ginger
1 garlic clove, chopped
1/2 lime
2 tbsp coconut cream
4 tbsp fresh or frozen peas
2 tsp light soy sauce
about 20 basil leaves

1. The broth can be made well in advance. Slice the shallots into very fine rings. In a casserole pan over a low heat, sweat them for 1 minute with a splash of oil. Add the two chopped chillies to the shallots.

2. In a pestle and mortar, grind all the spices to a powder and add these to the pot. Now pour in the coconut milk and the chicken stock and bring to a simmer. Simmer for about 8 minutes.

3. Cook the fish in a ribbed griddle pan. Heat the pan and add a splash of oil. Place the fish in skin-side down and cook for 4 minutes. Turn the fish over and give it another 4 minutes.

4. When the fish is almost cooked, prepare the lettuce by removing most of the outside leaves, leaving just the hearts. Cut these crosswise into chunks.

5. Heat 1 tablespoon of water in a wok and add the ginger and garlic. When the mixture is boiling, add the lettuce and turn over in the liquid. After 1 minute, drain the lettuce, catching the ginger and garlic as well. Make a pile of lettuce in each serving bowl.

6. Finish the broth by bringing it back to a simmer and adding the lime juice, the coconut cream, the peas and the soy sauce. Finally, lightly pound the basil leaves in the pestle and mortar and add to the broth.

7. Put the cooked sea bass on top of the lettuce in the bowls and spoon a generous amount of broth around the fish. Serve straight away.

Tangy Grilled Chicken with Spicy Coleslaw
serves 4

This is meant to be nothing grander than a midweek store cupboard special. It's one of those things I knocked up using ingredients I had kicking around – as far as I remember, the only thing I bought was the chicken.

There's no need to leave the chicken marinating for any length of time before you get grilling. The coleslaw is crunchy and spicy. Make it and eat it right away – it doesn't keep.

4 skinned chicken breast fillets

For the marinade
2 tsp soy sauce
2 tsp sweet chilli dipping sauce
2 tsp syrup from a jar of stem ginger
a few drops of Tabasco
1 garlic clove, finely chopped
5cm (2in) piece of fresh root ginger, peeled and finely chopped

For the coleslaw
1/2 head of Chinese leaf cabbage, quartered and finely shredded
1 red onion, halved and finely sliced
2 red chillies, cut into fine rings
2 carrots, peeled, sliced and shredded into fine matchsticks
1 yellow pepper, cut into very fine strips
2 tbsp light olive oil
a small blob of wasabi paste
1/2 tsp cracked black pepper
pinch of sugar
1/2 tbsp white wine vinegar

1. First, prepare the marinade. In a glass bowl, mix the soy sauce, sweet chilli sauce, ginger syrup, Tabasco, garlic and chopped ginger.
2. Lay a chicken breast on a board and use a very sharp knife to make ten cuts across the breast, each about 1-2mm (1/16in) deep. This will help the marinade to penetrate the chicken. Once you have scored all the breasts, put them in the bowl and work the marinade all over them with your fingers.
3. Heat a griddle pan to a fairly fierce heat, then cook the chicken fillets quickly. Give them 5 minutes on one side and another 5 minutes on the other. Check that they are cooked thoroughly and allow them to rest for a few moments whilst you make the coleslaw.

4. Place all the prepared coleslaw vegetables in a bowl and mix them up well.
5. Whisk together the oil, wasabi paste, cracked pepper, sugar and vinegar. Pour this over the vegetables and mix in well.
6. Serve the chicken breasts with the spicy coleslaw on the side.

Sheila's Marinated Chicken Drumsticks

serves 4

When I was asked to organise a barbecue on behalf of the Blondin Allotment Committee, it was Sheila who came to the rescue. We had to provide food for 40 very hungry plot holders who had spent the morning clearing paths, digging over the compost heap and generally tidying up the site.

These chicken drumsticks were the star attraction at lunch, so it is my duty to share the recipe with the world.

1kg (2lb 4oz) chicken drumsticks

For the marinade
2 tbsp sunflower oil
2 tbsp red wine vinegar

2 tbsp tomato purée
6 red chillies, chopped
1 tbsp Worcestershire sauce
2 tsp caster sugar
salt and pepper

1. Firstly, slash each drumstick with a knife a couple of times – this allows the marinade to penetrate and will also speed up the cooking.
2. Mix all of the marinade ingredients together and then pour over the drumsticks.
3. Leave this to marinate overnight. Next day, fire up the coals and when they are nice and hot start cooking the chicken. Check the drumsticks are cooked right through before serving.

Tea-smoked Chicken Breast on Vegetable and Noodle Stir Fry serves 4

This is a novel way to cook chicken breasts. When I made a similar dish on *Ever Wondered About Food*, it triggered every fire alarm in the street! So do remember to open the windows before you start. Your kitchen will end up smelling like a smoky tent at the Isle of Wight Festival, so expect funny looks from the neighbours.

The vegetables listed here are suggestions only. Use whatever you fancy; just cut them up nice and fine so that they can be cooked quickly in a wok. *Kecap manis* is a sweetened, thick soy sauce available from supermarkets.

For the smoky chicken
4 chicken breasts 2 tsp syrup from a jar of stem ginger
1 tbsp *kecap manis*
120g (4¼oz) raw rice
120g (4¼oz) brown sugar
3 teaspoons Darjeeling tea leaves

For the noodle stir fry
4 sheets medium dried egg noodles
15 mangetout

3 spring onions
2 carrots
1 red pepper
1 courgette
10 shiitake mushrooms
1–2 tbsp sesame oil
1 tbsp soy sauce
1 garlic clove, chopped
1 red chilli, chopped
1 tbsp chopped coriander

1. An hour or so before cooking make four slashes, each of a 2mm (¹⁄₁₆in) depth, across the chicken breasts. Mix the ginger syrup and *kecap manis* together and rub over the scored breasts.
2. Line a wok with a layer of foil and on this put the raw rice, brown sugar and tea leaves. Sit a rack over this, on which you can cook the chicken without it coming into contact with the rice and sugar.
3. Place the chicken breasts on the rack and cover the wok with a lid, then put on a full heat until you see smoke rising from the wok. At this point, turn down the heat and continue smoking for 15 minutes. Check that the chicken is cooked – if not, return to the wok for a bit longer.
4. Finely slice all the vegetables for the stir fry.
5. Cook the noodles as per the instructions on the packet. Give them a stir whilst cooking and rinse them under cold water when done.

6. Heat another wok over a high heat and add the sesame oil. First chuck in the vegetables that will require most cooking (in my list, these would be the carrots and pepper). Keep adding the vegetables until they are all in the wok, then add the noodles and finish with the soy sauce, garlic, chilli and coriander. Continue to stir-fry for another 30 seconds, then divide the noodles and vegetables between four plates and serve with the chicken breast on top.

One-pot Chicken and Vegetable Stew
serves 4–6

I cook this for the family and it's a real favourite – nothing glamorous, just a good healthy supper. A heavy-based casserole pan is the ideal cooking vessel.

2 onions, cut into large dice
3 garlic cloves, finely chopped
8 rashers bacon, each cut into 4
1 sprig of thyme
1.2 litres (2 pints) water
1 chicken stock cube
4 skinned chicken thighs (bone in)
4 skinned chicken breast fillets (cut in half)
2 carrots, peeled and cut into large chunks

1 parsnip, peeled and cut into large chunks
1/2 swede, peeled and cut into large chunks
12 whole button mushrooms
1/2 Savoy cabbage, cut into 3cm (11/4in) dice
3 tbsp pre-cooked flageolet beans – tinned or dried
75g (3oz) butter, diced
crusty bread, to serve

1. Quickly fry the onions, garlic and bacon in the casserole pan – they should brown only slightly. Then add the sprig of thyme. Now pour in the water and crumble in the chicken stock cube. Bring to a gentle simmer, then add all the chicken. Bring back to simmering point and cook for about 5 minutes.
2. Add the carrots, parsnip, swede and mushrooms. Leave this to simmer very gently, for about 10 minutes. Taste the stock as it develops and season as necessary.
3. By now, the chicken should be cooked. Add the diced cabbage and stir it in well. Add the flageolet beans. Finally, add the diced butter to enrich the stew.
4. Season, then serve at once with crusty bread.

Mum's Pork Belly Curry

serves 4

I was born in Zanzibar – a small island just off Tanzania in the Indian Ocean. The island has a rich and varied history. It has strong African, Arabic, Indian and European influences, which are obvious in the architecture and cuisine. My mum learned to cook on the island, and as a result her cooking has always been eclectic, to say the least!

She has a friend from those Zanzibar days called Bunny, whose family originally came from Goa. Every now and then, Bunny and my mum get together for a day's cooking. This curry is the result of one such a day.

It is easy to make and the result is fabulous: the richness of the pork belly is perfectly foiled by the sourness of the vinegar.

White mustard powder can be hard to find, so instead you could use yellow mustard seeds and grind them in a pestle and mortar.

6 tbsp white wine vinegar
2–3 tsp chilli powder (heaped if mild)
1½ heaped tsp turmeric
1 tsp ground white mustard
   seeds/powder
1 tsp cumin seeds
750g (1lb 10oz) pork belly (skinned
   but with fat left on), cut into 3cm
   (1¼in) dice

2 onions, chopped
3 garlic cloves, crushed
2cm (¾in) fresh ginger, grated
2 tbsp vegetable oil
Cucumber, Green Tomato and Mint
   Raita, to serve (see page 281)

1. Pour the vinegar into a bowl and add the chilli powder, turmeric powder, mustard powder and cumin seeds. Whisk all of these together and add the pork belly. Mix the meat in well and leave to soak overnight in the fridge.

2. When you're ready to make the curry, lightly fry the onion, garlic and ginger in a little oil. You want the onions to colour only slightly.

3. Add the marinated meat and bring to simmering point. Allow it to simmer for about 10 minutes.

4. Add a little water, about 100ml (3½fl oz), and simmer for about 1 hour. Check occasionally to see if more water is needed, and if so add another 100ml (3½fl oz) Cook until the meat is really tender.

5. Serve with rice, accompanied by the raita

Lamb Stew with Allotment Vegetables and Spinach and Ricotta Dumplings serves 4

This is a wonderful, heart-warming stew!

Middle neck and scrag end are both cuts taken from the neck of lamb. The meat requires slow, gentle cooking, but the result melts in the mouth. Any decent butcher should be able to provide these cuts of meat. Ask him to trim away some but not all of the fat, and tell him to leave the meat on the bone; the cuts will look like irregular cutlets.

This is a fairly light stew with a stock rather than a sauce. You can use whatever vegetables are available – I've chosen summery ones for this recipe.

I prefer the cherry tomatoes to be peeled when they go into the stew. The best way to peel them is by quickly scorching them with a blowtorch and picking off the skin. You could, of course, add them with the skin on.

I like to serve Spinach and Ricotta Dumplings (see opposite) in the stew, but mash or boiled new potatoes served on the side also work well.

20 pieces middle neck or scrag end
    of lamb
about 2.4 litres (4 pints) water
1 chicken or lamb stock cube
1 onion, peeled
1 sprig of thyme
1 sprig of rosemary
1/2 head of garlic
1 carrot, peeled

To finish the stew
1 carrot, peeled and cut into 3cm
    (1¼in) cubes
¼ swede, peeled and cut into 3cm
    (1¼in) cubes
1 courgette, peeled and cut into 3cm
    (1¼in) cubes
100g (3½oz) sugar snaps
12 cherry tomatoes
large handful of fresh or frozen peas,
    about 1 tbsp per person
10-12 Spinach and Ricotta
    Dumplings (see opposite)

1. Lightly brown the lamb all over in a casserole pan, then pour in the water. Next, crumble in the stock cube, then add the whole onion, herbs, garlic and carrot and very slowly bring to a simmer.

2. Once at a simmer, cook the meat very gently for about 1½ hours, by which time the lamb should be tender, and the cooking liquor should have an intense lamb flavour.

3. Pick the carrot, onion, garlic and herbs out from the stew and discard. At this point, the lamb and stock can be cooled and stored in the fridge, to be reheated when needed.

4. Reheat the lamb and the stock, then drop in the cubed carrot and swede. Allow these a few minutes to cook before adding the rest of the vegetables and the dumplings. Serve the stew straight from the pot as soon as the vegetables are done.

Spinach and Ricotta Dumplings
makes 10–12 dumplings

These little dumplings can also be served as gnocchi with chopped tomato, olive oil and garlic.

500g (1lb 2oz) spinach
250g (9oz) ricotta
1 egg yolk

2 tbsp grated Parmesan
125g (4½oz) flour,
salt and pepper

1. Blanch the spinach for 30 seconds in boiling water, then plunge into iced water. Drain, then squeeze really dry in a clean cloth. Lightly chop the spinach, and set aside.

2. Bring a shallow pan of water to the boil. Now set a glass or metal bowl over it. Put the ricotta into the bowl and add the egg yolk. Beat this together gently as it heats up, for 3–4 minutes, then sprinkle in the Parmesan. Mix well and remove from the heat.

3. Add the flour and, finally, fold in the spinach. Season the whole mix with salt and pepper.

4. Pat flour onto the palms of your hands and then roll the mixture into balls and cook in simmering water for 2–3 minutes. Alternatively, if serving in a stew, drop the balls directly into the stock and simmer for about 3 minutes.

Dilly's Sri Lankan Curry

serves 4

Dilly is well known for her curry skills. This is a fairly typical Sri Lankan curry and you will notice the ingredients call for Sri Lankan curry powder. I have given the recipe for this distinctively flavoured powder on the opposite page.

Curry leaves are typical of Sri Lankan cookery. They are not hot but do have a wonderful flavour. If you are struggling to find any of the ingredients, try an Asian supermarket.

2 tbsp sunflower oil
1 chicken, cut into breasts, thighs and drumsticks
6 garlic cloves, finely sliced
2 onions, finely chopped
20 fresh curry leaves
2.5cm (1in) ginger, peeled and finely chopped
2 tsp chilli powder
1cm (½in) cinnamon stick

4 cardamoms
4 cloves
1 tsp turmeric
2 tsp Sri Lankan curry powder (see opposite)
1 green chilli, chopped
3 tomatoes, chopped
300ml (½ pint) chicken stock
400ml (14fl oz) coconut milk
rice, to serve

1. Heat the oil in a heavy-based casserole pan over a medium heat. Fry the chicken until golden brown, then set it to one side.
2. Now add the garlic and onions to the pan and allow them to colour slightly. Add the curry leaves and fry for 1 minute, then add all the spices (including the curry powder), the chilli and the tomatoes. Allow this to cook for about 2 minutes.
3. Put the chicken back in the pan and stir it around so that it is coated with the contents of the pan.
4. Pour in the chicken stock and coconut milk and cook for about 40 minutes on a medium heat or until the chicken is cooked. Serve straight away with rice.

Sri Lankan Curry Powder

makes 250g (9oz)

This curry powder recipe may look daunting but it wil yield enough for
several batches of curry. Store in an airtight container and use within
a couple of months.

10g (1/3oz) chilli powder
75g (3oz) coriander seeds
10g (1/3oz) fennel seeds
25g (1oz) cumin seeds
25g (1oz) fenugreek seeds
6 cardamoms
2 tsp mustard seeds
6 cloves
5mm (1/4in) cinnamon stick
15g (1/2oz) cracked black pepper

25g (1oz) cashew nuts
40g (13/4oz) rice
40g (13/4oz) shredded fresh
　coconut (not desiccated)
8 sprigs of curry leaves
7.5cm (3in) rampe leaf
5cm (2in) lemon grass, finely sliced
15g (1/2oz) ginger, finely sliced
1/2 tsp turmeric

1. Lightly pan-fry the chilli powder, all the dry seeds, the cloves, cina-
   mon stick and the pepper in a dry heavy-based pan, then set aside.
   Pan-fry the cashews until they are hot – this will release their oils. Set
   aside.
2. Now add the rice to the dry pan, and heat until brown. Do the same
   with the coconut.
3. Finally, dry out the curry leaves, rampe leaf, lemon grass, ginger and
   turmeric in the pan. Leave all the ingredients to cool, then grind
   together into a powder.

Slow-roasted Shoulder of Lamb Studded with Garlic and Rosemary serves 4

This is real Sunday lunch stuff. In my view, shoulder of lamb is far superior to leg or even saddle. Don't be frightened to cook this nice and slowly for a couple of hours – it really doesn't need to be served medium rare. Ask your butcher to select the best shoulder he has (different breeds will be available at different times of the year), and ask him to tie the lamb with string, rather than putting it in a net as they sometimes do.

I recommend serving this with the Caramelised Shallots (see page 220), Roasted Root Vegetables (see page 219) and Onion Purée (see page 219).

1 whole shoulder of lamb
3 garlic cloves
1 branch rosemary
2 tsbp corn or sunflower oil

900ml (1½ pints) brown stock
  (a stock cube is fine)
salt

1. Preheat the oven to 160°C/325°F/Gas Mark 3.
2. Using the tip of a sharp knife, make a little incision in the flesh of the lamb and push a slice of garlic inside. Repeat this all over the lamb and then do the same with the rosemary, breaking off a small sprig and pushing it into each cut.
3. Rub the shoulder with 2 teaspoons of salt. Put the oil in a frying pan and, when hot, add the lamb, turning until it is brown all over.
4. Next, transfer the lamb to a roasting tray and pour over the stock.
5. Place the tray in the middle of the oven and roast for at least 1½ hours, turning the meat over as it browns. By the time the lamb is cooked, the stock should have reduced a little and taken on an intense flavour and will be perfect to serve as gravy.
6. Allow the shoulder to rest for 10 minutes before carving.

Doug's Prize-winning Moussaka

serves 4

This classic Greek dish was given to me by Doug, our allotment neighbour, who is a construction engineer. Stacking up different vegetables in a sure and safe fashion is right up his street.

olive oil

2 big aubergines, cut into slices 1cm (1/2 in) thick

600g (1lb 5oz) medium-sized potatoes, peeled

1 onion, finely chopped

4 garlic cloves, chopped

600g (1lb 7oz) lamb mince

sprig of thyme

sprig of marjoram

400g (14oz) tinned tomatoes, or the equivalent weight of fresh, chopped tomatoes

2 tbsp tomato passata

150g (5oz) grated Cheddar

For the white sauce

up to 600ml (1 pint) milk

60g (2 1/4 oz) butter

50g (2oz) plain flour

salt and pepper

1. To make the white sauce, first warm the milk in a saucepan. In another pan, melt the butter over gentle heat and add the flour. Stir together for about 2 minutes to make a roux. Add the warm milk to the roux little by little, allowing the sauce to return to a simmer each time. This allows the starch in the flour to thicken the sauce.

2. When you have a sauce the consistency of thick double cream, turn off the heat, season to taste, and allow the sauce to cool. Cover with clingfilm whilst cooling to avoid a skin.

3. For the moussaka, heat a generous amount of olive oil in a frying pan and fry the slices of aubergine. A little colour is fine, but you don't want crispy aubergines. When cooked, drain well on kitchen paper.

4. Meanwhile, bring a pan of water to the boil and boil the potatoes until they are just cooked. Drain, cool them and cut into slices about 1cm (1/2 in) thick. Set aside.

5. Heat 2 tablespoons of oil in a deep-bottomed saucepan. Add the chopped onion and garlic and fry over a medium heat until pale golden in colour, then add the lamb mince. Cook for a couple of minutes and then add the herbs, tomatoes and passata. Continue

cooking over a gentle heat for about 45 minutes, until rich and thick. Preheat the oven to 170°C/340°F/Gas Mark 3½.

6. Pour half the mince mixture into a baking dish and spread out evenly. Put a layer of potato over this, followed by a layer of aubergine. Repeat these layers and then pour over the white sauce.

7. Sprinkle with Cheddar and bake in the oven for about 40 minutes. Turn up the heat to 190°C/375°F/Gas Mark 5 and bake for 5 more minutes or until golden brown.

Braised Ox Cheek with Dauphinoise Potatoes

serves 4

Here is a cut that is a restaurant favourite but seldom cooked at home. I am not sure why – ox cheek requires little preparation and is not all that expensive. One cheek is a generous single portion but not big enough for two.

Dauphinoise potatoes are the perfect accompaniment to rich, tender braised ox cheek. They are also a fairly simple dish if you are given a few tips. This recipe is slightly different to the conventional method because the potatoes are cooked prior to baking. This is because I find the traditional method can be a bit hit and miss, leaving the potatoes dry and/or tasting too 'baked'.

I leave you to answer the cheese question. I don't usually add cheese, but the potatoes are equally good, though different, with the addition of cheese. Remember too, that you serve the potatoes in the dish in which they are cooked. A shallow porcelain dish is perfect.

4 ox cheeks
2 tbsp sunflower or olive oil
4 shallots
2 garlic cloves
4 tomatoes
375ml (13fl oz) full-bodied red wine
3 litres (5 pints) beef stock (either make your own or buy some 'real' beef stock from your butcher)
1 star anise
10 peppercorns
1 sprig of thyme

For the dauphinoise potatoes
8 large potatoes peeled – Maris Piper, King Edwards and Desirée all work well
600ml (1 pint) double cream
500ml (17fl oz) full fat milk
3 garlic cloves
100g (3½oz) Gruyère cheese (optional)
salt and pepper

To finish the dish
12 button mushrooms, quartered
20 button onions
2 tsp chopped tarragon

To cook the ox cheeks

1. First, trim the ox cheeks of any sinew with a sharp knife.

2. Heat the oil in a large casserole pan over a high heat, then fry the ox cheeks. What you are doing here is browning them all over, so make sure the pan is hot and keep rolling them over. The process will take 5–6 minutes. Once browned, put the cheeks to one side.

3. Roughly chop the shallots and garlic and add them to the pan.
   Lightly colour the shallots and garlic –
   this will take about 2 minutes over a moderately high heat.
4. Meanwhile, roughly chop the tomatoes and add them to the shallots
   and garlic.
5. Turn the heat down low and allow the tomatoes to cook for a few
   minutes. Now, pour in the red wine. Bring the wine to the boil and
   reduce it until only a quarter of the original amount remains.
6. Pour in the stock and drop in the browned ox cheeks, star anise,
   peppercorns and thyme. Very slowly, bring the stew back to a simmer.
   This slow reheating allows the meat to retain its juices. When the
   stew has reached a simmer, allow it to cook
   for 1 hour.

To make the dauphinoise potatoes
1. While the stew is cooking, make the dauphinoise potatoes. Preheat
   the oven to 180°C/350°F/Gas Mark 4.
2. Slice the potatoes very finely – ideally about 2mm (^{1}/16 in) thick. A
   mandolin is useful here, though nifty knife skills can do the job.
3. Pour the cream and milk into a pan. Bring to a simmer over a
   gentle heat. Crush two of the garlic cloves, then add to the cream
   and milk. Heat for about 3 minutes.
4. Add the potatoes to the cream and milk mixture and simmer for
   about 4 minutes, or until 'just' cooked but still intact as complete
   slices. Remove the potatoes using a slotted spoon and leave to cool
   for a minute. Reserve the cream and milk mixture.
5. Use the remaining garlic clove to rub around the inside of a
   medium-sized oven dish. Layer the potatoes in the dish. For every
   2–3 layers, pour over about 3 tablespoons of the cream mixture,
   then season.
6. On the top layer, add the grated cheese, if using.

continued overleaf

To assemble the dish

1. When the stew has been cooking for half an hour put the potatoes in the preheated oven. Bake them, uncovered, for about 40 minutes. When ready, the top should be browned and slightly crispy.
2. Once the meat has cooked for 1 hour it should be very tender (if not, cook it for a little longer). Since it is so tender, remove it from the pan carefully. Put it to one side (covered with a tiny amount of the stock) whilst you finish the sauce.
3. Pass the remaining stock through a sieve to remove all the bits. Return to the pan, put on a high heat and bring to the boil. Allow the stock to reduce to about half its original volume. This will take about 15 minutes.
4. Meanwhile, the potatoes will probably be ready so turn the oven to a low heat and leave the potatoes to keep warm whilst you finish the stew.
5. The stock should have thickened slightly to the consistency of double cream. It should also have an intense meaty flavour. When you are happy with the sauce, cool it slightly and pour it back over the cheeks.
6. Finally, fry the mushrooms and onions in separate pans for 3–4 minutes; a little colour is nice on both. When they are cooked, drop them into the warm sauce. Add the chopped tarragon, stir, and serve with the dauphinoise potatoes.

A Few Words on Meat

While our allotment project has been about vegetables, there was no way I could write a cookery book without mentioning meat at all. I am a big fan of meat – both cooking and eating it. MJ, however, has never eaten much meat and what meat she does enjoy is usually in the form of small pieces, for example in a casserole or a stir-fry. For her, the thought of a large slab of steak is a real turn-off. My daughter Ellie has inherited this unfortunate gene. On the other hand, our son Richie is a committed carnivore who eagerly tucks into rare steaks, large roasts and mixed grills. That's my boy! Unfortunately, the girls rule in our house so meat is something of a treat.

For many years I simply enjoyed the experience of meat without giving too much thought to the issues of where it came from, what breed it came from, the animal's diet, the conditions in which the animal was kept or how it was slaughtered. In the last few years, though, I have come to think far more about all the food we consume as a family.

In my view, the rise of the supermarket and the, not-unrelated, fall of the high street butcher has done much to alter our nation's perception of meat. I despair at the supermarket packaging of meat: everything is done to distance the consumer from the bare fact that what they are buying is a dead animal – dead because they demand it. The French are far less squeamish about this and consequently they have a more profound respect for what they buy and eat. I have tried to educate my children on the grisly facts of meat eating. Occasionally I will bring a whole pheasant home and we will pluck it and gut it (having a look at the heart, the liver and what's in the stomach) before we cook it for lunch. They think I am a cruel, heartless Dad, but my hope is that it will give them a sense of respect for the animal or bird they are eating.

We all need to be exposed to the realities to some extent. I have visited several abattoirs and chicken slaughterhouses. It isn't pleasant, I don't enjoy seeing animals killed and I don't mind if I never see it again; it is, however, an experience that ultimately leaves me with respect for the sacrifice that is necessary for me to continue my carnivorous lifestyle.

When I was young my Dad was fond of mentioning (practically every time we ate meat) that, when he was a boy, meat was expensive and a luxury. He would say that his mother cooked a joint on a Sunday and it was then served cold on a Monday before reappearing on a Tuesday as a casserole or in a minor role in a 'use-up' dish like Toad in the Hole. I found this speech incredibly dull and pitied the poverty I presumed he had been born into.

Now, however, I find myself re-evaluating his view of what was a fairly widespread example of 1940s post-war home economy. In 'them' days meat (especially chicken, according to his recollection) was an expensive part of any meal and thus an ingredient not to be taken for granted. Contrast that with today: I can buy four chicken breasts for little over £2 whilst a leg of lamb can be bought for just £4. The vegetable part of a meal can often be more expensive than the protein.

The question is: should we praise a world where meat is so cheap? Or should we question the economic demands on production that give us this low price? Most foodies recognise that meat production has cut a lot of corners in its quest to provide ever-cheaper protein. We will tell anyone who will listen – and regularly those who won't – that good meat costs money primarily because it takes so much longer to produce quality. We will also claim, rightly in my opinion, that traditionally, and therefore ethically, reared meat tastes better. Let the animal live that little bit longer and allow it some open space and you will produce a superior meat in terms of texture and flavour. All this applies without even considering the welfare of the beast in question. I have friends who are hugely concerned that the animal had a decent life – and who is to say they are wrong? Surely if treating an animal with respect is an option then it would be wrong not to.

However – and I won't win any friends at the *Observer Food Monthly* by saying this – I feel there is a genuine argument against the above ideals. These £2 packs of chicken breasts are purchased in vast quantities. And it is precisely because they are so cheap that makes them popular. Meat is now something that is available to everyone, not just the well off. Surely, if we improve the quality of life for a chicken then we increase the price of the dead bird – and that in turn means that those on a lesser income may have to go without. The socialist within me senses a dilemma. Should we consider the animal or the human?

So, I am firmly of the belief that properly reared animals yield the best meat. However, if it were up to me to ban cheap meat, I would struggle to do so simply because I think that a situation where those who can afford to eat great meat do so at their leisure and those who can't go without smacks of elitism. The answer, I feel, is to change people's general eating habits and encourage a diet less reliant on meat so that we all view meat as a thrice-weekly treat worth spending money on – maybe my Dad was right after all!

So, with that balance in mind, there are a few general pointers to take into account when buying meat.

Ditch the supermarket and find a real butcher. If you can strike up a relationship with your butcher you will have a constant stream of recommendations and sound advice. The BSE crisis forced huge changes in the way beasts were logged and recorded. Now traceability is a legal requirement. What this actually means is that there is a variety of information on every animal slaughtered – its diet, where it was reared, who reared it, where it was killed and when it was killed – all of which will give an indication as to the quality of the meat on offer. So ask your butcher what the animal was fed on. When it comes to cattle, the term 'grass fed' is a good indication of quality. Lush pastures taste good and influence the taste of the meat. (Of course, this information only goes so far: the 'lush pastures' of the Yorkshire Dales probably taste great but those alongside the M1 may be less tasty.)

And so to death. If the Buddhist faith is right we will all end up back here as something else. If I come back as a cow I would choose a small family-run abattoir for my dispatch over a huge industrial slaughterhouse since, in my experience, those animals from small abattoirs are treated well up to the last.

Once dead, the meat is in the hands of a butcher. This is a crucial period, especially in the case of beef. A dead cow is cut into four – two hind and two fore quarters. A decent butcher will let the carcass hang in its quartered state for at least 21 days before butchering it into primal joints – the large bits of meat. These are hung again for a period of about a week, allowing the meat to 'age'. This actually means it is starting to decay, but don't panic – this develops the flavour.

The breed of the animal is also a selling point. A friend once asked me if it was immoral to eat a 'rare' breed as, surely, if it is rare, it should be preserved. Actually, the opposite is the case. All breeds of farmed animals have been developed over many years by cross-breeding to produce a beast fit for the table. Many have eventually been deemed less economical than others, have been bred less and have faded away. Recently, however, some farmers have realised that the rarity of a breed may be what makes it popular so many breeds have been resurrected and marketed as superior precisely because they are not the popular breed. For me the jury is still out on this one – I have eaten some fantastic rare breed meat, but is this because of the breed or the fact that those rearing it are the type who farm properly and would have produced good meat whatever the breed? Nonetheless, our enthusiasm for rare breeds is taking hold and some, such as Gloucester Old Spot pig, are selling so well and becoming so widely available, you can't help wondering if 'rare' is still the right word.

Finally, when buying meat at the butchers or in a restaurant it is important to see the distinction between a named breed and the all-too-common tendency of naming the general area from whence it came. In my bit of west London we are well served with great gastropubs. Many of them put their menus up on a chalkboard – 'Cornish' lamb, 'Scottish' beef or 'Yorkshire-reared' pork all appear – but this actually tells us nothing. Animals are crap at geography and taste much the same from anywhere, but find out the breed, its life history and its treatment at the butchers and you should know what you're getting.

preserves
and sauces

Pickled Red Cabbage

makes about 4 x 300g (10oz) jam jars

Red cabbage should be eaten more often – it's a lovely vegetable. The classic way is to braise the cabbage slowly in the oven, which is indeed a fine way of eating it, but you should also try this raw pickling method. Don't wait until you need it – make a batch when red cabbage is in season and it will be ready to eat whenever you want. Do make plenty because it will keep for a long time in a sterilised kilner jar in the fridge. It goes really well with rich meats like pork, duck and goose as the acidity balances the fattiness of these meats. I also serve it with roasted game, ham, pâté and cold smoked fish.

1 red cabbage	4 tbsp red wine
1 clove	200ml (7fl oz) red wine vinegar
1 star anise	4 tbsp honey
2.5cm (1in) cinnamon stick	100g (3½oz) demerara sugar

1. Wrap up the three spices in a small piece of muslin and secure with string. Put aside for later.
2. Prepare the pickling liquor by pouring the wine, vinegar, honey and sugar into a pan. Bring this to a boil and add the muslin bag. Boil the mixture until it is reduced by half.
3. Taste the contents of the pan and assess the flavour. There should be sharpness due to the vinegar but it should be balanced by the sugar and honey. Adjust the mixture if you feel it needs it but remember that it won't be as strong once mixed with the red cabbage.
4. Meanwhile, prepare the cabbage by cutting it into quarters through the core. Remove the core completely from each quarter and then very finely slice the cabbage into a bowl.
5. Pour the warm pickling mixture over the cabbage. It won't submerge the cabbage so give it a mix every so often. When the liquid has cooled, transfer the cabbage to the fridge and leave overnight.
6. The next day, pour off most of the excess liquid and pack the cabbage into a sterilised jar (see opposite). Return to the fridge to store.

Courgette Pickle

makes 3 x 400g (14oz) jars

The courgette harvest on our allotment was fantastic. For weeks, we were eating courgettes in some form every day. Although they don't freeze well, they can be preserved by pickling and I love this recipe. It's tangy rather than spicy and goes well with all sorts of meats and cheeses. I have given the quantities for a decent-sized batch because it's the sort of thing you only make once a season, when there are plenty of courgettes around.

To sterilise a jar, simply place in a saucepan of boiling water for 15–20 minutes or in a hot oven for an hour.

10 courgettes	50g (2oz) brown sugar
1 red onion	1/2 tsp turmeric
1 red pepper	1/2 tsp mustard seeds
4 green chillies	2 tsp cumin seeds
25g (1oz) flaked sea salt	2 garlic cloves, finely chopped
175ml (6fl oz) white wine vinegar	ground black pepper

1. Cut the courgettes into thin slices on a slight angle, finely slice the red onion, and cut the pepper and chillies into julienne (very fine) strips.
2. Rub the sea salt into the mixture fairly vigorously. Allow the vegetables to sit for 5 minutes with the salt and then rinse off and pat dry.
3. Meanwhile, put the remaining ingredients in a pan and bring to the boil. Cook for 3 minutes and then allow to cool very slightly, before pouring over the vegetables.
4. Cool the pickle at room temperature. Pour off any excess liquid and store in a sterilised jar in the fridge.

Green Tomato Chutney

makes 5 x 400g (14oz) jars

Many years ago I worked for Gary Rhodes. We used to make a fabulous pork terrine served with a green tomato chutney. Until then, I had never realised that green tomatoes could have any use in the kitchen.

Certainly, our allotment churned out a lot of green tomatoes, and this recipe gave us a great way to use them up. The chutney is great with cheeses, terrines or on a simple ham sandwich.

2.25kg (5lb) green tomatoes, chopped roughly into 2cm (3/4in) dice
2 cooking apples, chopped as above
600ml (1 pint) malt vinegar
5 onions, chopped
100g (3 1/2oz) sultanas
350g (12oz) demerara sugar
2 tsp mixed spice
2 tsp ground cinnamon
2 tsp ground ginger
salt

1. Throw all the ingredients into a saucepan and turn on the heat. Start on a high heat and let the mixture boil for about 20 minutes. At this point, turn down the heat to maintain a simmer.
2. Every so often, stir the pan to prevent the mixture catching. When almost all the liquid has cooked off, turn off the heat. You should be left with a thick, dark brown, rich chutney. Cool and store in sterilised jars.

Green Tomato Salsa with Spring Onion and Green Chilli makes about 500ml (1 pint), enough for six people

This is a quick and simple salsa that goes really well with grilled bass or bream. If you like your salsa hot, retain the seeds in the chillies.

6 green tomatoes, very finely diced
2 green chillies, finely chopped
4 spring onions, sliced into very fine rings
4 tbsp olive oil
8 mint leaves, finely chopped
pinch of rock salt

1. Put all the ingredients in a bowl and mix well.
2. Cover with clingfilm and store in the fridge for up to 2 days.

Tomato and Chilli Jam

makes about 4 x 400g (14oz) jars

This is not your conventional jam: I wouldn't suggest using it to spread between Victoria sponges!

As our mountain of ripe tomatoes got bigger, we started to think past dinner and came up with ways to make our tomatoes last beyond the season. A large batch of this stored in the fridge will keep for ages, though you'll be amazed at how quickly you use it up.

I've been making this sweet, spicy jam for years and I love it. It benefits so many dishes – fish, meats and even cheese.

1.5 kg (3lb 5oz) ripe tomatoes
   (any varieties)
475ml (16fl oz) water
300ml (1/2 pint) white wine vinegar

750g (1lb 10oz) caster sugar
3 garlic cloves
2 heaped tsp dried chilli flakes

1. Cut the tomatoes into chunks. To give an idea of size, I cut an average plum tomato in half and then cut each half into four.
2. Put all the ingredients into a large heavy-based pan and bring to a simmer over a medium heat. Continue cooking the mixture until it starts to reach a thick, jammy consistency. At this point, reduce the heat and give the jam an occasional stir to avoid it catching on the bottom of the pan.
3. To test whether the jam is ready, put a little on a cold plate and then chill in the fridge. If it sets after a few minutes, it has reached the right consistency.
4. Pour into sterilised jars (see page 275), then leave to cool. Store in the fridge.

Aubergine, Tomato and Coriander Salsa

makes about 425ml (3/4 pint)

This is a great dressing for meat, particularly lamb or chicken. I often take a rump of lamb and rub it with a mixture of ground cumin, olive oil and ground coriander. I then roast it, and serve it dressed with this salsa. Alternatively, serve the salsa as a dip with flatbread or pitta.

I don't go along with the theory that aubergines should be salted before cooking to remove any bitterness. In fact, the salt just makes them emit water, with the result that they are impossible to brown in a pan. Simply use firm aubergines, and they shouldn't be bitter.

200ml (7fl oz) light olive oil, for frying
1¹/2 medium aubergines (avoid large ones as they often turn to seed inside)
2 red chillies

4 ripe tomatoes
2 garlic cloves, finely chopped
salt and pepper
2 heaped tbsp chopped coriander

1. Pour the oil into a wok and heat to about 130°C/250°F (see page 211 for testing oil temperature).
2. Meanwhile, prepare the aubergines by cutting them into 1cm (¹/2in) dice. Then chop the chillies and finely dice the tomatoes.
3. Fry the aubergine in the oil in three batches. Each batch should be golden brown and even slightly crispy when done. Allow the aubergine to drain on kitchen paper, and leave the oil to cool for about 10 minutes.
4. Place the drained aubergine in a bowl and pour over 100ml (3¹/2fl oz) of the cooled oil. Add the chillies, tomato and garlic, then season to taste. Mix together and leave to cool completely before stirring in the coriander. The mix should be slightly suspended in the olive oil, so add a little more oil if necessary.

Red Onion Jam

makes about 4 x 400g (14oz) jars

We had a great crop of red onions – over 250! As we were already using our own shallots for cooking, the red onions were earmarked for salads, but with so many of them we had to think about other uses.

In my professional kitchens, I have always kept a tub of red onion jam in the fridge. It's easy to make, lasts for ages and has multiple uses. It's great with pâtés and terrines, you can serve it with cheese, and it can be mixed into a salad or served with roast meats such as belly of pork.

There is no point in making small amounts of this; if you are going to go to the bother of chopping onions, you may as well make a large batch when your harvest of onions is ready.

20 red onions	350g (12oz) demerara sugar
750ml (1¼ pints) red wine	200g (7oz) redcurrant jelly
180ml (6½fl oz) red wine vinegar	120ml (4fl oz) port

1. Peel all the onions and cut them in half through the root. Lay each onion, cut side down, on the chopping board and slice out the section with the root in it. Now slice the rest of the onion very finely.

2. When all the onions are sliced, heat a saucepan and toss them in. Let them sizzle gently for a moment in the dry pan and then pour in the wine and vinegar.

3. Bring to the boil, pour in the sugar and redcurrant jelly and boil until the liquid has almost completely reduced. This will take 1–2 hours. By now, the onions will be soft and stained a deep claret colour. What moisture remains should be thick and syrupy – now is the moment to add the port.

4. Drop the temperature right down and stir regularly to prevent the onion mixture from sticking to the bottom of the pan. Continue cooking until the liquid is all but gone, then remove the pan from the heat. Allow to cool completely, then decant into sterilised jars.

Strawberry Jam

makes about 5 x 300g (10 oz) jam jars

This is a quick and easy strawberry jam recipe that I made with part of our summer crop. It also works well with raspberries and blackberries.

1.5kg (3lb 5oz) strawberries
1kg (2lb 4oz) jam sugar

150ml (5fl oz) water
1 tsp pectin powder

1. Put everything into a pan and simmer over a medium heat until the sugar has dissolved. Increase the heat and cook rapidly for about 20 minutes. The mixture by this point should look like a loose jam.
2. Take the pan off the heat and test the jam by putting a small amount on a plate in the fridge. If it sets nicely, turn off the heat, then spoon into sterilised jars (see page 275). Once cool, store in the fridge.

Mint Sauce

makes 250ml (8¾fl oz) of mint sauce base

When we planted mint at the allotment, I didn't really have mint sauce in mind. I thought a bit of fresh mint would be good for yoghurt raitas and couscous or even the odd jug of Pimm's. It was soon obvious that to keep up with our flourishing mint plantation we were going to have to drink an obscene amount of Pimm's or come up with a plan B. That plan turned out to be this recipe

This recipe is for a basic syrup which can be stored and to which you can then add fresh mint whenever you want mint sauce. Although it doesn't really matter what type of vinegar you use here, personally I prefer to use malt vinegar

400ml (14fl oz) malt vinegar
400g (14oz) demerara sugar

a few mint stalks

1. Place all the ingredients in a pan over a medium heat and bring to a boil. The mixture will need stirring at first until the sugar dissolves.
2. Keep the pan boiling until the mixture is reduced by at least half. The point at which it must be removed from the heat is hard to call, but you will notice that the sauce begins to take on a glossy appearance and is denser than when you started. Don't expect a thick, gloopy syrup, but you will notice a certain richness.

3. At this stage taste a spoonful of the syrup, first allowing it to cool for a few seconds. It certainly won't be good enough to drink, but it should have a nice balance between the acidic vinegar and the sugar.

4. If you are happy with the flavour, leave the syrup to cool. Pour it into a jar and mark as 'mint sauce base'. Whenever you need some mint sauce, simply pick and chop as much mint as you want and pour over enough syrup just to cover.

Cucumber, Green Tomato and Mint Raita

makes about 300ml (½ pint), enough for 4 people

This cooling raita is the perfect accompaniment to spicy dishes. Yoghurt is the best thing to cool the mouth when eating hot food, so this simple raita will spare you during those spicy moments! It's definitely better than desperately gulping water, which simply spreads the heat around the mouth.

½ cucumber
3 green tomatoes
10 mint leaves, chopped
250ml (9fl oz) plain yoghurt

¼ tsp cumin seeds
pinch of chilli powder
pinch of ground ginger
pinch of salt

1. Cut the cucumber in half lengthways and remove the seeds with a spoon, then discard. Dice the seeded cucumber into 1cm (½in) cubes and throw them into a small bowl.

2. Now finely dice the tomatoes and add them to the cucumber with the chopped mint.

3. Mix all the remaining ingredients in a separate bowl and then pour over the cucumber, tomato and mint and mix together.

Pesto

makes 2 x 300g (10 oz) jam jars

I have used many different pesto recipes over the years. Some chefs like to toast the pine nuts, others don't – personally, I like to brown them in olive oil. This recipe was given to me by a chef I met whilst on holiday in Italy. He insisted that real pesto should be made by hand, using a pestle and mortar. If you need the exercise, then that's certainly the way to go. Frankly, I think a food processor will get the job done equally as well.

Pesto keeps well in the fridge as long as you pack it into a jar and ensure there are no air pockets. It is also worth putting a layer of olive oil over the top to prevent the pesto from discolouring.

about 300ml (1/2 pint) best-quality, extra virgin olive oil
100g (3 1/2 oz) pine nuts

1 large bunch (150g/5oz) basil
125g (4 1/2 oz) fresh Parmesan, grated
3 garlic cloves

1. Put 100ml (3 1/2 fl oz) of the olive oil in a pan and tip in the pine nuts. Place the pan over a gentle heat and allow the pine nuts to slowly turn a light golden brown colour. Remove from the heat and cool.

2. When the pine nuts are cool, pour into a food processor and add the basil, Parmesan and chopped garlic. Blend for a minute or so. Then, with the machine still running, slowly add the rest of the oil until a rich thick paste is achieved.

Herb Oil
makes 400ml (14fl oz)

Most professional chefs will use herb oil from time to time. Not only does it have a lovely flavour, but it also gives a finished dish a wonderful visual lift. Any mixture of soft green herbs can be used for this recipe and the result should be a beautiful emerald green oil, which can be drizzled over cooked meats and fish or over the surface of a soup or sauce.

I keep the oil in a squeezy bottle in the fridge, where it will last for a couple of weeks.

a 1.2 litre (2 pint) measuring jug   olive oil
    stuffed full of green herbs

1. Bring a large pan of water to the boil and stand a bowl of cold water ready beside it. Blanch the herbs in small batches to ensure the water remains boiling. As each batch goes in, count to ten before removing it from the boiling water and plunging into the cold water. This quickly stops the cooking process.
2. When all your herbs are blanched, take them out of the cold water and squeeze them dry with a clean tea towel. They must be really dry before the next step of the recipe.
3. Now all that remains is to blend the herbs with the oil. A liquidiser will work, up to a point. However, the best machine I have found for making this oil at home is a coffee grinder. Place the herbs in the machine of choice and pour in enough oil to just cover the herbs. Blitz thoroughly to mix together. Do this in small batches: if you blend a large amount, the machine will have to run for longer, which could heat the oil and destroy the colour. When blended, pass the mixture through some muslin. Pour the strained oil into a bottle and keep refrigerated.

Flavoured Butter

makes 250g (9oz)

Here is a flavoured butter that can be frozen and taken out to use when needed. Play around with different herbs and use them with various meats and fish. Dill, chive and lemon go very well with grilled white fish whilst shallot, thyme, garlic and parsley are great with a steak.

Store the butter as a block in the fridge or roll up into a log in clingfilm so that you can cut slices when needed.

250g (9oz) unsalted butter
4 tbsp fresh herbs, chopped
salt and pepper

Variations
cracked black pepper, parsley and
   garlic
basil and grated lemon zest
shallot and thyme
cayenne pepper, chopped chilli, garlic
   and coriander

1. Leave the butter out to soften. It should be soft enough to easily push a knife through, but not so warm that it starts to look oily. When soft, put it in a bowl and mix in the herbs. Season and refrigerate.
2. If you wish to add chopped shallots or garlic, finely chop both and then sweat them in a little butter. Leave to cool, then add to the soft butter and herbs.

Granny's Vinaigrette

makes about 250ml (9fl oz)

Granny would never have called this vinaigrette. She called it 'oil and vinegar' and, of course, that's all it is.

In my opinion a salad is dull without a dressing and I use various dressings for different salads. Balsamic vinegar and olive oil makes a simple tasty dressing to which various other ingredients can be added, such as fresh herbs, chopped shallots or garlic and lemon.

At other times, I make more elaborate concoctions involving oil infused with chillies, rosemary or truffle and vinegars from Chardonnay or Cabernet Sauvignon.

continued overleaf

These are all great, but the one I come back to time and again is Granny's simple, quick and cheap dressing. I often quadruple the quantities given below to make a litre (1³/4 pints) at a time and then keep it in the fridge.

Although I have indicated specific measurements, vinaigrette is very much about personal taste, so play with the same ingredients in varying ratios until you hit on the one you like best.

5 heaped tsp English mustard
200ml (7fl oz) vegetable oil
50ml (1³/4 fl oz) white wine vinegar
6 tsp sugar

plenty of coarsely ground black pepper
a little salt

1. Put everything into a jam jar, secure the lid tightly and shake like an enthusiastic percussionist in a New Orleans jazz band.
2. Taste, and adjust if you like.

Beurre Blanc

makes 400ml (14fl oz), 4 generous portions

Beurre blanc is simply a butter sauce. The butter is gently heated and emulsified and a selection of fresh herbs added.

This is the perfect accompaniment to fish, chicken or vegetables such as asparagus or artichokes. Even better, it only takes 5 minutes to make.

300ml (¹/2 pint) meat, vegetable or fish stock
250g (9oz) unsalted butter

2 tbsp any fresh herbs you fancy
salt and pepper

1. Bring the stock to a simmer in a pan. Meanwhile cut the butter into dice and then add it to the stock, whisking whilst you do so.
2. Once all the butter has been incorporated, blend with a stick blender.
3. Finally, season the sauce and add the herbs of your choice.

Neil's Sweet Chilli Dipping Sauce

makes 250ml (1/2 pint)

I love sweet chilli sauce, but had never really considered making my own because I assumed the shop-bought stuff was as good as it gets.

One afternoon, I popped round to see my friend, Neil, and found him busy in the kitchen. He had made some sweet chilli sauce and asked if I would like to try it. It was fabulous, and I immediately demanded the recipe.

Neil uses Japanese pickled root ginger in his version, which I think is the winning ingredient: it adds a depth of flavour that is missing in the shop-bought version.

The amount of chilli you use obviously has an effect on the resulting heat. The hottest part of a chilli is not, in fact, the seeds but the white membrane, or 'placenta', that attaches the chilli flesh to the seeds. So, to reduce the heat further, take this part of the chilli out – but if heat is this much of a concern, perhaps chilli sauce is not for you!

2–6 hot red chillies
1 red pepper
1 yellow pepper
175g (6oz) caster sugar
225ml (8fl oz) water

6 tbsp white wine vinegar
90g (3¹/₄oz) Japanese pickled root
   ginger
a little salt

1. Chop the chillies roughly with a knife and place them in a food processor. Remove all the flesh from the peppers and chop roughly, then add it to the chilli. Turn on the machine and whiz until the pepper and chilli are finely chopped but not reduced to a purée.
2. Now make a stock syrup from the sugar and the water. Put both ingredients into a pan and simmer for about 10 minutes, or until the volume is reduced by about half.
3. Add the chopped peppers and chillies to the syrup, then pour in the vinegar and simmer for a further 10 minutes.
4. Chop the Japanese root ginger finely into small dice. Put in the pan, add the salt and simmer until the whole mixture starts to thicken.
5. Remove the pan from the heat and allow to cool. Pour into sterilised jars and store in the fridge.

Easy Tomato Pasta Sauce
makes 8 portions

This is home cooking, not restaurant food! We found that summer on the allotment yielded far too many tomatoes for one family to eat, so as well as chutneys and soups we made batches of tomato sauce to freeze. This recipe can form the base of many a pasta meal the whole year through.

8 shallots
2 tbsp olive oil
6 garlic cloves

1 red chilli
20 ripe red tomatoes
salt and pepper

1. Peel the shallots and cut them in half, then slice them up very finely.
2. Heat the olive oil in a saucepan (make sure you have a lid that fits). Add the shallots and allow to sweat over a gentle heat; this basically means cooking them without allowing them to colour.
3. Meanwhile, chop the garlic cloves and the chilli as finely as possible, then add this to the shallots.
4. Prepare the tomatoes by using a sharp knife to remove the 'eye' (the bit where they attach to the vine). Then cut each tomato in half and cut each half into about six pieces. Size is less important than uniformity – make sure you cut the tomato evenly.
5. Add the tomatoes to the shallots and put the lid on the pan. Bring to a simmer and cook for about 35 minutes, stirring occasionally.
6. After this time, you should have a fairly wet mixture and the tomatoes should have broken right down. Remove from the heat and season before leaving to cool completely. Once cool, pour into freezer bags and store in the freezer.

Serving suggestions
1. The easiest method: simply defrost a bag, reheat the sauce, then mix with pre-cooked pasta.
2. Pour some reheated tomato pasta sauce onto some fried bacon lardons, then finish with feta cheese and torn basil.
3. Reheat some sauce, then add some fresh washed clams and mussels along with chopped rocket and a pinch of saffron.

puddings and sweet things

Steamed Spiced Plum and Walnut Sponge

serves 4

English food at its very best! This steamed sponge is the perfect pudding for a lazy Sunday in the middle of winter, when visiting the allotment just seems like a bad joke.

The plum jam used here could be shop-bought, but I recommend making your own. Alternatively, try serving this with Roasted Plums (see opposite).

For the plum jam
15 plums
6 tbsp jam sugar

For the sponge
175g (6oz) unsalted butter, plus extra
  for greasing

175g (6oz) self-raising flour
175g (6oz) caster sugar
3 eggs
1/2 tsp mixed spice
1 tsp ground cinnamon
about 50ml (1³/4oz) milk
2 tbsp finely chopped walnuts

To make the jam

1. Cut the plums into quarters and remove the stones. Throw the plums into a pan over a high heat, then sprinkle on the sugar. Very quickly, in about 2 minutes, the heat and the sugar will turn the plums to a wet mulch. As the temperature in the pan rises, the mixture will start to look more glossy and jam-like in consistency.

2. Keep stirring the jam to avoid it catching on the bottom of the pan. Test the mixture by setting a small amount on a plate in the fridge. If it doesn't set at all, keep heating, and test again. For this pudding, though, a looser jam works well.

To make the sponge

1. Put the butter, flour, sugar and eggs in a mixer or food processor and whisk or blend well until combined.

2. Add the mixed spice, cinnamon and half the milk and blend again until the mixture is a thick pouring consistency. You may need to add more milk at this point if you feel the mix is a little thick. Now stir in the chopped walnuts.

3. Butter a 1.2-litre (2-pint) pudding basin and then cut a circle of grease-proof paper and place it in the bottom of the basin. Pour

2 tablespoons of plum jam into the basin. Now three-quarters fill the basin with the sponge mixture. It is important to leave a gap for the sponge to rise. Put a piece of buttered foil over the top of the pudding basin, then tie it securely with string.

4. Place a large pan of water on the stove and bring to the boil. There should be enough water to reach two-thirds of the way up the pudding basin when it is sat in the pan.

5. Before putting the pudding in the pan, take a piece of foil and fold it into a strip that you can lay under the pudding basin and up the inside of the pan – this will make it easier to get the basin out of the hot pan.

6. Steam the sponge for about 1½ hours. A good way to test if it's done is to slide a metal skewer into the sponge: if it comes out clean and hot, it's ready.

7. Serve with more plum jam or roasted plums (see below) and plenty of custard.

Roasted Plums serves 4

Here's a lovely way to serve plums through the late summer months. Try them like this with mascarpone or a good vanilla ice cream – or even as compôte with Greek yoghurt, for a nice breakfast.

12 ripe plums
50g (2oz) butter
1 tbsp golden caster sugar

½ tbsp water
1 star anise
1 small cinnamon stick

1. Cut the plums in half and remove the stones.
2. Melt the butter in a heavy-based casserole pan over a medium heat. Add the sugar, and allow this to start caramelising, then put in the plums, flat side down. Pour in the water, add the spices and cook for 5 minutes, occasionally turning the plums over.
3. Remove from the heat and allow to cool at room temperature.

Mum's Apple Snow

serves 4–6

I don't think my mum invented this dish, but I have to say I've never known anyone else to serve it. The best way to describe it is as an apple trifle but with none of that jelly nonsense.

Apple snow is easy to make and I think it's one of the nicest puddings I know. Mum insists that any apple will do, be it eater or cooker, so there really is no excuse not to give it a go.

For the custard, it's fine to use good old custard powder and milk.

4–6 apples	up to 600ml (1 pint) custard
4 tsp sugar	2 tbsp milk
1 packet trifle sponge fingers	1 egg white

1. First of all, you need to make an apple purée, which can be done well in advance. Peel and core the apples and chuck them into a saucepan with 3 teaspoons of sugar. (Adjust the amount of sugar depending on your taste, but don't make it too sweet.) Stew the apples well and, if they don't yield their own liquid, add a little water – but only if absolutely necessary.

2. Once stewed, the apple should be puréed using a hand blender or food processor and then left to cool.

3. Break up the sponge fingers into large pieces and lay them in the bottom of a serving bowl – a glass bowl is best. Alternatively, you could use individual glasses.

4. Now make up the custard, as directed on the packet. Once the custard is made, add the milk, just to keep it on the thin side of stodgy. Then, whilst the custard is still hot, pour it over the sponge fingers, which will start to absorb it.

5. Meanwhile, whisk the egg white to a stiff peak, adding 1 teaspoon of sugar towards the end of the whisking to help stabilise the egg white foam. Gradually pour in the apple purée whilst continuing to whisk. (My mum, poor woman, does all this by hand, but it's fine to use an electric whisk!) Then pour the combined apple purée and egg white foam over the custard and sponge.

6. Refrigerate for at least 2 hours before serving.

Emergency White Chocolate Cheesecake with Summer Berries serves 4–6

This is an 'emergency' dessert because it is so quick and simple. I guarantee you will be able to knock it up with minimum fuss and to maximum effect. Although, obviously if you're involved in a real emergency I would not suggest a cheesecake as a feasible solution!

For the shortbread base
225g (8oz) unsalted butter, diced
   and chilled
90g (3¼oz) caster sugar
15g (½oz) cornflour
225g (8oz) plain flour
pinch of salt

For the cheesecake filling
150g (5oz) white chocolate, broken
   into chunks
175g (6oz) ricotta
225g (8oz) mascarpone cheese
fresh summer berries, to serve

1. To make the shortbread base, put the butter and sugar in a mixing bowl and beat until the sugar has been incorporated. Don't overbeat at this stage – if using a machine, the whole process will only take a couple of minutes.
2. Next, combine the cornflour, flour and salt. Add this to the butter and sugar mixture and again beat in just enough to combine.
3. Choose a tin for your cheesecake – a 20–25cm (8–10in) flan tin will be fine for these quantities, or you could make individual tarts in tins of about 10cm (4in).
4. Take the raw shortbread mix and spoon into the chosen tin. Smooth it down until you have a layer about 2cm (3/4in) thick across the bottom. Place this in the fridge to set for about 30 minutes.
5. Meanwhile, preheat the oven to 160°C/325°F/Gas Mark 3. Once the shortbread layer has set, place the tin in the oven for about 20 minutes, or until the shortbread is a very pale golden brown. Remove and set aside to cool.
6. For the filling, melt the white chocolate in a heatproof glass bowl over a pan of steaming water.

7. Meanwhile, beat together the ricotta and mascarpone in another glass bowl. Pour in the melted white chocolate and mix everything together.
8. Spoon the cheesecake mix on top of the cooled shortbread and put in the fridge to set.
9. To serve, remove the cheesecake from the tin, slide onto a plate and heap with the fresh summer berries.

Berries Dipped in White Chocolate
serves 4–6

I make these at home with the kids; they love them. And chocolate-covered berries are a cool petit four to round off a meal. It's crucial to freeze the berries first. Once the berries have been dipped in the white chocolate, they can be left in the fridge for a couple of hours.

1 punnet each of raspberries, blueberries and small strawberries

250g (9oz) white chocolate
cocktail sticks

1. Find a tray that fits in your freezer and place the berries on it, making sure that none are touching. Freeze them for about 1 hour.
2. Break up the white chocolate and put it into a heatproof glass bowl. Place the bowl over a pan of simmering water and allow the chocolate to melt. Once it's melted, you can turn off the heat but leave the chocolate in the bowl over the pan to keep it soft.
3. Take a frozen berry and stick it on a cocktail stick. Holding the stick, dip the berry in the chocolate, which should set against the frozen berry immediately. Place the coated berries on a plate. After coating a batch of ten berries, put the plate in the fridge.
4. Complete the remaining berries, working in batches of 10, until all the berries are coated. Keep in the fridge until ready to serve.

Mum's Meringue Cake
serves 4–6

As children, my sister and I were allowed to choose our birthday meals. Looking back, I realise I gave my mum quite an easy ride: it wasn't a poached medallion of veal with a morel consommé and a slice of foie gras that I wanted; my favourite meal at the time was macaroni cheese. For dessert, I always chose this. The mixture of meringue, fresh cream and raspberries remains one of my all-time favourite puddings.

Having learnt a bit over the years about making meringues, I know to cook meringues at a very low temperature. So I was a little shocked to read in Mum's recipe that she cooks it at 120°C/250°F/Gas Mark ¹/2 for 15 minutes and then turns it down to 100°C/210°F/Gas Mark ¹/4 – this flies in the face of all accepted wisdom. I can only presume that she knows something the rest of us don't. Follow her advice; you won't regret making this. Prepare the meringue and cream cake at least 3 hours before you wish to serve it.

4 egg whites
225g (8oz) caster sugar

600ml (1 pint) double cream
400g (14oz) raspberries

1. Preheat the oven to 120°C/250°F/Gas Mark ¹/2. Find 3 baking trays of a similar size and lay a piece of baking parchment on each. (I think silicon paper is best, because it won't stick.) On each tray, draw a circle about 20–23cm (8–9in) across.
2. Pour the egg whites into a mixer and use the whisk attachment to whisk them into a stiff foam. This will happen quickly - it takes about 2 minutes. (Alternatively, you can whisk by hand, which takes a little longer.) As the whites begin to stiffen, slowly pour in the sugar.
3. Divide the meringue into three and spread a third onto each circle drawn on the parchment.
4. Place the trays in the oven and bake for 15 minutes. Then reduce the temperature to 100°C/210°F/Gas Mark ¹/4, and bake for at least another 1³/4 hours. As a guide, the meringues should peel away from the paper easily when fully cooked.
5. Lift the cooked discs of meringue off their trays, and allow them to cool completely.
6. Meanwhile, whip the cream to what my mum calls a 'sloppy'

consistency – only just firm enough to spread over and sandwich the meringues. She points out here that the consistency of the cream can make or break the pudding, so don't overwhip the cream.

7. Spread the cream over the first meringue and place the second meringue on top. Spread more cream over that second meringue, then put the third meringue into position. Finally, just for good measure, spread cream over the top meringue.
8. Serve with a generous bowl of raspberries.

Crème Anglaise

serves 4

Let me say that there is nothing wrong with custard powder, but some desserts deserve a more refined approach. For that reason, I include a recipe for *crème anglaise*, which is really just posh custard.

Incidentally, it's worth pointing out that the full flavour of vanilla is only obtainable through the use of both the pods and the seeds. The overall flavour of vanilla is the sum of both parts, so don't do as some books suggest and simply scrape the seeds into your mix. And whilst we are on the subject: 'No, Mum, you can't use vanilla essence instead!' Vanilla extract possibly, but never essence.

6 egg yolks
120g (4¼oz) caster sugar
400ml (14fl oz) milk

100ml (3½fl oz) double cream
4 vanilla pods

1. First, beat the egg yolks and sugar together in a bowl.
2. In a saucepan, bring the milk and cream to a boil.
3. Halve the vanilla pods and scrape out the seeds. Add both the seeds and the pods to the milk and cream.
4. Pour the boiling milk and cream over the egg and sugar mixture and then return to the pan.
5. Cook slowly over gentle heat until the mixture thickens, stirring regularly with a wooden spoon. At this point, it's important not to let the liquid return to the boil, or it will scramble.
6. Once the mixture has thickened, pass it through a sieve to strain, and then allow to cool. Gently reheat before serving or serve cold.

Warm Baked Victoria Sponge with Red Berries and Whipped Cream serves 4

This simple dessert is based entirely on the theory that nothing tastes as good as a freshly baked cake, particularly if the cake in question is accompanied by fresh berries and lots of cream. By cooking the cake mixture in ramekins you can pass it off as a dessert, but really it's just a great excuse to have your cake and eat it!

3 large eggs
100g (3¹/₂oz) golden caster sugar,
    plus 1 tbsp for sprinkling on top
70g (2¹/₂oz) plain flour
15g (¹/₂oz) cornflour

20g (3/4oz) melted butter

To serve
600ml (1 pint) cream
400g (14oz) red berries

1. Preheat the oven to 190°C/375°F/Gas Mark 5.
2. Bring a shallow pan of water to the boil and place a large heatproof round-bottomed bowl over the steam. Reduce to a simmer and then place the eggs and sugar in the bowl and whisk continuously to form a frothy creamy mass (this is known as a 'sabayon'). The process may take 10 minutes or more, but keep whisking to avoid the eggs cooking too quickly and forming lumps.
3. Remove the bowl from the steam and continue whisking for a couple of minutes before folding in the flour and the cornflour. It is important to 'fold' rather than to mix otherwise you will knock much of the trapped air out of the sabayon and the cakes won't rise. So gently turn the mixture over with a spatula until the flour is incorporated. Then fold in the melted butter.
4. Butter four 10cm (4in) individual ramekins and three-quarters fill them with the sponge mix. Bake in the oven for about 12 minutes, or until cooked through.
5. Remove from the oven and sprinkle the browned surface with the extra caster sugar.
6. Serve the cakes in the ramekins with lots of cream and fresh berries on the side.

Custard Tart with Rhubarb Compote

serves 4

I love custard tart, but I am a little fussy about its composition. It has to be dusted with freshly grated nutmeg and it must have a good, eggy flavour. This is achieved through the use of milk as well as cream. Avoid recipes that claim to be luxury versions containing double cream – they will only disappoint.

Do give the pastry a go: in my professional cooking, I always make sweet shortcrust pastry from scratch. But if you can't be bothered to at home, I reckon it's fine to use a slab of shop-bought (weighing about 500g/1lb 2oz).

For the sweet pastry
175g (6oz) butter
75g (3oz) icing sugar
2 egg yolks
250g (9oz) plain flour
up to 2 tbsp water

For the custard
150ml (¼ pint) full fat milk
300ml (½ pint) single cream
2.5cm (1in) cinnamon stick

2 large eggs
2 egg yolks
50g (2oz) caster sugar
grated nutmeg

For the rhubarb compote
8 rhubarb stalks
about 4 tbsp caster sugar
1 tsp chopped stem ginger
zest of 1 orange

To make the sweet pastry

1. In a large bowl, cream the butter and sugar until it's a pale colour. Add the egg yolks and beat them in well. Mix the flour in thoroughly and then add enough water so that the mixture comes together to form a dough. Beat for 2 minutes, and then leave to rest in the fridge for at least 1 hour.

2. The next stage, whether using home-made or shop-bought pastry, is to blind bake the tart case. Sprinkle a work surface with flour, then roll out the pastry – it should be about 5mm (¼in) thick and large enough to fill the base and sides of a 25cm (10in) tart tin.

3. Lay the pastry into the tin and carefully push it into the edges. Trim any excess pastry. Now lay a piece of clingfilm over the layer of pastry and fill the tart up with baking beans. Close the clingfilm over the top to contain the beans.

4. Rest the case in the fridge for 1 hour. Meanwhile, heat the oven to 170°C/340°F/Gas Mark 3½.

5. Bake the pastry case for about 15 minutes. (Don't worry, the clingfilm won't melt.) Take out of the oven and remove the beans. Return the case to the oven for a further 5 minutes until it is golden brown all over. Set aside to cool.

To prepare the custard

1. Heat the milk, cream and cinnamon in a saucepan over a gentle heat. Bring to simmering point.
2. Meanwhile, beat the eggs, yolks and sugar together in a large bowl. Pour the milk and cream onto the beaten eggs and whisk it all together. Strain the mixture into a jug.
3. Preheat the oven to 130°C/270°F/Gas Mark 3/4. Place the cooked pastry case (still in its tin) on a baking tray, then slide it onto a shelf in the oven. Pull the shelf out slightly so that you can carefully pour the custard into the cooked tart case right up to the top. Now grate a little fresh nutmeg over the surface of the tart. Gently slide the tray right into the oven, taking care that no custard spills over the edge. Bake in the oven for 35 minutes.
4. At this point, the tart is ready to come out of the oven. The custard will not be set solid. In fact, it should be slightly wobbly.
5. Allow the tart to stand for a couple of hours, then carefully remove it from the baking case. Usually, I let it stand for another hour in the fridge before cutting it into slices. Take the slices out of the fridge a while before serving as the tart is better eaten at room temperature.

To make the rhubarb compote

1. Whilst the tart is standing, cut the rhubarb into 2.5cm (1in) chunks and throw the pieces into a saucepan. Sprinkle over the caster sugar and then place over a low heat.
2. Gently bring the rhubarb up to a simmer, then add the ginger. Simmer the mixture until it is well stewed – about 15 minutes. The rhubarb will break up, but don't worry about this.
3. Finally, grate the zest of the orange into the rhubarb. Taste and adjust the sweetness. Leave to cool and then store in the fridge ready to servze with the custard tart.

Hot Doughnuts with a Jam Injection
makes about 20

These are an absolute winner in our house. This recipe is for a large batch of doughnuts but I promise none will go to waste. The jam is injected using the type of syringe that is sometimes used to feed very small babies. They can be easily bought at a chemist (a syringe, not a baby!).

For the dough
225g (8oz) strong flour
5g (1/8oz) salt
15g (1/2oz) fresh yeast
25g (3/4oz) sugar
25g (3/4oz) butter
100ml (31/2fl oz) water

500ml (18fl oz) sunflower or corn oil
4 tbsp caster sugar mixed with 2 tsp
   ground cinnamon
175g (6oz) strawberry jam

1. Place all the ingredients for the dough into a mixer. Using the dough hook attachment, mix well at a medium speed for about 3 minutes. (Use a bowl and your muscles if you don't have a mixer, but be prepared to knead for at least 10–15 minutes).

2. Now remove the mixer bowl, then cover with a damp cloth and leave it to stand for about 25 minutes at room temperature. This will allow the dough to prove, which means the yeast is getting to work, and the dough will rise and double in size.

3. Once the dough has risen, it needs to be 'knocked back', which simply means gently pummelling it with your knuckles to disperse the trapped air.

4. Cut the dough into small pieces about the size of a walnut. Roll these bits of dough into neat balls and allow them to prove again. If you want your doughnuts ready quickly, let them stand at room temperature for 20 minutes. However, if you can hold off for an hour or two, allow them to prove on a tray in the fridge.

5. To cook the doughnuts, fill a deep heavy-based saucepan with oil to a depth of 20cm (8in). Bring the oil to a temperature of about 175°C/350°F and drop in a few dough balls. You can test the temperature by dropping in a small piece of dough – it should sink

continued overleaf

half way, then rise back to the surface and sizzle before gently browning. Allow them to fizz and roll around until they are golden brown – 6 minutes maximum. Remove and then roll them in the sugar and cinnamon mixture sprinkled on a tray.

6. Gently warm the jam in a small saucepan; if it has fruit pieces in it, strain these out before using it.

7. Carefully pour some jam into a syringe and inject into the middle of each doughnut. Serve warm with vanilla ice cream.

Dilly's Bakewell Tart

serves 4

Here is one of my all-time favourite puddings. Actually I hadn't eaten it for years until Dilly turned up at the allotment with a few slices one afternoon – now I can't stop making it.

In my view, this is best served warm, not hot, and with a generous helping of double cream.

500g (1lb 2oz) sweet shortcrust pastry
175g (6oz) raspberry jam
175g (6oz) ground almonds
175g (6oz) caster sugar
75g (3oz) butter
4 eggs, beaten
1^1/$_2$ tbsp self-raising flour
handful of flaked almonds

1. Preheat the oven to 170°C/340°F/Gas Mark 3^1/$_2$.

2. Prepare the tart case. Sprinkle a work surface with flour, then roll out the pastry – it should be about 5mm (^{1}/$_4$in) thick and large enough to fill the base and sides of a 25cm (10in) tart tin. Lay the pastry into the tin and carefully push it into the edges. Trim any excess pastry.

3. Pour the jam into the empty raw tart case and spread across the base evenly.

4. Beat together the ground almonds, sugar, butter, eggs and flour until well combined. Pour this mixture on top of the jam until the case is three-quarters full. Sprinkle the flaked almonds over the surface.

5. Bake in the oven for 35–40 minutes or until firm to the touch and golden brown on top.

MJ's Fruit Crumbles

serves 4

Here is the dessert that MJ makes more than any other! She is actually quite territorial about it. I wouldn't dare to make a crumble because she is the in-house crumble maker; but if I did, I would make it with white flour and white sugar. MJ, though, says this is too refined – she likes a more rugged crumble, and I have to admit that it does taste good.

For the crumble
125g (4½oz) plain flour
175g (6oz) butter
75g (3oz) soft dark brown sugar
50g (2oz) Demerara sugar
50g (2oz) stale biscuits, shortbread or digestive
100g (3½oz) oats

Fruit variations
Apples and sultanas work well – peel and dice 4 Bramley apples and cook in a little butter and sugar until soft. Add a handful of sultanas. Cool slightly before use.
Blackberry and apple – you could use blackberries on their own but they are quite soggy, so combining with apple gives the mixture some depth. Peel and chop 4 Bramley apples into a pan with about 20 blackberries to each apple. Cook until the apple is soft and the blackberry juice has been absorbed.
Rhubarb – my favourite: chop up 12 rhubarb sticks and cook in a pan with about a teaspoon of sugar per stick of rhubarb. Allow the mixture to reduce a little so that it's not too wet. If I am coming round, please add a little chopped stem ginger, a vanilla pod and, at the last moment, some orange zest!

1. Put the flour in a bowl and rub in the butter until the mixture resembles breadcrumbs. Mix in the sugars.
2. Crumble the biscuits and add them to the bowl, then mix in the oats.
3. Preheat the oven to 180°C/350°F/Gas Mark 4.
4. Take your prepared fruit and pour into the base of an ovenproof dish. Generously spoon plenty of crumble mixture over the top.
5. Bake in the oven for about 30 minutes or until piping hot and bubbling at the edges.

Anton's Pear and Almond Croustillant with Pear Crisps serves 4

This recipe takes a little effort to make, but it's well worth it. Anton was my trusted assistant in the restaurants where I was the head chef. He was at my side both times that I gained a Michelin star, and that's no coincidence. I include this recipe to acknowledge his immense talent but also because it's a bloody good pudding!

2 conference pears
50g (2oz) caster sugar
50g (2oz) unsalted butter
2 tbsp pear eau de vie (optional)
8 sheets filo pastry, 14 x 14cm
   (4$^{1}/_{2}$ x 4$^{1}/_{2}$in) square
200g (7oz) butter, melted
200g (7oz) frangipane
50g (2oz) flaked almonds

vanilla ice cream
4 pear crisps (see page 308)

For the frangipane
125g (4$^{1}/_{2}$oz) butter
125g (4$^{1}/_{2}$oz) icing sugar
125g (4$^{1}/_{2}$oz) ground almonds
25g (1oz) plain flour
3 eggs

To make the frangipane
1. Cream the butter and sugar until it is pale in colour. This can be done easily in a mixer but is also possible by hand.
2. Add the almonds and flour, then mix both well into the butter mixture.
3. Beat the eggs together, then slowly add to the mixture.

To make the croustillant
1. First peel the pears, then cut lengthways into four and remove the core. Roll them in the caster sugar.
2. Melt the unsalted butter in a frying pan and, when hot, add the pears to caramelise. This will take about 2 minutes; be careful not to burn the sugar. At this point, add the pear eau de vie, if using. This will create a little syrup in the pan. Remove the pear from the syrup and drain. Some juice may drip from the pears as they cool; add this to the syrup in the pan and keep warm.
3. Lay out four of the filo sheets lengthways and brush with melted butter, then lay another filo sheet on top of each. Pipe or spoon a sausage size amount of frangipane lengthways down the middle.

Lay two pieces of pear on top and roll up like a sausage roll, being careful not to squeeze any of the mix out of the ends. Press the ends down well and brush with more melted butter. Sprinkle with the almonds and refrigerate for 2–3 hours.

4. Preheat the oven to 180°C/350°F/Gas Mark 4, then bake the parcels until brown and crispy. Remove from the oven and leave them to rest somewhere warm for 5 minutes; do not cover.

5. Cut each croustilliant in half and serve with vanilla ice cream, pear crisps and, if you wish, a little of the reserved syrup.

Pear Crisps

makes 10–12 crisps

Not all restaurant tricks are complicated, these crisps are simple to make and also work well with apples.

200g (7oz) caster sugar
200ml (7fl oz) water

juice of 1 lemon
1 firm(ish) pear

1. First you need to make a 'stock syrup', which simply consists of equal amounts of sugar and water simmered for a few minutes. Chuck the sugar in a pan and pour in the water. Bring to a boil, then turn the heat down and simmer for about 5 minutes. Leave the stock syrup to cool completely before using it for the crisps. Once it is chilled, add the lemon juice to the syrup.
2. Using a mandolin or a very sharp knife, cut the pear into slices about 1mm (1/16 in) thick. Soak them in the stock syrup for a few seconds and then remove them and let any excess syrup drain off.
3. Lay the slices on a sheet of non-stick silicon paper and place the paper on a flat baking tray.
4. Put the tray in the oven at 80°C (175°F) for 2–3 hours, or until the slices are dried out and crisp. If your oven does not go as low as this, just set it to its lowest temperature and prop the door open slightly with a wooden spoon.
5. Any extra stock syrup can be kept in a container in the fridge until it turns up once more in another recipe.

Tarte Tatin

makes a 25cm (10in) tart, serves 4–5 people

A friend and I run a weekend cookery course in south-west France. We take groups of foodies off to local markets, as well as going truffle-hunting and wine-tasting. The weekend also features a couple of cookery demonstrations by yours truly, and this dish is by far the most popular demo request.

For this tart, you will need an ovenproof frying pan -one which you can rely on not to stick! I keep a pan at home specifically for this job!

600g (1lb 5oz) quality, shop-bought puff pastry
75g (3oz) unsalted butter

120g (4¼oz) caster sugar
6–8 Granny Smith apples
cream or vanilla ice cream, to serve

1. First of all, roll out the pastry to about 3mm (¹/8in) thick and cut it into a circle slightly bigger than the base of your chosen pan. Prick the pastry with a fork several times – this will allow steam to escape as the tart is cooking. Put the pastry on a tray, then leave to rest in the fridge.

2. Slice the butter finely and cover the base of a cold frying pan. Sprinkle over the sugar.

3. Peel the apples, cut them into quarters and remove the cores. Arrange the apples on top of the butter or sugar so that they fit tightly, covering the base of the pan. Put the pastry on top of the apples and push it in around the edges.

4. Preheat the oven to 190°C/375°F/Gas Mark 5.

5. Meanwhile, place the pan on a medium heat to caramelise the apples – this will take about 10 minutes. Shake the pan lightly every now and then while the apples are cooking. Now place the pan into the preheated oven, to cook for 20 minutes.

6. Remove from the oven and allow the pan to cool very slightly. Then place a plate over the pan. Carefully turn both the plate and pan over so that the tart drops onto the plate, revealing the apples lying on top of the pastry. The apples should be deeply caramelised.

7. Serve warm with cream or vanilla ice cream.

Index

Page numbers in **bold** denotes an illustration

USING THE PLOT

Acknowledgements

The fact that I have managed to write a book will amuse many of those who know me well. The truth is that I could not have written it at all without the help of certain people.

Firstly I would like to thank the 'on site' allotment team – MJ, Ellie, Richie and our allotment neighbours Dilly, Doug, Eddie and Sylvie. Thanks also to Chris and Stella Williams for on-going practical gardening advice.

Thanks to everyone at Blondin Allotments for help, friendship and encouragement.

On the book side of things I want to thank Jenny Heller and Lizzy Gray at HarperCollins for encouraging me to be myself and write from the heart – without your belief, I would have given up long ago. Thanks also to my wonderful editors Kirstie Addis and Caroline Curtis, plus designers Anna Martin and Bob Vickers.

My business partner Greg Bellamy also needs a mention. I was supposed to be working on a restaurant project for much of the time that I was actually 'shovel in hand' and he picked up all the extra graft.

Thanks to Yas for interpreting all my recipes and testing them so thoroughly.

Thank you to my Dad, Colleen, my Mum, my sister Ali, my brother-in-law Chris, and Janet and Malcolm for support, advice and encouragement when the going got tough.

Finally, thanks to my grandparents Dick and Marjorie Merrett whose approach to food, gardening and life in general inspired my desire to write. I very much hope you would have enjoyed the read.

Picture acknowledgements
The publishers would like to thank the following people for their photographs:

Marie-Louise Avery pp180, 193, 194, 196, 201, 205, 215, 230, 235, 238, 243, 246, 255, 263, 265, 283, 293, 299, 302, 307; Mary-Jane Curtis pp2, 14, 34–5, 42, 56, 71, 74, 91, 105, 120, 133, 144, 157, 161, 168–9, 174; Jonathan Gregson pp6–7, 176, 187, 188; Paul Merrett p11; Jenny Heller pp8, 129.